SPSS

IN SIMPLE STEPS

Authored by:

Kiran Pandya, Smruti Bulsari, Sanjay Sinha

&

DT Editorial Services

Published by:

dreamtech PRESS

IN SIMPLE STEPS

ISBN: 978-93-5004-251-9

Reprint Edition: 2026

Printed at: Raj Kamal Press, Delhi.

Dedicated to

The loving memory of my dear brother

Jyotindra Pandya

And

My mother, **Hasumati Pandya**

And

My wife, **Archana** and daughters, **Prita** and **Lekha**

– Kiran Pandya

"Scientific laws are not advanced by the principle of authority or justified by faith or medieval philosophy; statistics is the only court of appeal to new knowledge".

– P C Mahalanobis

My parents

Bakul Bulsari and **Asha Bulsari**

– Smruti Bulsari

Preface

Statistics is despised by most of the students in social science for obvious reasons that they have a non-mathematical background. Proliferation of research activities and necessity of empirical verification have led to increasing use of statistics. The students are required to learn a specific set of skills about data analysis so that they can understand the experimental literature and do analysis on fresh data. Familiarity with statistics has become very important in the world dominated by quantitative data. Statistics is not only the number game, but also a useful tool to understand our world.

Sometimes, even brilliant students are found to be apprehensive of numbers and simple calculations. With the advent of scientific calculators and computers, basic data analysis has become very easy. Many statistical packages have been developed in the last couple of decades to facilitate the use of statistics and empirical verification in research for those who are afraid of statistics. Special statistical packages such as Statistical Package for Social Sciences (SPSS)/Predictive Analytics SoftWare (PASW) are now considerably easier to use and have made possible to do even complicated analysis.

The main objective of this book is to help students and researchers to undertake statistical analysis with the help of computer using PASW 18.0. We have used concepts and technical terms in this book, which may not sound very rigorous from the point of view of a statistician. Some very good books on statistics and research methodology are available in the market. The users/readers of this book are advised to refer to those books for better understanding of statistical concepts and techniques.

The concept of this book arose from our experience of teaching and applying research methods. We have gained a lot of knowledge from the interactions with participants of various training programmes and workshops on research methodology, statistical analysis, and SPSS organized at university campus and other institutions. During these programmes and workshops, it was felt that there is a need to make statistical methods more accessible and understandable to students who are undertaking research work or project work for their post-graduate courses and dissertation. We have tried to keep the text clear and simple in order to make the students easy to understand the subject matter.

SPSS/PASW is a widely used and popular statistical package. The use of statistical package has become almost indispensible for statistical analysis and research. It is difficult to make optimum use of the software unless students undergo training or have access to the manual. In this book, we have tried to provide an overview of SPSS/PASW and explain the basic commands necessary for statistical analysis. The book deals with presentation, analysis, and interpretation of quantitative data. It makes use of elementary statistical techniques that are explained and put into use with the help of lucid examples. We are sure that the students with little background in statistics and some exposure to windows will be able to do meaningful analysis in different branches of knowledge.

SPSS/PASW has many other interesting features, some of which require understanding of advanced statistics and programming. We have tried to cover most of the topics that are required by research students in performing primary statistical analysis. Once the students are familiar with the techniques covered in this book, it will be possible for them to learn advanced features on their own.

While developing the structure underlying this book, many people offered valuable advice and are engaged in useful exchange of information concerning the applications of statistics in social science research. Our many thought-provoking discussions have enriched the contents of this book. The decision of which topics to be covered has been one of the most difficult aspects in the preparation of the book

We here, take the opportunity to thank our friends – Dr Prashant Joshi, Dr Akash, Acharya, Dr Gaurang Rami, Dr Jayesh Desai, Neha Sheth, Dr Krishnaraj Chudasama and Bhavesh Vanparia, with whom we interacted at length to know the requirement of researchers and making this text book helpful to young researchers, especially in social sciences.

During last couple of years, we had opportunity to interact with Jignasu Yagnik, Dr Neeraj Hatekar, Prof. Umesh Naik, Dr A S Rao, Dr P Marvania, and Dr Vivek Belhekar. They helped us in improving the presentation and coverage of the statistical tools that are useful in research.

We thank SPSS®, Inc., 123 S Wacker Drive, Chicago, for giving necessary permission to use various images generated by SPSS.

We would like thank Mr. R Raman Kandpal and the editorial board at Wiley for providing outstanding support. The reviewers offered many constructive and valuable suggestions. We gratefully acknowledge their help.

Thanks to respective family members for bearing negative externality emanating from writing this book.

We have made every endeavor to make the book error-free. We take the sole responsibility for any error that might have gone unnoticed.

Kiran Pandya

Smruti Bulsari

About the Authors

Dr Kiran Pandya obtained the M. Phil. degree from Gokhale Institute of Politics and Economics, University of Pune, Pune. He was awarded the degree of Philosophy by the University of Sussex, East Sussex, U.K., and the Academic Staff scholarship by the Commonwealth Commission in U.K. to pursue his doctoral studies.

Currently, he is working as a Professor and Head in the Department of Research Methodology and Interdisciplinary Studies in Social Sciences, Veer Narmad South Gujarat University, Surat, Gujarat. He has more than twenty-eight years of teaching and research experience. Dr Pandya has published a number of papers in national and international journals and also has co-authored books on quantitative methods. He is actively involved in research and carrying out sponsored projects in the area of human development.

Dr Smruti Bulsari obtained the Master's degree in management and economics. She also holds a PG Diploma in Research Methodology and a Diploma in Computer Technology. She has obtained her doctoral degree and has more than ten years of teaching and research experience. She is currently a faculty in MBA programme of Veer Narmad South Gujarat University, Surat, Gujarat. Dr Bulsari has published papers in national and international journals. She has also co-authored books on Statistical Package for Social Sciences (SPSS) and other subjects. She is associated with many research projects. She has delivered lectures in State-level and National-level workshops and training programmes in SPSS.

Prof. Sanjay Sinha holds the M. Phil. degree in Financial Management, Advanced Diploma in Financial Management, MBA in Financial Management, M. Sc. Degree in Statistics, and B. Sc. Degree in Physics, Mathematics, and Statistics. He is currently attached to ITM Business School, Kharghar, Navi Mumbai, as an Associate Professor and pursuing doctoral degree programme. He has also undergone a certificate programme in Capital Markets, Regulation and Compliance from the University of Reading, Reading, U.K. He has around 12 years of corporate experience in different capacities in various organizations, primarily in the Banking, Financial Services and Insurance (BFSI) segment. He quit the corporate world in 2006 when he was in the Vice President cadre and joined ITM group of Institutions as faculty in the area of Finance and Quantitative Techniques. He is currently heading the Department of Quantitative Techniques and teaches several courses in the areas of Finance as well. Prof Sinha has publications in various international journals.

IN SIMPLE STEPS

Table of Contents

Chapter 1

Overview of PASW Statistics

In this Chapter:

Man is continually attempting to quantify more and more characteristics about self, and the world surrounding him. Statistics may be causing undue anxiety in the minds of college students. The ranges of readily available statistical computing packages have greatly increased accessibility to statistics. A step-by-step approach followed in this book will make learning both – statistics and this software package – simple and fun.

Statistical Package for the Social Sciences (SPSS) is one of the most widely used statistical software. IBM acquired SPSS Inc. in 2009 and revamped the GUI of this software. The modules for direct marketing, spectral analysis of time series data, forecasting etc. were added and the software was renamed as IBM SPSS Statistics or Predictive Analytic Software (PASW) Statistics. In this chapter, you get acquainted with concepts of PASW; and explore the User Interface (UI) of PASW Statistics. You also learn the basic steps for performing statistical procedure.

1.1 Introduction to PASW

PASW Statistics covers a broad range of statistical procedures that allow you to summarize data (that is, compute means, standard deviations and other measures of central tendency and dispersion), determine whether the differences between groups are statistically significant or not (for example, t-tests, analysis of variance), examine relationships among variables (for example, correlation, multiple regression), defining complex relationships among variables (for example, modeling using Neural Networks), time series analysis (examples: seasonal decomposition, autocorrelation, ARIMA), Survival Analysis and graphs (example: bar charts, line graphs). PASW contains several tools for recoding data, computing new variables, merging and aggregating datasets as well as manipulating data. This chapter focuses on the characteristics of the PASW software, different menus, and terminology used by PASW.

Note

PASW Statistics is now onwards referred to as PASW.

PASW consists of four different windows, each associated with a particular PASW file type. The discussion in this book is limited to the three windows most frequently used in analyzing data in PASW, the **Data Editor,** the **Output Viewer** and the **Syntax Editor** windows. The Data Editor is the window, which launches when an SPSS session commences. Moreover, the Data Editor is used to insert as well as store data in a spreadsheet format. The Output Viewer opens automatically. When command is executed, a graph is created using dialogue box or command syntax. The Output Viewer stores the consequences of statistical studies and graphical demonstration of data. The Syntax Editor is a text modifier, which allows you to create PASW commands. When the commands are created, you can submit them to the PASW processor. The Output Viewer shows the result of these commands. You can save the contents of any of these windows. By using the **Window** menu, make sure that the particular window is active (to save contents). After it's confirmed, click on **File** and then **Save**. The contents of each of these windows can be printed by activating a window and clicking on the **Printer** icon (or open the **File** menu and click on **Print**).

PASW automatically adds a three-letter suffix to the end of the file name (".sav" for data editor files, ".spv" for output files, and ".sps" for syntax files). Thus, with a particular data set, it is probably wise to use a single name for the prefix of all three files and let the suffix distinguish between the different file types. Basic information on these files is summarized in table 1.1:

Table 1.1: Functions of PASW Editor Windows

Window	Suffix	Function
Data Editor	.sav	Helps define, enter, and edit your data and to run statistical tests
Output Viewer	.spv	Contains the results of the statistical procedures. The earlier versions of SPSS had .spo as its suffix. SPSS 16.0 and onwards, the suffix is .spv.

Table 1.1: Functions of PASW Editor Windows		
Window	**Suffix**	**Function**
Syntax	.sps	Records the sequence of the operations that are "pasted." This window is activated when you click on the Paste function and although this is beyond the goals of these lessons, you may want to know that PASW commands can actually be run from this window.

Note

Draft Viewer Window, which was available till SPSS 15.0, is not supported in PASW 18.0. Instead Export to text document can be used from the Output Viewer Window. Other windows like Chart Editor, Pivot Table window can be activated from the Output Viewer Window by double-clicking the chart and the table respectively. Script window is used to write scripts using command statements of PASW (called Sax Commands).

Now we shall discuss some of the important features of the PASW that help the user to facilitate data processing.

1.2 Menus

Menus appear on the top most portions of the window and just below the title bar. Clicking on any of the menu items produces a pull-down sub-menu displaying several options which can be selected to perform different tasks as per requirements. The title bar, command menu, main menu and sub-menu are shown below in Fig.PASW–1.1:

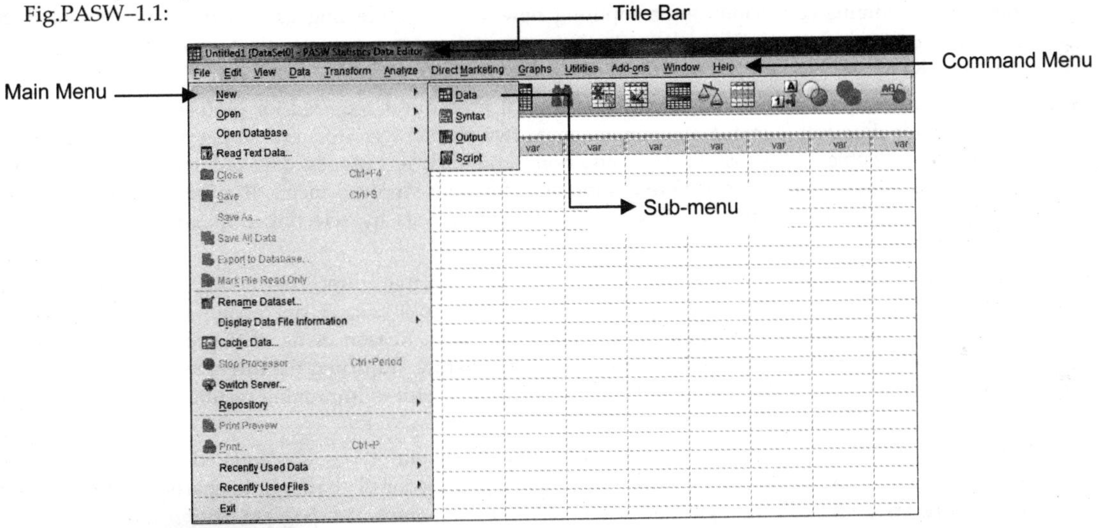

Fig.PASW–1.1

The command menu options that appear on command bar are briefly described as follows:

- **File:** Contains commands for opening a new or an existing file, saving a file and exporting data from a file which is different from the data file of PASW format. This PASW menu not only gives options for displaying file properties but also provides features for interface with other packages like MS-Excel, SAS, STATA, MS-Access, with text files and even with files stored on server, internet or any other repository that the user has access to. This means, it provides facilities for opening many other file types or data sources.
- **Edit:** Contains commands for finding a particular case from a large dataset, going to a particular location in file, inserting cases or variables etc.

Note

In PASW, each row uniquely identifies the characteristic of one respondent or any other unit of observation. This unit of observation is referred to as case in PASW.

Edit menu contains options for copying data from one location in the same data file or from other data file and then pasting it at appropriate location in the working / active data file. You can find and replace data through Edit menu.

- **View:** Contains commands for viewing data labels, tool bars, status bar, grid lines, changing fonts etc. You can change the fonts in the data editor window through View menu. In the output viewer window, the commands for showing detailed results, or just the result titles (expand and collapse commands by clicking on + and – signs respectively), the commands for showing or temporarily hiding the results are also available in View menu. You may customize the sub-menus through Menu Editor Command of View menu.
- **Data:** Contains commands for data manipulation like defining properties of variables, copying properties of data; also, sorting, aggregating, splitting and merging files, selecting cases, etc. Identification of duplicate cases and unusual cases (outliers or any cases that deviate significantly from the properties of all other cases) is possible through data menu. You may define multiple response sets as well as create and view orthogonal designs (similar to advanced statistical procedures like factor and conjoint analysis) using this Data menu.
- **Transform:** Contains commands for computing new variables, creating groups from ungrouped data, ranking cases, replacing missing values etc. You may define, and generate time series using Transform command. Random Numbers are generated using Transform command.
- **Analyze:** Contains commands for executing statistical procedures required for performing data analysis; commands for descriptive statistics, comparison of two or more groups, examining association between two or more variables. Analysis of data using non-parametric techniques, data reduction, quality control etc. all these are possible using different sub-menu items of Analyze menu. It is possible to undertake regression analysis, and define models in time series analysis by selecting different commands from Analyze menu.
- **Direct Marketing:** Used for analyzing data obtained through direct marketing research. Different techniques like Recency, Frequency and Monetary (RFM) analysis, cluster analysis, prospect profiles, propensity to purchase etc. are used for analyzing this data. Reason being, that proactive steps can be undertaken on the basis of the results of these analyses, before launching the direct marketing campaign. This module has been added in the PASW software and is useful in improving results of direct marketing campaigns.
- **Graphs:** Contains commands to construct and display several types of charts, diagrams and maps. Different types of charts like histograms, line charts, quality control charts, hi-lo charts for stock market analysis etc. are generated through the Graphs menu. Pie diagram, bar diagram, scatter diagrams etc are also generated using graphs menu. Maps can be created to display the similarities and differences across different indicators like rainfall, forest cover, literacy level etc. for a given geographical area, usually, a country, state, district etc. PASW requires the geoset (blank map in the format required by PASW) for the geographical area for which the map is to be created. Maps can then be generated, using Graphs menu.
- **Utilities:** Contains sophisticated data manipulation tools required for advanced statistical analysis.
- **Add-ons:** Contains commands for adding required programs for advanced statistical analysis which are not already installed in PASW.
- **Window:** Contains commands for switching over from one window to another or, for resizing (maximizing, minimizing and restoring) windows.
- **Help:** It gives information pertaining to various commands and its usage. Like any other windows-based program, this can be viewed by clicking the F1 key or by clicking **help**.

1.3 Tool Bar

Tool bar is located below the menu bar and gives quick access to frequently used sub-menu items. It works as a short cut. Tool bar as shown below in Fig.PASW–1.2:

Fig.PASW–1.2

1.4 Dialogue Box

When you select any command through command menu for data transformation, data management or, for performing any statistical test, a small window with a list appears. This drop down list of, variables, some radio buttons, check boxes, and some push buttons appears on the currently active window. Appropriate variables for any given analysis, options and tests can be chosen from this dialogue box. A dialogue box looks like the one shown below in Fig.PASW–1.3:

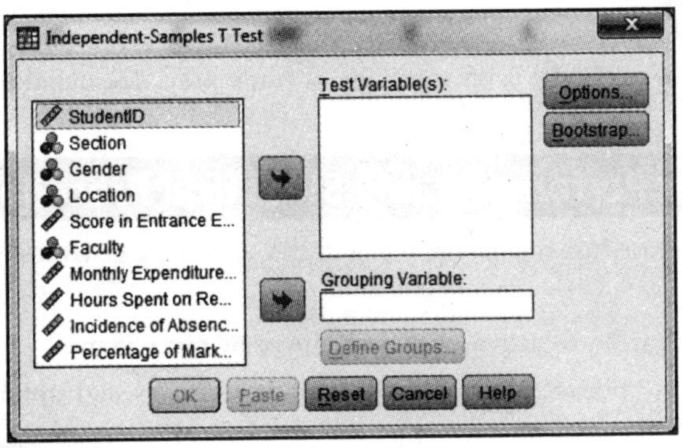

Fig.PASW–1.3

Once you select appropriate variables and options, **OK** button gets enabled. In order to execute the command click the **OK** button. The buttons are referred as Push Buttons. Clicking on some of the push buttons will open up a new dialogue box; that is, clicking Options in the dialogue box (Fig.PASW–1.2) opens up dialogue box as shown below in Fig.PASW-1.4:

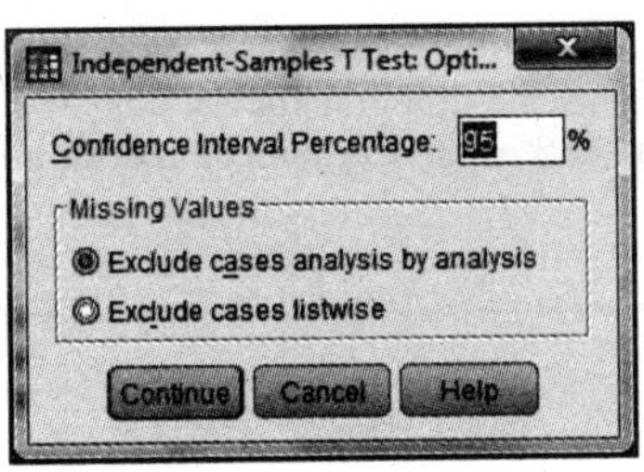

Fig.PASW–1.4

In a dialogue box, if you want to select more than one variable it can be done simply by, holding the **Ctrl** key of the keyboard and clicking on multiple variables. If the variables are consecutive, they can be selected by holding **Shift** key instead of **Ctrl**.

1.5 Designate Window

It is possible to have two or more output (viewer) and syntax editor windows open at a time. Note that only the latest versions of SPSS / PASW allow you to open more than one Data Editor Window simultaneously. By default, the last open window is the designated window. You should not get confused between the designated window and the active window. You may activate a window just by clicking anywhere inside that window, however to designate a window, you need to perform the following procedure:

1. Click output viewer or syntax editor window to make it an active window.
2. Click the blue colored rectangle with a star on it as shown in Fig.PASW–1.5:

Fig.PASW–1.5

Once you click on the blue rectangle with star sign, it turns grey. The window with that grey icon is the designated window.

1.6 Basic Steps for Performing any Statistical Procedure

To perform any statistical procedure or analysis using PASW, following general steps should be performed:

1. Load your data set.
2. Keeping the data editor window active, click on appropriate menu item.
3. Once the dialogue box appears, select the appropriate variables and options to do required statistical analysis.
4. Click on **OK** to execute the command.
5. Click on the output viewer window to see the generated results.

Statistical procedure can be performed using syntax file also. Following steps should be performed to use syntax file.

1. Open syntax file containing commands. If you have not included the command for opening the data file, first open the data file.
2. Run appropriate or required syntax for doing statistical analysis. You can also run all the commands or select particular command syntax and run it. Certain commands are required to be executed in sequence.

Summary

In this chapter we learnt:

- The concept of PASW.
- The UI of PASW.
- The basic steps for performing statistical procedure, while using the command menu and the syntax command file.

Chapter 2

Data Management

In this Chapter:

Once the data for the research is collected, the next stage is to enter the collected data in appropriate form to facilitate statistical analysis. Precautions taken at this stage can save researcher from possible hassles at a later stage of research. Understanding structure of data, number of data files to be created and definition of variables is very important in the initial stage of data entry. Predictive Analytic Software (PASW) provides an easy interface for data entry, storage of data, retrieval of stored data, adding more data that may be required at different stages of data entry and analysis. Checking for duplicate entries and errors in data entry is desirable before using data for analysis. Some studies carry out disaggregated analysis. In such case, conditional analysis may be useful which is done by presenting data in a different form or, selecting some cases matching a particular condition. This chapter discusses procedures for entering data, storing data, retrieving stored data, sorting data, checking for duplicate entries, data aggregation and other related procedures.

2.1 Creating a Data File

The first step in working with PASW is to enter your data and create a PASW data file .Do keep in mind that PASW can read data files created by other programs such as Microsoft Excel, SAS, STATA, Lotus 1-2-3, Microsoft Access, ASCII files and those created in earlier versions of SPSS.

When you first open up PASW, you will be prompted to make a decision about running the tutorial, typing in new data or opening up an existing file as shown below in Fig.PASW–2.1:

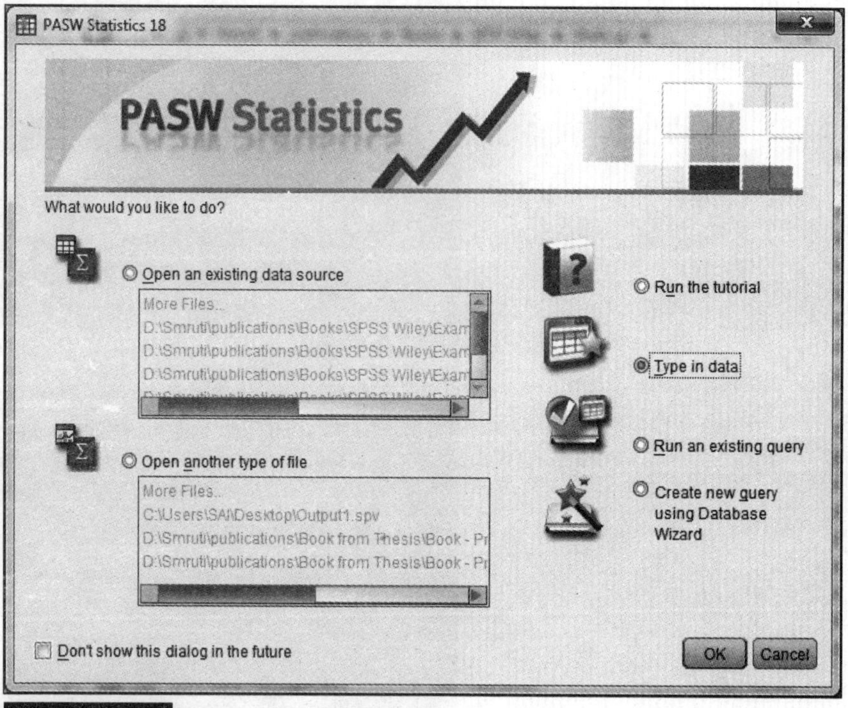

Fig.PASW 2.1

You will be creating a new data file as you are unfamiliar with PASW. To create a new data file, click **Type in data** and then click **OK**. This should open data editor window, as shown below in Fig.PASW–2.2:

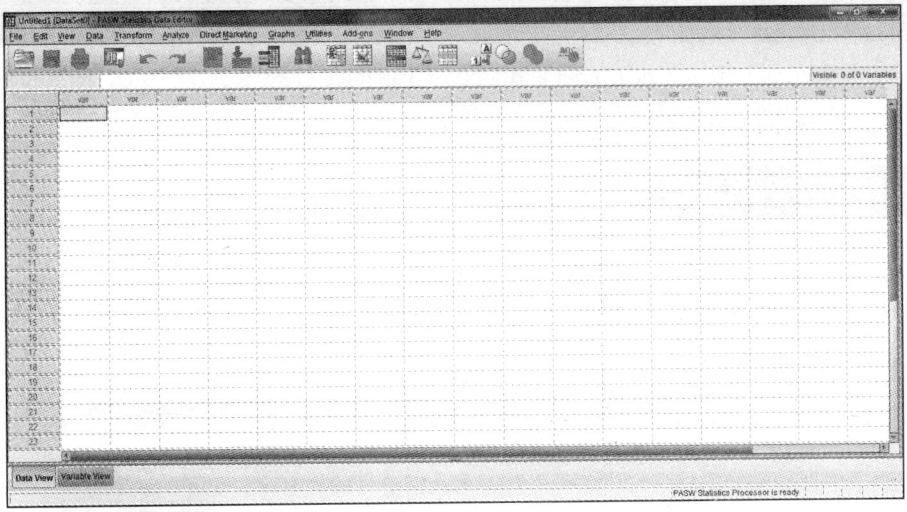

Fig.PASW–2.2

PASW treats each row as respondents or case. The data on each respondent should be entered in a separate row.

Example

Assume that you are interested in developing a profile of students studying in a professional course. To do this, you collect information about 60 students of that course as a sample. The details of some of these students are given in Table 2.1:

Table 2.1: Information of Students of a Professional Course

Student ID	Section	Gender	Location	Score of Entrance Examination	Faculty of Graduation	Expenditure on Education	Hours of Reading	Percentage of Marks Scored in First Year
1	1	Male	Local	65	Science	500	8	69
2	1	Male	Commuter	50	Arts	700	5	60
3	1	Female	Commuter	55	Arts	250	2	55
4	1	Male	Commuter	60	Commerce	400	9	69
5	1	Male	Local	54	Science	800	3	56
6	1	Male	Commuter	56	Science	350	5	54
...	1	Male	Commuter	68	Science	300	9	60
60	1	Male	Local	65	Science	520	4	59

Points to Keep in Mind

- Rows are used for entering information on respondents or cases. Here, students are respondents.
- Columns are used for entering variable information. Here, we will use six columns, one for each of the following variables (Student ID, Section, Gender, Location, Score of Entrance Examination, Faculty of Graduation, Expenditure on Education, Hours Reading, and Percentage of Marks Scored in First Year).

- Assign numerical code for the gender and location variables. Here, we will assign the values 0 to Males and 1 to Females. Similarly, we assign 0 to Locals and 1 to Commuters. For the variable Faculty, 1 is assigned to Arts, 2 to Commerce and 3 to Science.

2.2 Defining Variables

In this section, we will describe the step-by-step procedure for adding variables to the data file:

1. Click either the **Data View** or **Variable View** buttons from bottom left corner of the data editor window. In our case, we have clicked the **Variable View** button. For entering the variables and their characteristics, you should work in the **Variable View** window. The relevant portion of the **Variable View** window is shown below in Fig.PASW–2.3:

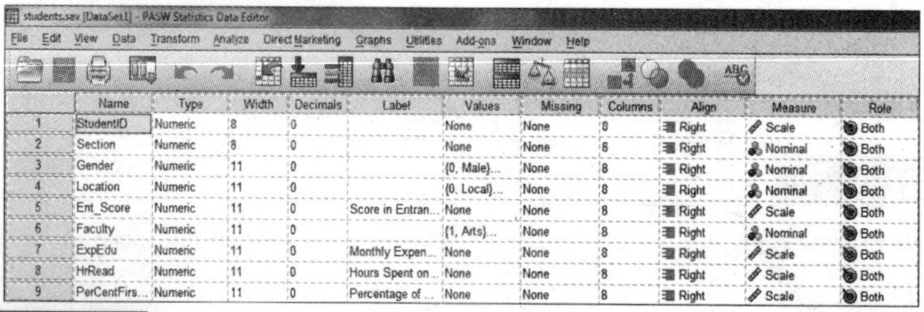

students.sav [DataSet1] - PASW Statistics Data Editor

File Edit View Data Transform Analyze Direct Marketing Graphs Utilities Add-ons Window Help

	Name	Type	Width	Decimals	Label	Values	Missing	Columns	Align	Measure	Role
1	StudentID	Numeric	8	0		None	None	8	Right	Scale	Both
2	Section	Numeric	8	0		None	None	8	Right	Nominal	Both
3	Gender	Numeric	11	0		{0, Male}...	None	8	Right	Nominal	Both
4	Location	Numeric	11	0		{0, Local}...	None	8	Right	Nominal	Both
5	Ent_Score	Numeric	11	0	Score in Entran...	None	None	8	Right	Scale	Both
6	Faculty	Numeric	11	0		{1, Arts}...	None	8	Right	Nominal	Both
7	ExpEdu	Numeric	11	0	Monthly Expen...	None	None	8	Right	Scale	Both
8	HrRead	Numeric	11	0	Hours Spent on...	None	None	8	Right	Scale	Both
9	PerCentFirs...	Numeric	11	0	Percentage of ...	None	None	8	Right	Scale	Both

Fig.PASW–2.3

In the space for **Name**, type the desired variable name. The first character must be alphabetic; the remaining can be alphabetic and/or numeric, but no spaces can appear in the variable name. So, in this case, let's type **StudentID**.

Note that Old versions of SPSS required that the variable name should not be more than eight characters.

2. Next press the **Tab key** (or **Enter key**) and you notice that PASW assigns default values to all the settings. You should go through the relevant column for that particular variable. Clicking on a column will turn it to a shaded area.

The functions and corresponding default values of each of these columns are given below in Table 2.2:

Table 2.2: Variable Characteristics and their Default Values

Variable Characteristics	Explanation	Default Value
Type	Data type – string, date etc.	Numeric
Width	Total number of characters	8
Decimals	Number of characters after decimal point (only in case of numeric data)	2
Label	Description of the variable in maximum 255 characters	None
Values	Give labels to different levels of a variable	None
Missing	Enables you to designate certain scores as missing	None
Columns	Maximum number of characters in a column	8
Align	Alignment of values in a given column	Right
Measure	Specifies the measurement scale of the variable	Scale
Role	Specifies the role of the variable ,its displayed at appropriate places Input role means that variable will be used as an Independent or predictive variable	Input

Click **Decimals** to change decimal places to **0**. Click **Label** to provide a label for the variable – for example; you might type **Gender of the Student**. Click Values column to specify the codes. Here, code **0** is used for **Female** and **1** for **Male.** To specify these codes, click Values column. A push button like will appear in the Values column. Type **0,** in the **Value** box and type **Females** in the **Label** box. Then create the label of **Males** using value **1**. Your final dialogue box should look like the one shown below in Fig.PASW–2.4:

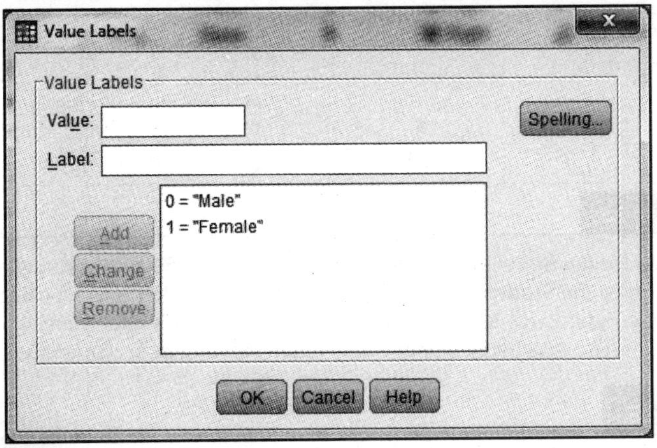

Fig.PASW–2.4

In the **Role** column (shown in Fig.PASW–2.3), select the option **Both,** for all the variables. Since a researcher may not be aware at this stage as to which statistical techniques he will use, it is advisable to specify **Both** in the Role column. The other options are **Input, Target, Partition** and **Split**. Other roles will require understanding of concepts of split file and regression analysis. These concepts are discussed at appropriate places in this chapter and, in the chapter on Regression Analysis. An overview of each of these roles is presented in Table 2.3:

Table 2.3: Variable Roles and their Meanings

Role	Meaning
Input	This will allow you to use the variable only as input (independent) variable for regression analysis.
Target	This role will allow you to use the variable only as dependent variable for regression analysis.
Partition	This role should be assigned to a variable when you want separate analysis for each group of the categorical variable.
Split	This role should be assigned if you want that the file should not be split on a particular categorical variable.

3. Follow the same procedure for entering the information of the next variable.
4. Now define each of the remaining variables. The details of other variables is given along with the dataset in the appendix – A.

2.3 Entering the Data

Defining variables is a very important procedure before beginning, entering of data. Variables information may be defined or modified even at a later stage. When the data is shared or more than one person is using the data, it is desirable to enter variable information before data entry.

1. Click the **Data View** button (lower left hand corner). You should see all of the variable names that you have entered, as shown below in Fig.PASW–2.5:

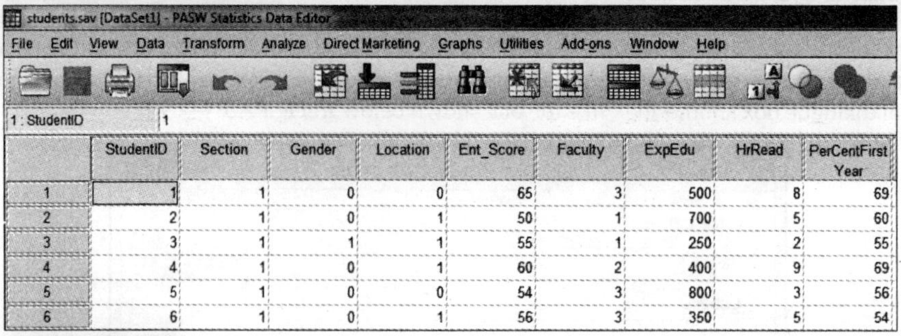

	StudentID	Section	Gender	Location	Ent_Score	Faculty	ExpEdu	HrRead	PerCentFirst Year
1	1	1	0	0	65	3	500	8	69
2	2	1	0	1	50	1	700	5	60
3	3	1	1	1	55	1	250	2	55
4	4	1	0	1	60	2	400	9	69
5	5	1	0	0	54	3	800	3	56
6	6	1	0	1	56	3	350	5	54

Fig.PASW–2.5

2. Now, type in data for the first six respondents in the data sheet. Start by clicking in the left-most column of the first row and type the **StudentID** (here, **1**). Press tab or enter key and type **Section** (here, **1**), then, press the Tab Key or the right arrow key and type the first student's **Gender** (here, **0**). Continue to do this until the data is typed in. The data for 60 students is given in the dataset of Appendix – A.

2.4 Saving Data

When you are through with entering data in your data file, save it. Click the **File** and **Save** options in sequence. This will open a dialogue box (like all other Windows-based programs) as shown below in Fig.PASW–2.6:

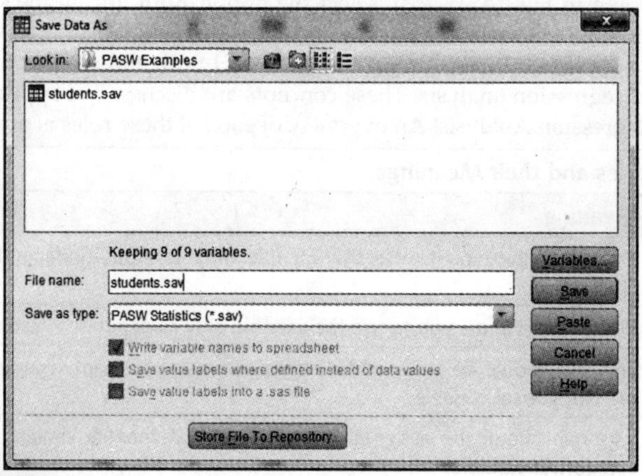

Fig.PASW–2.6

Type **Students** (or whichever name you want) in the **File name** box and click the **Save** button (Fig.PASW–2.6). Note that PASW automatically adds the **.sav** suffix to your file name. This is the PASW suffix that is used to designate data files

2.5 Opening an Existing Data File

1. Click **File**, **Open** and **Data** in sequence. This will open the dialogue box on the active screen, as shown in figure 2.7:

Note that a recently used file can be opened by clicking **File**, **Recently Used Data** and **Filename (students.sav)** in sequence. It gives a list of the 10 recently used files.

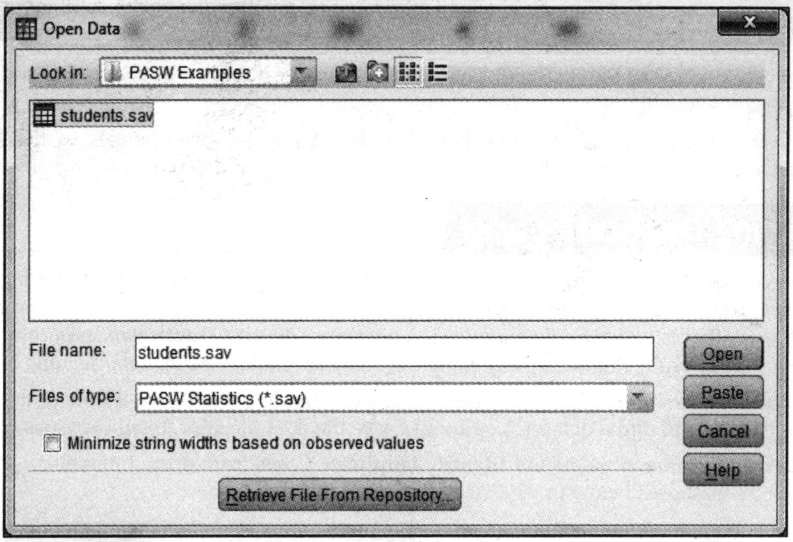

Fig.PASW-2.7

2. Select **students** (or, the name you have saved the previously created data file) from the list and click **Open** to continue further.

2.6 Inserting Variables

In the dataset **students.sav**, you have already entered the **Percentage of Marks Scored in First Year**. To update your dataset with the **Incidence of Absence**, you are required to create a variable for **Incidence of Absence (Absence)**.

If you are in the **Data View** window:

1. First click the column next to Hours of Reading (here, Percentage of Marks Scored in First Year) and then click Data.
2. Then click Insert Variable.

If you are in the **Variable View** window,

1. First click the row next to Hours of Reading (here, Percentage of Marks Scored in First Year) and then click Data.
2. Then click Insert Variable.

This will create a column prior to the column **Percentage of Marks Scored in First Year** with name **var0G01**. You can then click the **Variable View** window and change its name (to **Absence**) as well as its other attributes (The attributes and data for this newly inserted variable **HrRead** is given in Appendix – A).

Now you need to save the changes in your data file by clicking on **File** and then on **Save**.

2.7 Inserting Cases

This command inserts a blank row just above the currently selected row, where relevant data can be entered. If you are in Variable View window, click the Data View window. This option will appear in disabled mode in Variable View window.

1. First click the row number 7 and then click **Data**.
2. Then click **Insert Cases**.

The contents of row 7 will shift to row 8 and a blank row will appear on row 7. The data to be entered on row 7 is given in Appendix – A).

Note that at every stage, you should click **File** and then **Save,** to save changes to the PASW data file. Alternatively an active file can be saved by clicking on the **Save** Icon on the toolbar or by using **Ctrl+S** keys.

2.8 Identifying Duplicate Cases

In survey research when a sample size is large, often data collection and data entry is done by different people. In such situations, there is a possibility of committing error in data entry. Existence of duplicate cases in a data file is one such error that is a commonly experienced problem .**Identify Duplicate Cases** command helps us in detecting these kinds of problems. Before any statistical analysis is undertaken, data cleaning is essential.

In order to understand the utility of this command, select the first five cases from the students.sav data file, and copy and paste it at the end of the dataset. You should save the data file after doing copy-paste.

1. Click **Data** from command menu and **Identify Duplicate Cases** from drop-down menu. This will open up a dialogue box, as shown below in Fig.PASW–2.8:

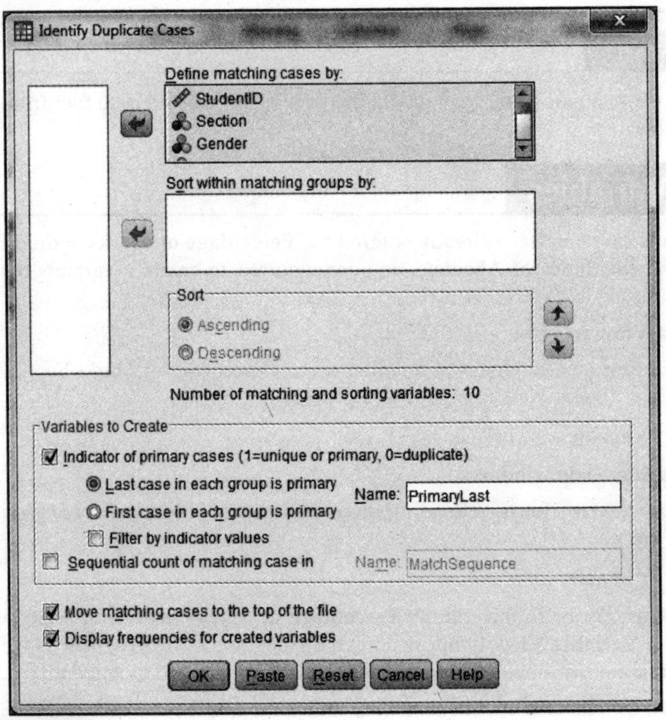

Fig.PASW–2.8

Select **all the variables** and move it to **Define Matching Cases by** list box. This means that the check for duplicates will be performed on all the variables. If values of all the variables are matching with corresponding variables of some other case in the same file, they will be identified as duplicate cases.

2. Keeping other options in the dialogue box unchanged, click **OK** button to execute the command. The output will be displayed in the output viewer window as shown below:

Frequencies

Statistics

Indicator of each last matching case as Primary

N	Valid	65
	Missing	0

Indicator of each last matching case as Primary

		Frequency	Percent	Valid Percent	Cumulative Percent
Valid	Duplicate Case	5	7.7	7.7	7.7
	Primary Case	60	92.3	92.3	100.0
	Total	65	100.0	100.0	

First, you will see the title **Frequencies** followed by two tables – **Statistics** and **Indicator of each last matching case as Primary**. **Statistics** table shows that all 65 cases were taken into consideration while finding the duplicate cases. **Indicator of each last matching case as Primary** table shows that there were 5 (which is 7.7 per cent of total cases) duplicates cases in the entire dataset of 65 cases. The cases identified as duplicate cases are placed at the top of the data file as shown below in Fig.PASW–2.9:

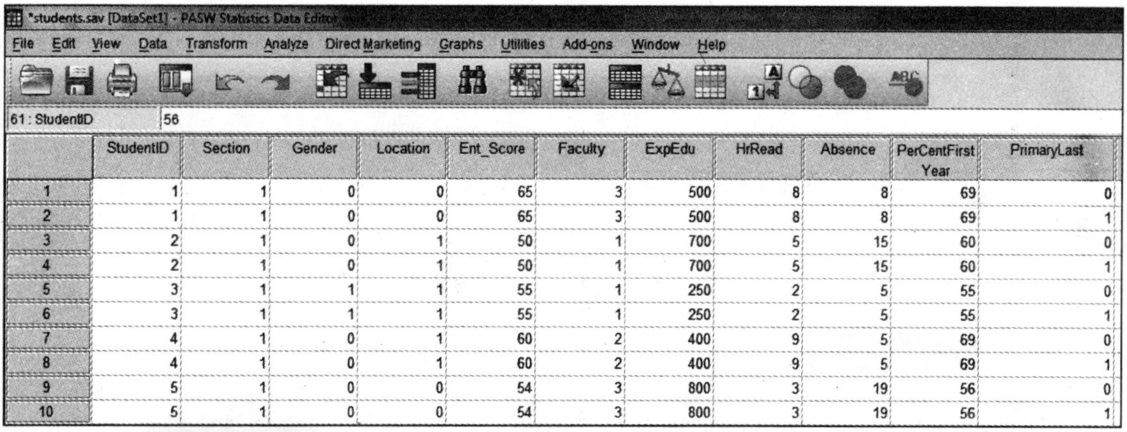

	StudentID	Section	Gender	Location	Ent_Score	Faculty	ExpEdu	HrRead	Absence	PerCentFirst Year	PrimaryLast
1	1	1	0	0	65	3	500	8	8	69	0
2	1	1	0	0	65	3	500	8	8	69	1
3	2	1	0	1	50	1	700	5	15	60	0
4	2	1	0	1	50	1	700	5	15	60	1
5	3	1	1	1	55	1	250	2	5	55	0
6	3	1	1	1	55	1	250	2	5	55	1
7	4	1	0	1	60	2	400	9	5	69	0
8	4	1	0	1	60	2	400	9	5	69	1
9	5	1	0	0	54	3	800	3	19	56	0
10	5	1	0	0	54	3	800	3	19	56	1

Fig.PASW–2.9

Fig.PASW–2.9 shows that five cases are identified as duplicate. The last column **PrimaryLast** is created on execution of **Identify Duplicate Cases** command. There are two values 0 and 1 in this **PrimaryLast** column. Since the default selection in the **Variables to Create** frame was **Last Case in each Group in Primary**, the case having value 1 in the **PrimaryLast** column is shown below the case having value 0. In the dialogue box of Fig.PASW–2.9, 1 indicates primary or unique case, and 0 indicates a duplicate entry of the same case.

As mentioned earlier, **do not save** the file. To discard all these changes, close the file without saving and reopen it.

2.9 Identifying Unusual Cases

This command is used to identify unusual behaviour of the samples selected for our analysis. For example, there could be different clusters of students with similar characteristics and there could be some students who deviate from the cluster norms to which they belong or are closer to. We can identify those students (cases) by using Identify Unusual Cases command.

1. Click Data and Identify Unusual Cases in sequence. This will bring up a dialogue box as shown below in Fig.PASW–2.10:

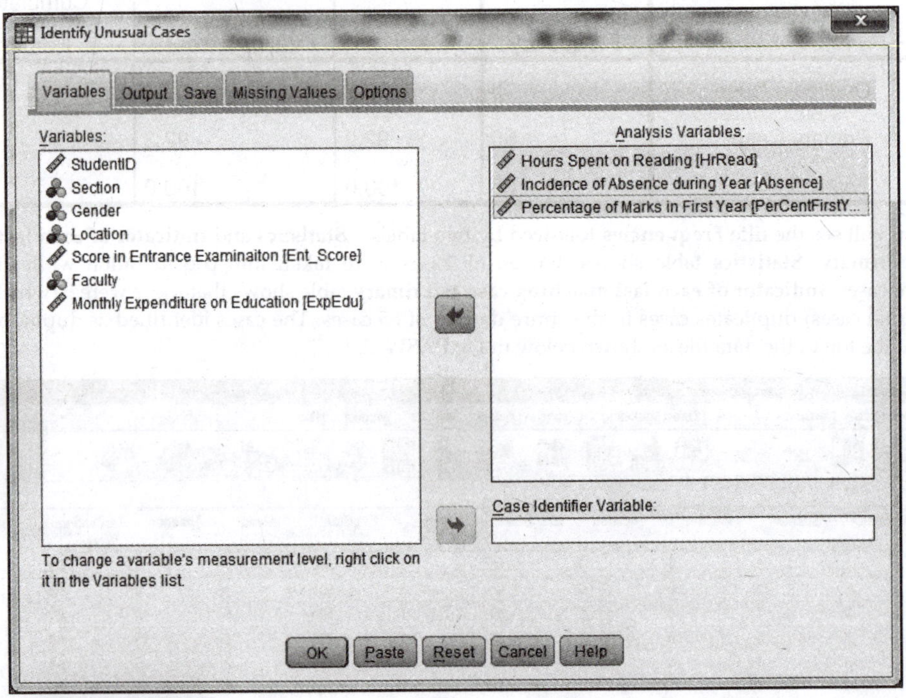

Fig.PASW–2.10

2. Since we are interested in identifying students on basis of their **Percentage of Marks Scored in First Year, Hours Spent on Reading** and **Incidence of Absence**, we select three variables and move them to the **Analysis Variables** list box.
3. Select **StudentID** and move it to the **Case Identifier Variable** text box.
4. Keeping all other options unchanged, click **OK** to execute the command. Following output is displayed in the output viewer window:

Detect Anomaly

Anomaly Case Index List

Case	StudentID	Anomaly Index
36	36	3.287
17	17	2.031

Anomaly Case Peer ID List

Case	StudentID	Peer ID	Peer Size	Peer Size Percent
36	36	1	41	68.3%
17	17	1	41	68.3%

Anomaly Case Reason List

Reason:1

Case	StudentID	Reason Variable	Variable Impact	Variable Value	Variable Norm
36	36	PerCentFirstYear	.773	89	62.85
17	17	Absence	.489	25	10.88

Detect Anomaly will be displayed as the title of the output. Under the main title **Detect Anomaly**, three tables will be displayed – **Anomaly Case Index List**, **Anomaly Case Peer ID List** and **Anomaly Case Reason List**. **Anomaly Case Index List** table gives details about case number, case identifier variable (in our example **StudentID**) and anomaly index.

Anomaly index is calculated by taking the ratio of Group Deviation Index (GDI) of the case, to GDI of the cluster to which the case belongs. Group Deviation Index is the variance of value of the case from, the mean value of observations of that variable belonging to the cluster under consideration. The distance from case value to the group mean for the given cluster, is calculated using log-likelihood method. When the data is measured on a continuous scale and follows a normal distribution, Euclidian distance could be a reasonably good measure for finding the distances. However, when the data measured on continuous scale is not normally distributed or, the variable is measured on categorical scale, Euclidian distances would not be an accurate measure, distance should be calculated using log-likelihood method. When distance is to be calculated uses more than one variable, log-likelihood provides more reliable and accurate estimates than Euclidian distances. Log-likelihood method is based on probability associated with deviation of case from its cluster's mean value. A cluster is a group of cases sharing similar characteristics and is identified using two-step cluster algorithm.

It can be seen that case numbers 36 and 17 differ from the peer groups. There are two peer groups. In our example, case number and **StudentID** are identical. Anomaly Index greater than 2 indicates that the cases identified as unusual cases are outliers. Thus both cases – 36 and 17 are unusual or outliers.

Anomaly Case Peer ID List table gives the anomalous cases, **StudentIDs**, peer group ID, size of peer group and percentage size of peer group in the entire sample. In our example, there are two peer groups, one with 41 cases (68.3 per cent of total cases) and second with 19 (31.7 per cent) cases.

Anomaly Case Reason List table presents the reason for anomaly, impact of that variable, the value of that variable and variable norm as per the cluster behaviour. Here, **Percentage of Marks Scored in First Year** is the reason for anomaly for case no. 36, **Incidence of Absence** is the reason for anomaly for case no. 17.

Take the reciprocal of total number of variables used for anomaly detection (in our example 3). This works out to 1/3 = 0.33. If the variable impact value is greater than the reciprocal of number of variables, the impact of this variable is said to be large. The Variable Impact for both – Percentage of Marks Scored in First Year and that of **Incidence of Absence** is greater than 0.33, which indicates that the impact of these two variables is large. Fourth column shows the value of that variable for the given case. The value of variable – **Percentage of Marks Scored in First Year** for case no. 36 is 89 and that for Incidence of Absence for case no. 17 is 25. Variable Norm is the average value of that variable for the cluster in which the anomalous cases lie. The mean score of **Percentage of Marks Scored in First Year** for peer group 1 is 62.85 and that for **Incidence of Absence** for peer group 1 is 10.88. This shows that both these cases are outliers for the respective variables.

Outliers can also be identified using the Explore Option of Descriptive Statistics in Analyze menu. This is discussed in detail in *Chapter–4: Describing Data Numerically.*

2.10 Sorting Cases

The cases are sorted in ascending or descending order as specified.

1. Click **Data** and then on **Sort Cases.** The dialogue box will appear as shown below in Fig.PASW–2.11:

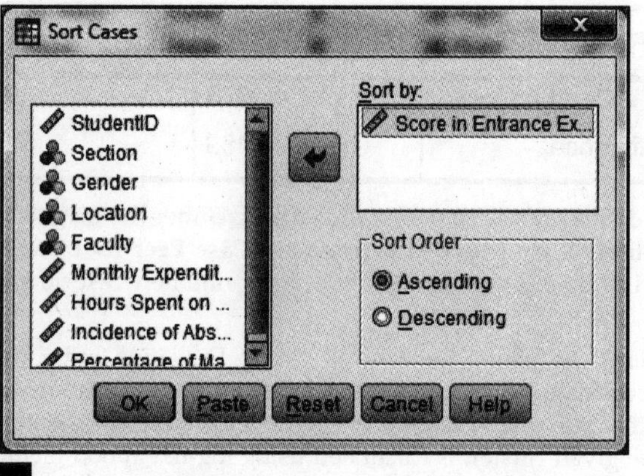

Fig.PASW–2.11

2. Next, select the variable Score in Entrance Examination and move it to the Sort by list.
3. Select the Ascending radio button in the Sort Order frame and click OK.

This will sort the cases in the file in ascending order of graduation marks. Similarly, to sort the cases in descending order, select **Descending** radio button in the Sort Order frame.

2.11 Merging a File

In researches involving large datasets, usually the task of data entry is carried out by two or more data entry operators. The task of data entry could be allocated on the basis of number of questionnaires for each operator. However, in case of long questionnaires, organized in two or more modules, it is likely that one module is allocated to each data entry operator. If all completed questionnaires are divided among data entry operators, we would have to merge the files containing data entered by different operators. Similarly, if modules are divided among data entry operators, the modules will have to be merged to get the full dataset. This section discusses merging of files for both these situations.

2.11.1 Add Cases

This option for merging a file is used when different operators are given different sets of full questionnaires for data entry. As discussed earlier, each respondent is a case. Thus, we will have to add cases to the master file in order to get the complete dataset. For adding cases,

1. Ensure that your active dataset is **students.sav**. Click **Data**, **Merge Files** and **Add Cases** in sequence. A dialogue box will appear as shown in Fig.PASW–2.12:

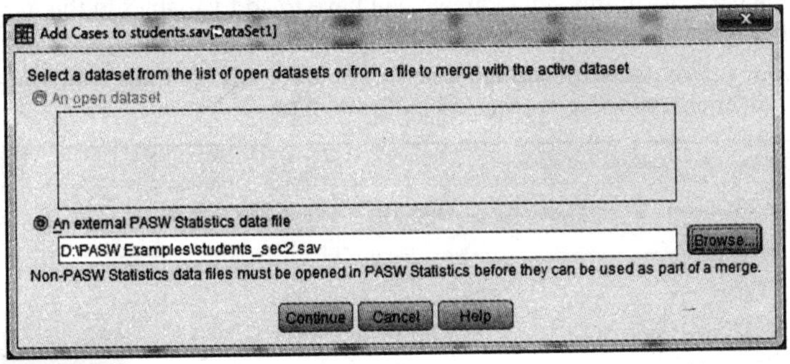

Fig.PASW–2.12

2. The default selection is **An external PASW Statistics data file**. Click Browse and select the file (here, **students_sec2.sav**; the details are given in Appendix – A) from which you want to add the cases. (Ensure that when you execute this command, **students_sec2.sav** is not open).
3. Click the **Continue** button (Fig.PASW–2.12). A dialogue box as shown below in Fig.PASW–2.13 will appear on the screen:

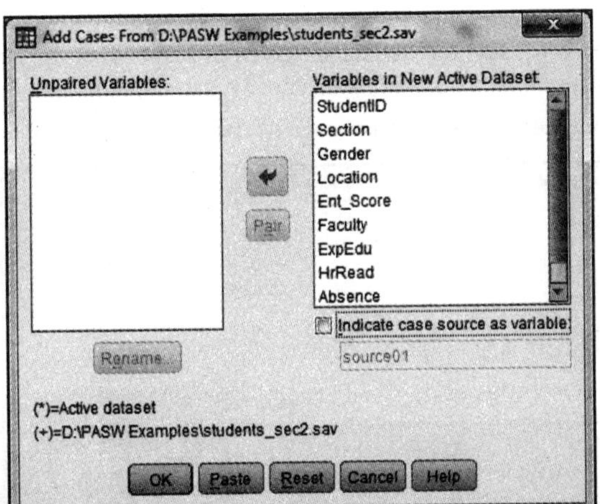

Fig.PASW–2.13

4. Variables in the **New Active Dataset** list box contain the list of variables that are present in the **students.sav** as well as in the **new dataset (students_sec2.sav)**. If there are any variables in the **students_sec2.sav** which are not in **students.sav**, those variables will appear in **Unpaired variables** list box.
5. Click the **OK** button to execute the command (Fig.PASW–2.13).

For a beginner, it is desirable that the number of variables and its sequence are identical in the active file and the file to be merged.

See in students.sav file, 60 new cases are added to the existing dataset.

2.11.2 For Adding Variables

When different data entry operators enter data of different modules of the questionnaire, all of them enter data for the same set of respondents (cases) but, for different questions. Each question of the questionnaire can be considered to be one variable. In this situation, we will have to add variables to the master file for getting the complete dataset. For adding Variables,

1. Ensure that your active dataset is **students.sav**. Click **Data**, **Merge Files** and **Add Cases** in sequence. A dialogue box will appear as shown below in Fig.PASW–2.14:

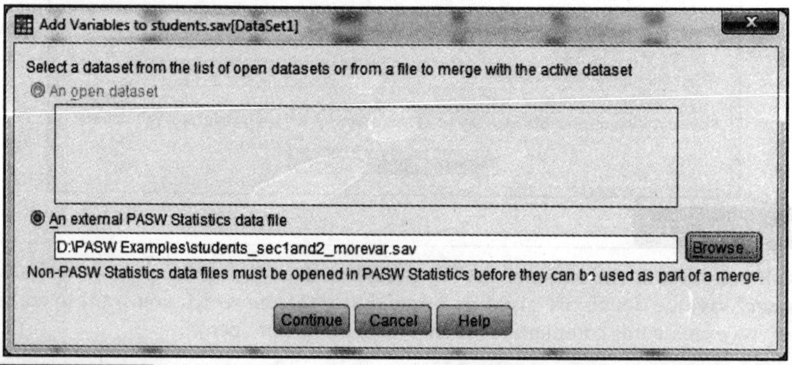

Fig.PASW–2.14

2. The default selection is **An external PASW Statistics data file**. Click Browse and select the file (here, **students_sec1and2 more var.sav**; the details are given in Appendix – A) from which you want to add the variables. (Ensure that students_sec1and2_morevar.sav is not open).
3. Click **Continue**. A dialogue box will appear as shown below in Fig.PASW–2.15:

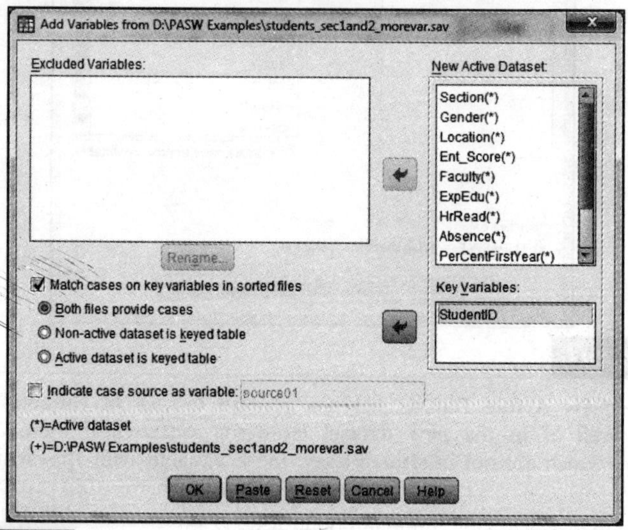

Fig.PASW–2.15

4. The list of variables that will appear in the new dataset after merging files is shown in **New Active Dataset** list box.
5. **StudentID** will appear in the list of **Excluded Variables**. This is because **StudentID** is common in both the files.
6. Select **Match cases on key variables in sorted files**.
7. Select **StudentID** and move it into **Key Variables** list box.
8. Click **OK** to execute the command.

The students.sav file will now have three more variables – Percentage of Marks Scored in Second Test, Beginning Salary and Parents' Income.

2.12 Data Aggregation

For your research, you might have collected data on individual incomes of family members but, collecting information on income of individual members might give a better idea about family incomes. Here, you will have to sum the income of individual family members to get the family income. Similarly, you are interested in knowing the highest level of education in the families. Here, you would ask the level of education for each family member and then select the highest level of education. Adding individual incomes to get family income or selecting the highest level of education is possible in PASW, using aggregate command. This command performs arithmetic or statistical operations on similar categories of respondents. Functions like sum, maximum, mean etc. can be computed for cases or respondents with similar attributes. The procedure for aggregate command is as under:

1. Click **Data** and then **Aggregate**. This will open a dialogue box as shown below in Fig.PASW–2.16:

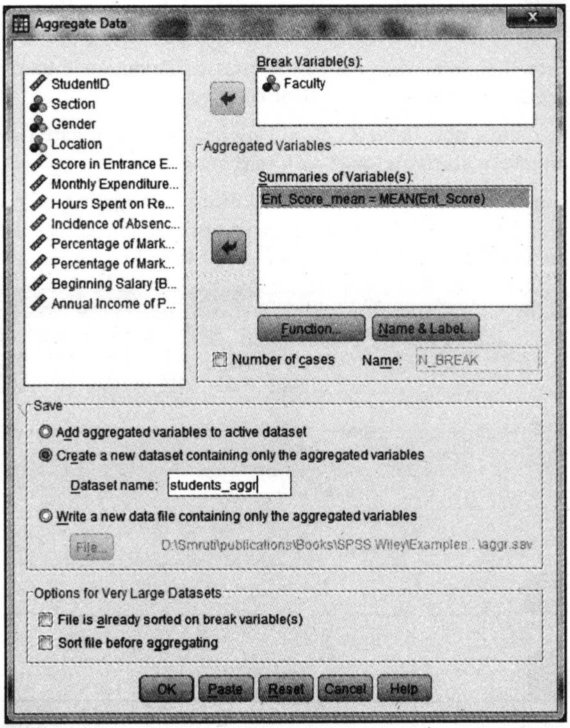

Fig.PASW–2.16

2. In **Break Variables**, specify the level variable (here, **Faculty**) on which aggregation is to be performed.
3. Select **Score in Entrance Examination** and move it to the **Summaries of Variables** list box. The default operation is **Mean**. You may change the aggregation command by clicking on **Function** button. Before doing this, once more select **Score in Entrance Examination** and move it to the **Summaries of Variables** list box.
4. Now click Function button. This will open a dialogue box as shown below in Fig.PASW–2.17:

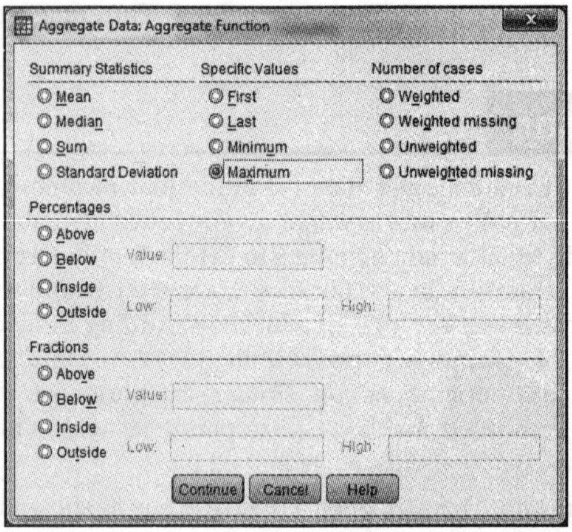

Fig.PASW–2.17

5. You may select the function (for example, **Maximum**) that you want to perform on the variable (here, **Score in Entrance Examination**) and click **Continue**.
6. In **Save** frame, select **Create a new dataset containing only the aggregated variables** and give name to the dataset. We call that dataset – **students_aggr,** as typed in text box.
7. In **Options for very large datasets**, select **Sort file before aggregating** (If your file is already sorted, you may select that option) and click **OK**. A new file will open on execution of the aggregate command. The relevant portion of the new file is shown below in Fig.PASW–2.18:

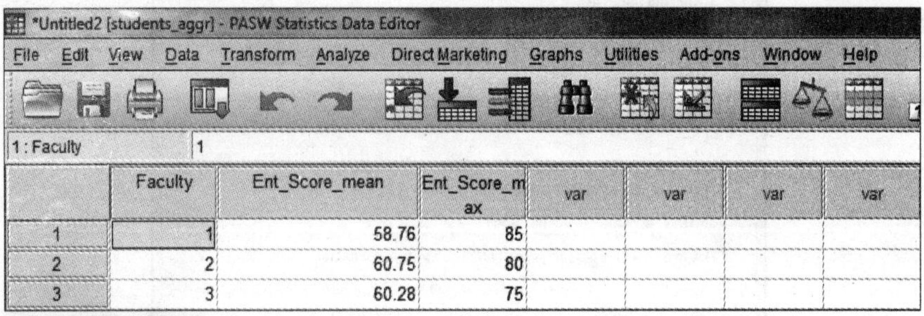

Fig.PASW–2.18

2.13 Splitting File

In Socioeconomic survey, data are collected on several characteristics of households and are grouped by gender, geographical location, income level, religion and such grouping variables. Split file command is useful for performing same statistical analysis on separate groups based on the values of one or more grouping variables.

Split File command has two options – **Compare groups** and **Organize output by groups** (Fig.PASW–2.19). You can choose the options as per requirement of presenting the output. We' ve chosen **Compare groups** option for illustration. For example, if you select **Gender** as grouping variable, you can find descriptive statistics like mean, mode, median, standard deviation separately for **Males** and **Females**. For splitting the file,

1. Click **Data** from the command menu and then **Split File** to get the dialogue box as shown below in Fig.PASW–2.19:

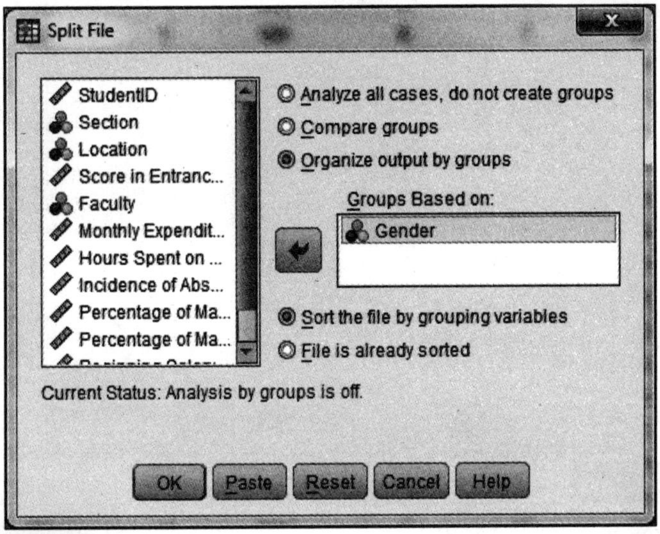

Fig.PASW–2.19

2. Select **Organize output by groups** and move **Gender** from the variable list box to the **Groups Based on** list box, then click **OK**.

The file will be sorted on the basis of Gender value in ascending order. To find the mean, maximum value, minimum value and standard deviation for age, income or any other variable, separately for males and females, one single command of descriptive statistics (described in detail in *Chapter – 4: Describing Data Numerically*) can be used to compute these statistical measures. Splitting the file eliminates the need for executing the same procedure separately for Males and Females. This command saves time and is convenient when same statistical operations are to be performed on different categories of respondents, in the same dataset.

Note

*While you execute this command, make sure that the option – **Sort the file by grouping variables** is selected. If you have already sorted the file by grouping variable, you may select – **File is already sorted**.*

2.14 Selecting Cases

Select Cases offers several methods for selecting a sub-group of cases from the data file based on criteria that includes variables, arithmetic or logical expressions. Random sample of cases can also be selected. For example, to randomly select a small sample from the Census data or a sub-sample from the data of National Sample Organization (NSSO), this command is useful. In this chapter, we will restrict our discussion to **If conditions.** For performing any statistical procedure on students with a score of 55 or more in entrance examination, it can be done with the help of Select Cases command. The procedure for Select Cases is described below:

1. Click **Data** and **Select Cases** in sequence. This will bring up a dialogue box as shown below in Fig.PASW–2.20:

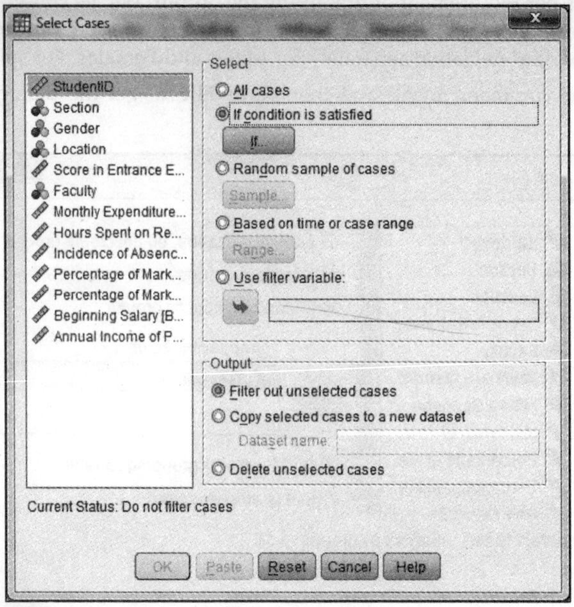

Fig.PASW–2.20

2. Click **If condition is satisfied** and **If** sequentially. This will open the dialogue box as shown below in Fig.PASW–2.21:

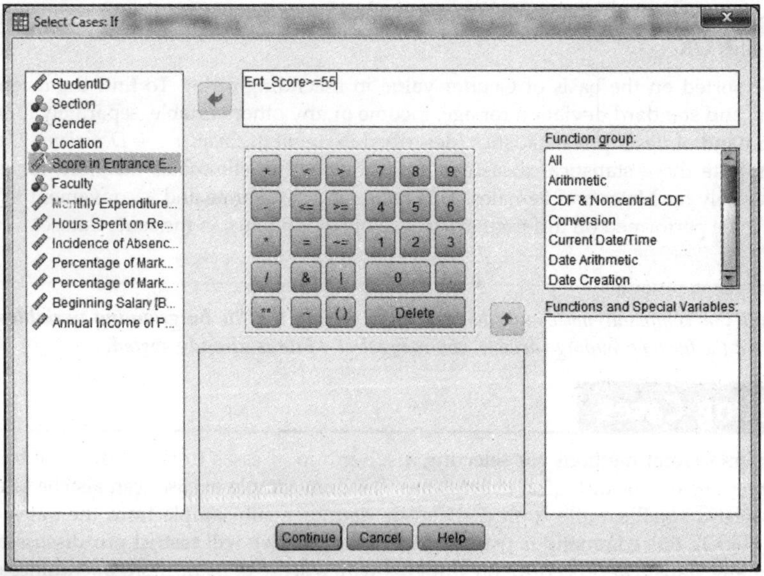

Fig.PASW–2.21

3. Then click **Score in Entrance Examination** and take it to the text area.
4. Click >= and then type **55**.
5. Next, click **Continue** to go to the previous dialogue box.
6. Below, in the frame of **Output**, click **Filter out unselected cases.**
7. Click **OK** to execute the command.

This will deselect all the cases where the graduation percentage is less than 55. Then any statistical test can be performed on these selected cases. This will look like the one shown below in Fig.PASW–2.22:

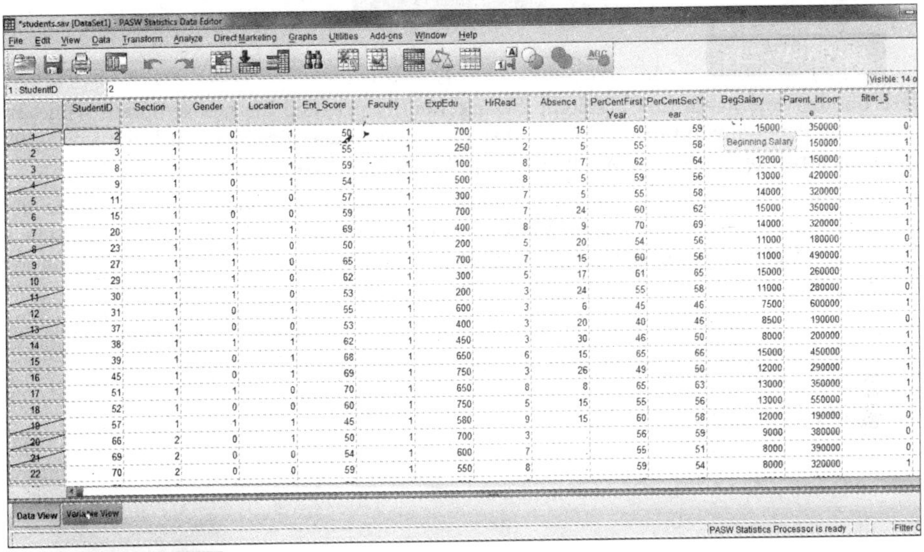

	StudentID	Section	Gender	Location	Ent_Score	Faculty	ExpEdu	HrRead	Absence	PerCentFirstYear	PerCentSecYear	BegSalary	Parent_Income	filter_$
1	2	1	0	1	50	1	700	5	15	60	59	15000	350000	0
2	3	1	1	1	55	1	250	2	5	55	58	Beginning Salary	150000	1
3	8	1	1	1	59	1	100	8	7	62	64	12000	150000	1
4	9	1	0	1	54	1	500	8	5	59	56	13000	420000	0
5	11	1	1	0	57	1	300	7	5	55	58	14000	320000	1
6	15	1	0	0	59	1	700	7	24	60	62	15000	350000	1
7	20	1	1	1	69	1	400	8	9	70	69	14000	320000	1
8	23	1	1	0	50	1	200	5	20	54	56	11000	180000	0
9	27	1	1	0	65	1	700	7	15	60	56	11000	490000	1
10	29	1	1	0	62	1	300	5	17	61	65	15000	260000	1
11	30	1	1	0	53	1	200	3	24	55	58	11000	280000	0
12	31	1	0	1	55	1	600	3	6	45	46	7500	600000	1
13	37	1	0	0	53	1	400	3	20	40	46	8500	190000	0
14	38	1	1	1	62	1	450	3	30	46	50	8000	200000	1
15	39	1	0	1	68	1	650	6	15	65	66	15000	450000	1
16	45	1	0	1	69	1	750	3	26	49	50	12000	290000	1
17	51	1	1	0	70	1	650	8	8	65	63	13000	350000	1
18	52	1	0	0	60	1	750	5	15	55	56	13000	550000	1
19	57	1	1	1	45	1	580	9	15	60	58	12000	190000	0
20	66	2	0	1	50	1	700	3		56	59	9000	380000	0
21	69	2	0	0	54	1	600	7		55	51	8000	390000	0
22	70	2	0	0	59	1	550	8		59	54	8000	320000	1

Fig.PASW–2.22

If you want to revert back:

1. Click Data and then on Select Cases.
2. Next, click All Cases and then on OK.

The deselection marks will disappear.

2.15 Listing Cases

Listing of Cases is useful as part of data cleaning and understanding the structure of data. Visual inspection of data helps in getting a feel of the data and detects any anomalies. It also helps in discerning patterns. The procedure for Listing Cases is not menu-driven and is available only through command syntax. The syntax for generating a list of cases should be written in the Syntax Editor window. The procedure for creating a Syntax File, writing the syntax and executing the syntax is described as under:

1. Click **File, New** and **Syntax** in sequence.
2. Then type the command as shown below in the Fig.PASW–2.23:

Note

The variable names shown in lower case below instruct PASW, which variables to list in the output. You can type in the command ALL in place of variables names, which will produce a listing of all the variables in the file. The subcommand /CASES FROM 1 TO 10, is an instruction to PASW to print only the first ten cases. If this instruction is omitted, all cases would be listed in the output.

Fig.PASW-2.23

3. To execute this command, first highlight the selection by pressing the mouse button while dragging the arrow across the command or commands that you want to execute. Next, click the icon with the black, right-facing arrow on it. Or, you can choose a selection from the **Run** menu.

Executing the command will print the list of variables: **StudentID**, **Gender** and **Ent_Score** in the above example, to the Output Viewer. The **Output Viewer** is the third window with which you should be familiar; all output would be displayed here. The output generated from running the **List** command from syntax file is shown below:

List

StudentID	Gender	Ent_Score
1	0	65
2	0	50
3	1	55
4	0	60
5	0	54
6	0	56
7	0	68
8	1	59
9	0	54
10	0	59

Number of cases read: 10   Number of cases listed: 10

Summary

In this chapter we learnt:

- Creating Data file.
- Defining Variables.
- Entering Data.
- Saving a data file.
- Opening an existing data file.
- Inserting Variables.

Chapter 3

Data Transformation

In this Chapter:

A researcher is often required to alter or modify dataset in some way. In case of both primary and secondary data, a researcher is required to modify datasets or create new variables by modifying existing data. Modification of variables is largely in form of mathematical operations on the existing variable, converting ungrouped data into grouped data or, assigning ranks to values. Predictive Analytic Software (PASW) offers advanced facilities for performing these operations. For example, you might have the values of monthly salary of some students and are interested in finding their annual salaries; or you could be interested in knowing the percentage of parents' income that is spent on education. In such situations data transformation commands can be undertaken by selecting appropriate options from, the Transform option of the command menu. In this chapter we shall study the uses of data transformation command and its PASW procedure.

3.1 Computing a New Variable

Compute Variable command is used to create a new variable by doing mathematical or statistical operations on the existing variable. We try to compute annual salary of the students from their monthly salaries that are entered in the students.sav file. We will have to multiply monthly salary by 12 in order to get the annual salary. Let us see how this is done in PASW:

1. Open students.sav.
2. Click Transform as shown in Fig.PASW–3.1:

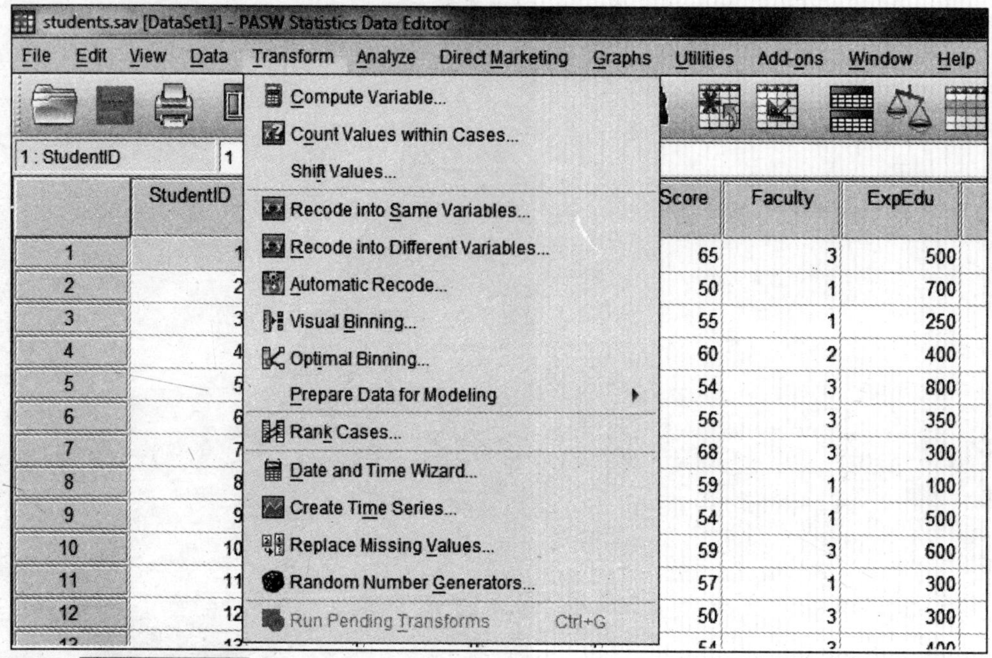

Fig.PASW–3.1

Note

We shall work with this menu throughout this chapter.

3. Now click on **Compute** from the **Transform** sub-menu. This brings up a dialogue box as shown in Fig.PASW–3.2:

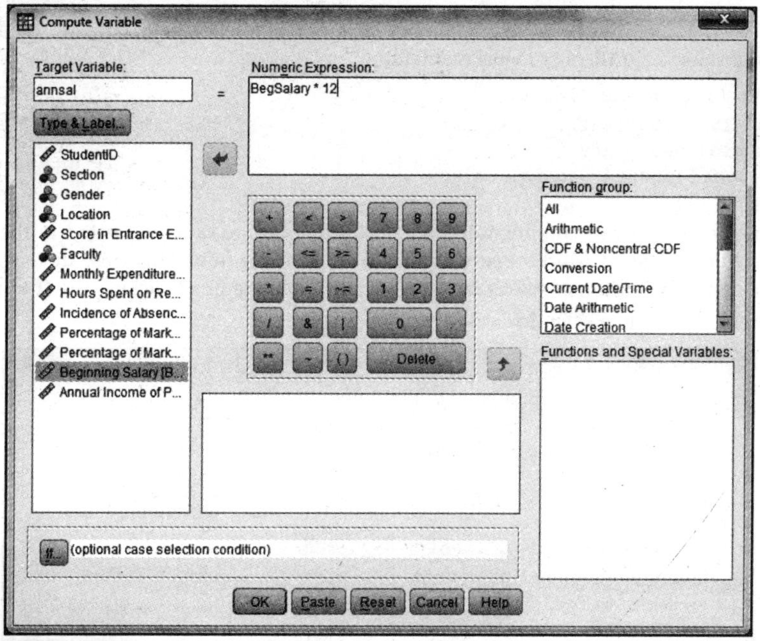

Fig.PASW–3.2

4. Type annsal in the Target Variable text box.
5. Select Beginning Salary from the list box of variables and move it into the Numeric Expression text box. Click on multiply (* sign) on the key pad and type 12.
6. Click Type & Label button and you see the dialogue box as shown in Fig.PASW–3.3.

   This is used to give Label (**Annual Salary**) to the new variable and specify the characteristics of the new target variable – **annsal**.

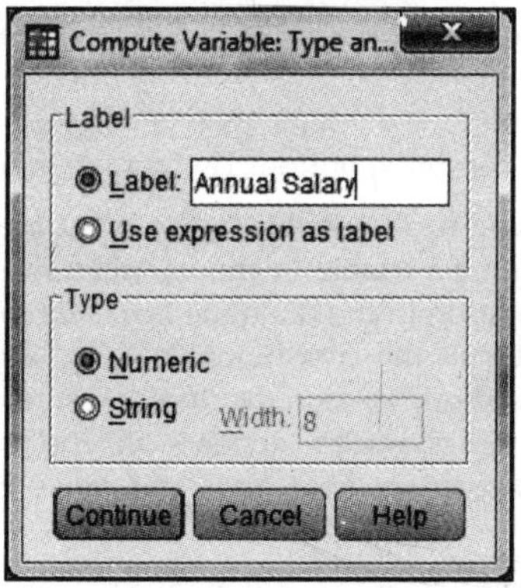

Fig.PASW–3.3

7. Click the **Continue** button to go back to the **Compute Variable** dialogue box. Now, click **OK** button to execute the command.

The example shown above demonstrates the computation of a new variable, **annsal (Annual Salary)** which appears in the rightmost column of the working dataset.

Command Syntax for Compute Variable

```
DATASET ACTIVATE DataSet1.
COMPUTE annsal=BegSalary * 12.
VARIABLE LABELS annsal 'Annual Salary'.
EXECUTE.
```

Variables can also be computed conditionally. For instance, you are only interested in the **Annual Salary** of students whose **Percentage of Marks Scored in Second Year** are more than **65**, the said condition can be specified by clicking on **If** button of the Compute Variable Dialogue Box. Clicking the **If** button will produce a dialogue box as shown in Fig.PASW–3.4:

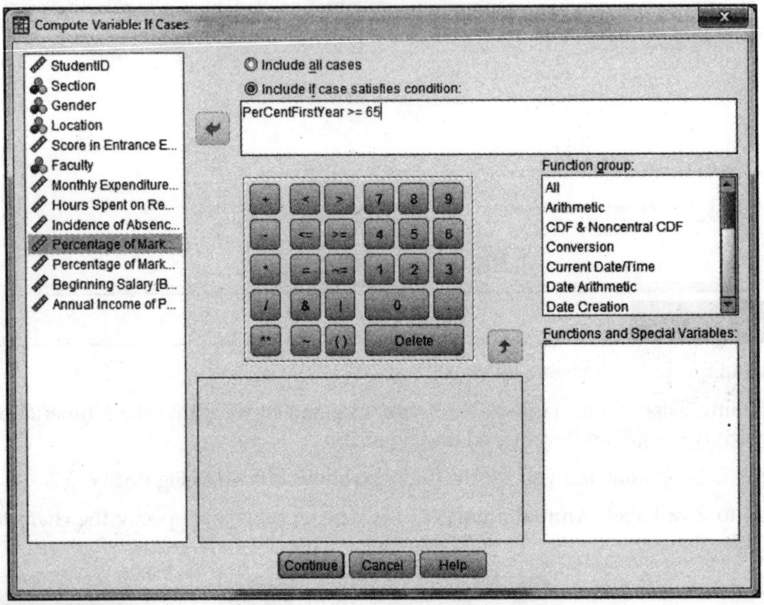

Fig.PASW–3.4

8. Click the Include if case satisfies condition button. The gray region of the dialogue box is activated.
9. Specify the condition to compute a fresh variable in the input box, which is situated at the upper right of the dialogue box. Click, either on a variable in the variable list, which is located on the left side of the dialogue box, or type in the condition in the dialogue box. Moreover, the buttons on the numeric pad can be used. You can enter variables in the conditional box by selecting and clicking on the name of the variable and clicking the arrow button between the two boxes. As soon as the buttons on the bottom left of the dialogue box is clicked, the character appears in the input box. For our example, click the variable **Percentage of Marks Scored in First Year** and move it to the condition text box as shown in Fig.PASW–3.4.
10. Click the **Continue** button to return to previous dialogue box and then click the **OK** button to execute the command.

Command Syntax for Conditional Compute

```
IF (PerCentFirstYear >= 65) annsal=BegSalary * 12.
VARIABLE LABELS  annsal 'Annual Salary'.
EXECUTE.
```

3.2 Recoding Variables

Recoding Variables command is used to change the earlier assigned codes to create new categories or collapse existing categories. Once the data file is created using survey data or secondary data, in future you may need to recode some of your data; you may want to convert the variable measured in ratio (continuous) scale to a variable measured in nominal or ordinal (discrete) scale. In light of some preliminary data analysis, you need to change the codes of existing variable or create new categories to allow you to undertake an additional analysis. We could do this manually, but it would be time consuming and errors might be committed if the data set is large. PASW provides the **Recode** command for this purpose. For example, in this dataset, if you want to classify the students on the basis of their marks scored in second year, this command will be useful. We create five classes (Distinction, First, Second, Third and Fail) based on the **Percentage of Marks Scored in Second Year** by these students.

Recode submenu of **Transform** menu (Fig.PASW–3.1) offers two options:

1. Into Same Variables, and
2. Into Different Variables.

When you choose **Into Same Variables** option, the original values of the variable are replaced with the new recoded values .It is advisable to use **Into Different Variables** option, because you may change your mind at a later date. If you recode it into different variables, you will still have the original values.

The procedure for Recoding Variables is described as under:

1. Click **Transform, Recode** and **Recode into Different Variables.** A dialogue box as shown in Fig.PASW–3.5 will appear on the screen.

   The procedure for Recoding Variables is described as under.

2. Click **Transform, Recode** and **Recode into Different Variables**. A dialogue box as shown in Fig.PASW–3.5 will appear on the screen:

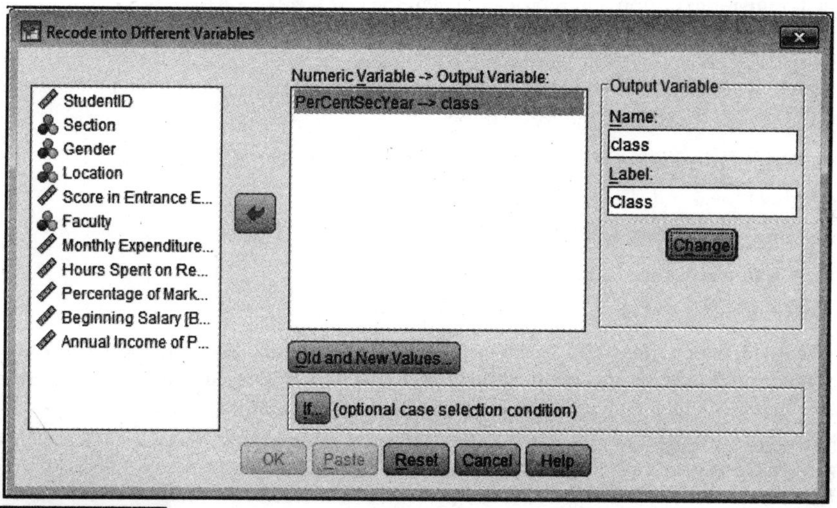

Fig.PASW–3.5

3. Click Percentage of Marks Scored in Second Year and take it to the Numeric Variable -> Output Variable text area.

4. Give the name of new variable class in the Name and Class in its Label. The Numeric Variable -> Output Variable text area displays PerSecYear -> class.

5. Click the Change button.

6. Click the **Old and New Values** button. A dialogue box as shown in Fig.PASW–3.6 will appear on the screen".

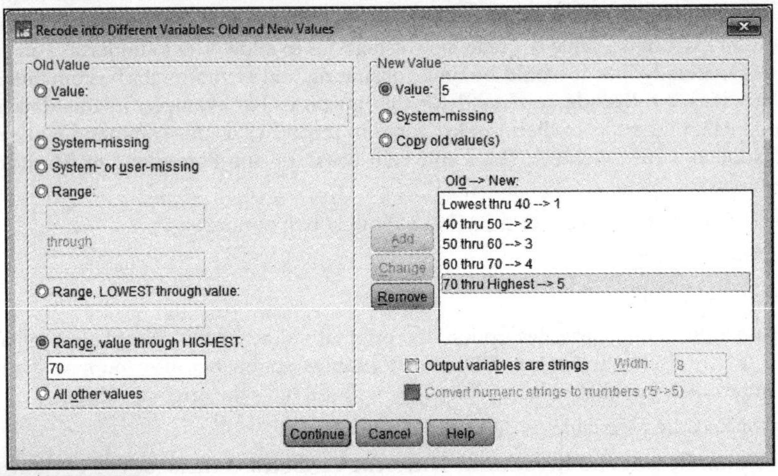

Fig.PASW–3.6

7. Click the **Range, Lowest through value** radio button and type 40 in the text box.
8. In **New Value** type **1** and click on **Add** button.
9. Click the **Range** radio button and type **40 and 50**in the text boxes.
10. In **New Value** type **2** and click the **Add** button.
11. Click the **Range** radio button and type **50 and 60** in the text boxes.
12. In **New Value** type **3** and click the **Add** button.
13. Click the **Range** radio button and type **60 and 70**in the text boxes.
14. In **New Value** type **4** and click the **Add** button.
15. Click the **Range, Value through Highest** radio button.
16. In the **New Value** box, type **5** and Click the **Add** button.
17. Click **Continue** and then **OK** to execute the command.

A new variable with name **class** will be created in the last column. You can then go to the Variable View window and then specify the groups by assigning value labels (as discussed in 2.2) for future reference.

Command Syntax for Recoding into Different Variable

```
DATASET ACTIVATE DataSet1.
RECODE PerCentSecYear (Lowest thru 40=1) (40 thru 50=2) (50 thru 60=3) (60 thru 70=4) (70
  thru Highest=5) INTO class.
VARIABLE LABELS  class 'Class'.
EXECUTE.
```

Values can also be recoded conditionally. The process for recoding values on the basis of a condition is essentially identical to the process for conditionally computing new variables discussed in the section 3.1. When you click on the **If** button in the main **Recode** dialogue box (Fig.PASW 3.5), a dialogue box as shown in Fig.PASW–3.7 will appear:

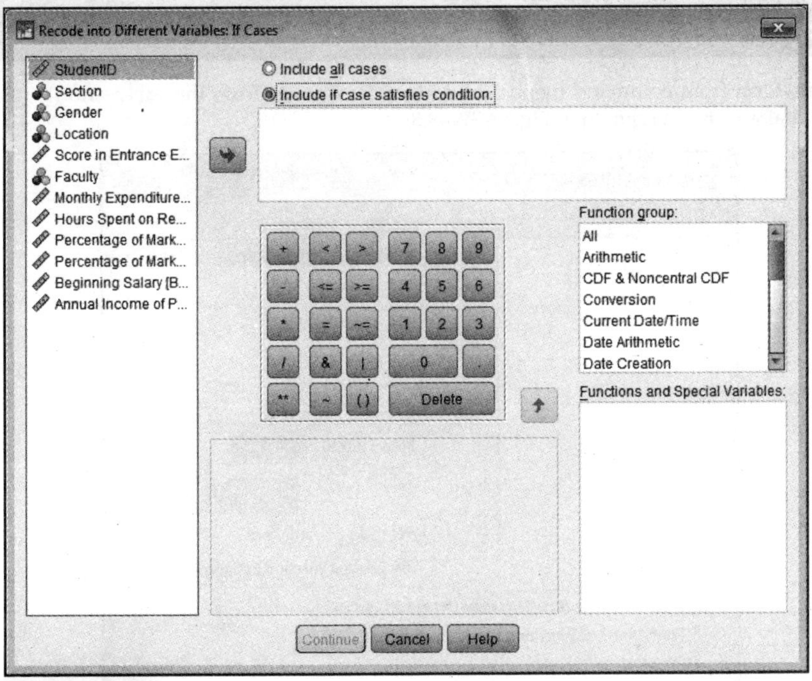

Fig.PASW–3.7

You can specify the conditions and then follow the procedure for recode.

3.3 Automatic Recode

Automatic Recode is used to convert string variables to categorical numeric variables. For example you have entered Females and Males as **F** and **M** respectively. **Automatic Recode** will convert **F** to **1** and **M** to **2**.

Open a new dataset.

Note

Remember to close the students.sav dataset .PASW allows you to keep more than one datasets open at a time but as a novice user, keep only one dataset open, in order to avoid confusions.

Create a variable – **Gender**. In the Variable View Window, select **String** in **Type** Column. Go back to the Data View Window and enter the data given in table 3.1 in the **Gender** column:

Table 3.1: Data for Automatic Recode

Case No.	Gender	Case No.	Gender	Case No.	Gender	Case No.	Gender
1	M	6	M	11	M	16	M
2	F	7	M	12	F	17	M
3	F	8	F	13	M	18	M
4	M	9	F	14	F	19	F
5	M	10	F	15	F	20	M

The procedure for Automatic Recode is as follows:

1. Click **Transform** from command menu and **Automatic Recode** from the sub-menu (Fig.PASW–3.1). You will get a dialogue box as shown in Fig.PASW–3.8:

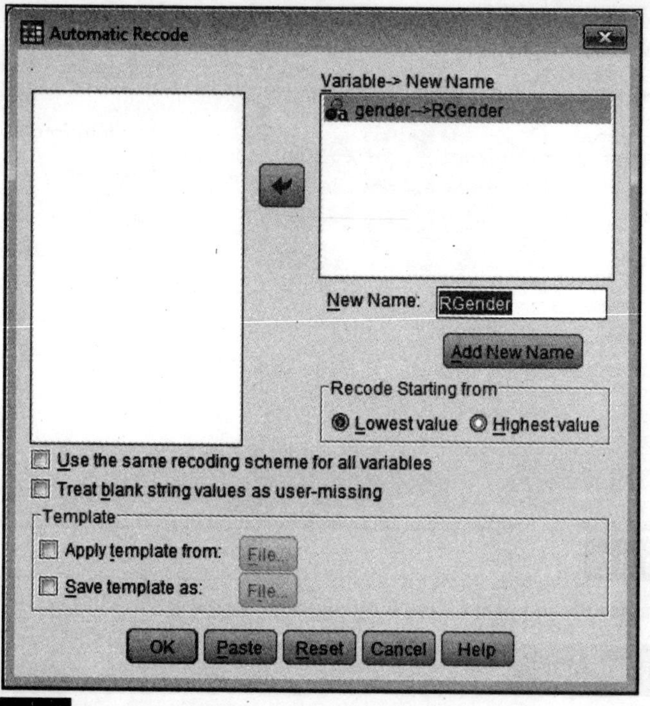

Fig.PASW–3.8

2. Select **Gender** and move it into the **Variable->New Name** box.
3. Type **RGender** in **New Name** box and click the **Add New Name** button.
4. Click **OK** to execute command.

A new variable – **RGender** will be created in the last column of the dataset.

Command Syntax for Automatic Recode

```
DATASET ACTIVATE DataSet2.
AUTORECODE VARIABLES=gender
  /INTO RGender
  /PRINT.
```

3.4 Visual Binning

Visual binning is used to convert ungrouped data into grouped data. Unlike **Recode** command (discussed in 3.2), you cannot collapse categories using **Visual Binning** command. For example, students can be categorised into five classes, with the help of **Visual Binning** command, on basis of the same variable – **Percentage of Marks Scored in Second Year**. The procedure for Visual Binning is discussed as under:

1. Click on **Transform** and **Visual Binning** in Sequence. A dialogue box as shown in Fig.PASW–3.9 will appear on the screen:

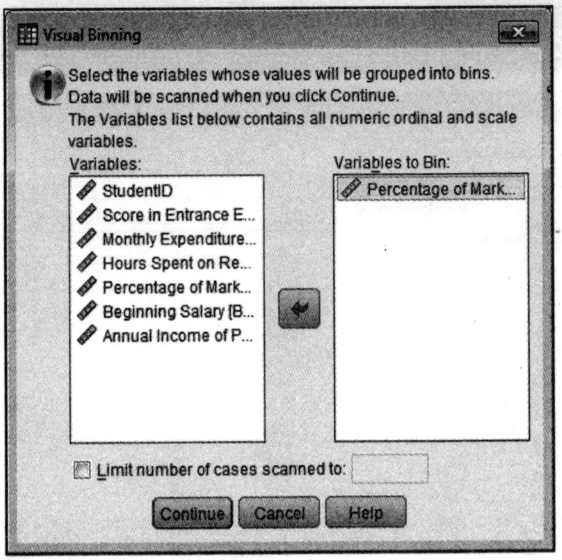

Fig.PASW–3.9

2. Select Percentage of Marks Scored in Second Year and move it to the Variables to Bin box.
3. Click the Continue button to get the dialogue box shown in Fig.PASW–3.10:

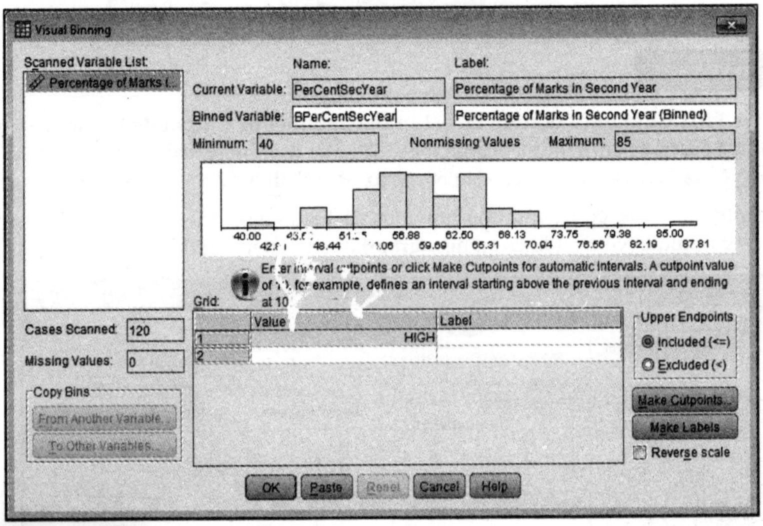

Fig.PASW–3.10

4. Click Percentage of Marks Scored in Second Year to activate the dialogue box.
5. Type BPerCentSecYear in the Binned Variable text box.
6. Click the Make Cutpoints button to specify the class intervals. A dialogue box as shown in Fig.PASW–3.11 will appear on the screen:

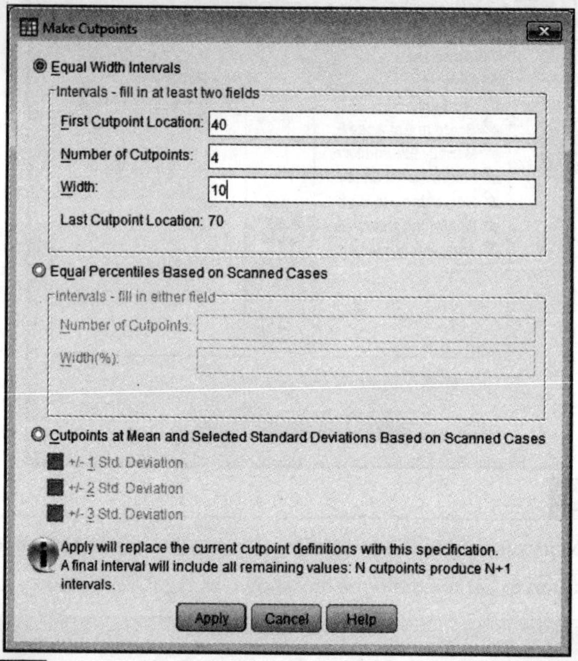

Fig.PASW–3.11

7. Type **40** in the **First Cutpoint Location** box, **4** in the **Number of Cutpoints box** and **10** in **Width** box. The **Last Cutpoint Location** will automatically show **70** (We are interested in making five groups – ranging from less than 40 as first group, 40-50, 50 to 60, 60 to 70 and above 70).
8. Click the **Apply** button to go back to the previous dialogue box. The histogram in the previous dialogue box will show cutpoints (vertical lines on histogram) as shown in Fig.PASW–3.12:

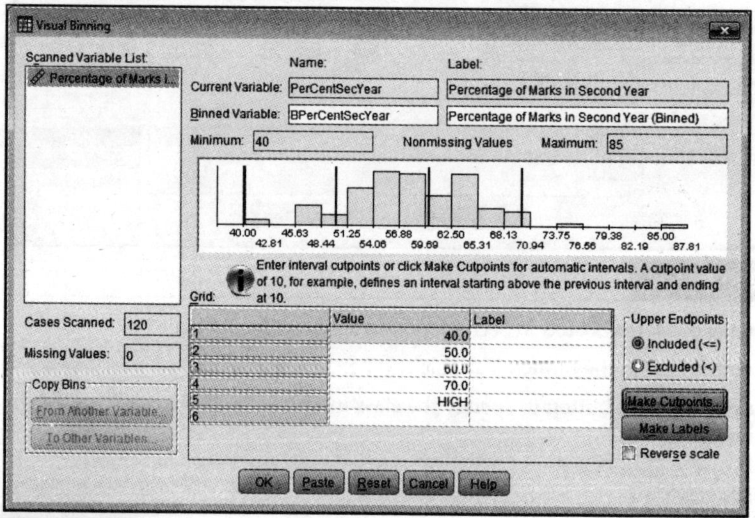

Fig.PASW–3.12

9. Click the **OK** button. A dialogue box with a warning as shown in Fig.PASW–3.13 will appear on the screen:

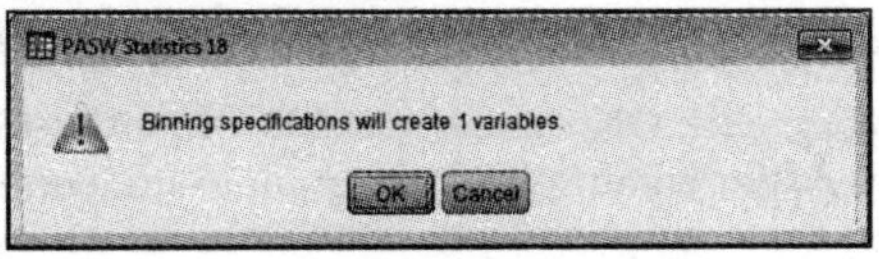

Fig.PASW–3.13

10. Click the **OK** button of Warning Dialogue Box (Fig.PASW–3.13) to execute the command.

A variable **BPerCentSecYear** appears in the last column. Here, **1** represents **less than 40 per cent** marks and **5** represents more than **70 per cent marks**. This variable is an ordinal variable.

Command Syntax for Visual Binning

```
DATASET ACTIVATE DataSet1.
* Visual Binning.
*PerCentSecYear.
RECODE  PerCentSecYear (MISSING=COPY) (LO THRU 40=1) (LO THRU 50=2) (LO THRU 60=3) (LO
  THRU 70=4)
    (LO THRU HI=5) (ELSE=SYSMIS) INTO BPerCentSecYear.
VARIABLE LABELS  BPerCentSecYear 'Percentage of Marks in Second Year (Binned)'.
FORMATS  BPerCentSecYear (F5.0).
VALUE LABELS  BPerCentSecYear 1 '' 2 '' 3 '' 4 '' 5 ''.
VARIABLE LEVEL  BPerCentSecYear (ORDINAL).
EXECUTE.
```

Note

The concepts about measurement scales – nominal, ordinal, ratio and interval are discussed at length in Chapter – 4.

3.5 Rank Cases

The **Rank Cases** command calculates ranks and generates a new variable that shows the ranks. We can rank in either ascending or descending order. For example, you want to find out who obtained first rank out of these 120 students of our dataset on the basis of who has scored maximum percentage of marks in second year and subsequent ranks in descending order.

This can be done in the following manner:

1. Click on **Transform** and then on **Rank Cases**. You will see a as shown in Fig.PASW–3.14:

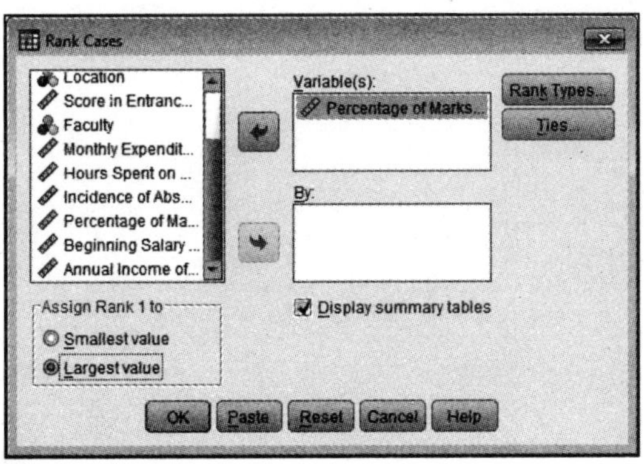

Fig.PASW–3.14

2. Select **Percentage of Marks Scored in Second Test** (for which ranks are to be obtained).

3. For obtaining the ranks in descending order, select **Largest Value** in the **Assign Rank 1 to** box.
4. Keeping all other default values, click **OK**. A new variable – **RperCentSecYear** is created and will appear in the last column of the Data Editor window. For two or more students having equal percentage of marks, mean ranks will be assigned. For example, 69 per cent marks are scored by two students. There are five students having more than 69 per cent marks. The ranks of these students will appear as 6.5 and 6.5.

Command Syntax for Ranking Cases

```
RANK VARIABLES=PerCentSecYear (D)
  /RANK
  /PRINT=YES
  /TIES=MEAN.
```

Summary

In this chapter we learnt:

- Computing Variables
- Recoding Variables
- Automatic Recode
- Visual Binning
- Rank Cases

Chapter 4

Describing Data Numerically

In this Chapter:

Numerical description of data is crucial for two reasons: it helps in understanding and discovering information and patterns hidden in data; also helps identify any errors in data entry. Tables and graphs are mainly used to describe data. Numerical description of data is called summary statistics or descriptive statistics. Summary measures like mean, median, mode and standard deviation, etc. are used to describe a variable and to study characteristics of data.

Data can be defined as the basic unit or raw material of information. In statistics, we represent data using numbers which are generated either by taking a measurement or by counting. The data generated as a result of measurement are continuous data and those generated as a result of counting are categorical data. In this chapter, we shall learn types of measurement scales and summarizing data – continuous as well as categorical using PASW.

4.1 Types of Measurement Scales

It is important to understand the scale on which data is measured so as to apply the right statistical technique for data description as well as analysis. In statistics, the term 'measurement' can be broadly defined as identifying objects or events, with the help of numbers on the basis of a set of rules. These sets of rules are categorized into four groups and hence, there are four types of measurement scales. These are described as follows:

1. **Nominal Scale:** When numerical labels are assigned to categories, the variable Gender is measured on nominal scale. For example, Males = 1 and Females = 2. Here 1 and 2 are labels assigned to two categories of Gender. Here, 2 is not necessarily greater than 1.
2. **Ordinal Scale:** When numerical labels are given to objects such that the categories can be ranked, it is measured on ordinal scale. For example, Age Group 0-25 = 1, 26-50 = 2, 51-75 = 3 and 75 and above = 4. Here, Age Groups are ranked with lowest as 1 and highest as 4. Other examples are, ranks of students in a class or, any variable measured on likert scaleor semantic differential scale etc.
3. **Interval Scale:** When an object or event is measured in a way that the distance between two data points can be obtained, for example, the difference between 40°C and 30°C temperature of a city can be measured and it is exactly equal to the difference between 50°C and 40°C. However, here 0°C does not mean absence of temperature. This means, in interval scale there is an arbitrary zero and not an absolute zero.
4. **Ratio Scale:** The only difference between interval scale and ratio scale is that in ratio scale, there is a true or an absolute zero. For example, height, weight, age, income etc. are measured on ratio scale.

Thus, the discussion on measurement scales clearly shows that, variables measured on nominal and ordinal scales are categorical; where as those measured on interval and ratio are continuous. In the following section, we shall discuss various summary measures and PASW procedures to obtain them.

4.2 Summary Measures

The measure of central tendency used to describe categorical data is mode (maximum frequency). For continuous data, mean (arithmetic mean, geometric mean and harmonic mean), median and mode are used. The measures of dispersion include range, standard deviation, average deviation, inter-quartile range, skewness, kurtosis etc.

4.2.1 Frequencies

Frequencies give the number of observations or cases that fall into each group or category. For example, you want to know the number of males and females in a faculty, or number of students in arts, commerce or science stream. Frequencies command is useful in such calculations. We try to find the number of students in each Faculty – Arts, Commerce and Science. The procedure for computing frequencies is described below:

1. Open students.sav.

2. Click Analyse to get the sub-menu as shown in Fig.PASW–4.1:

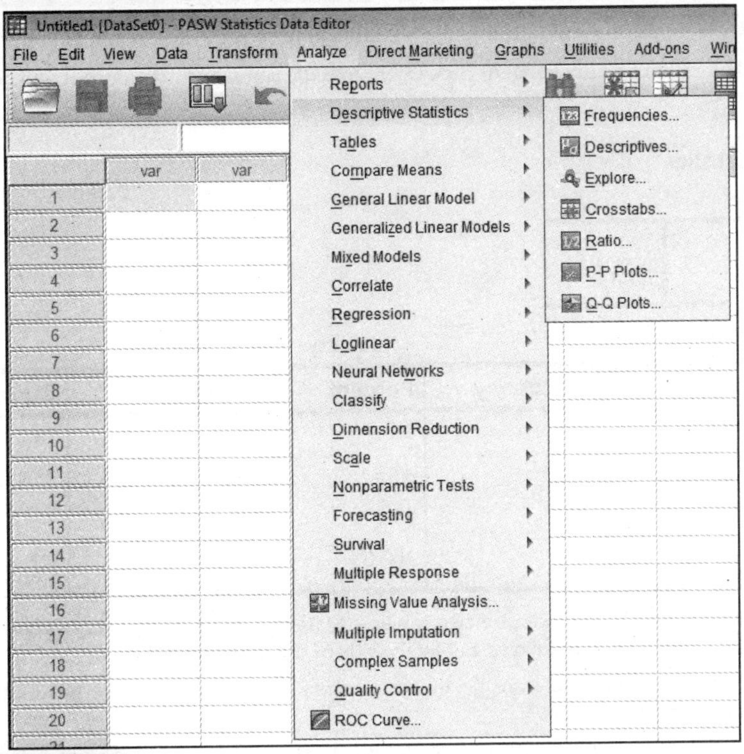

Fig.PASW–4.1

3. Now click **Descriptive Statistics** and **Frequencies** from the **Analyse** sub-menu. You will get a dialogue box as shown in Fig.PASW–4.2:

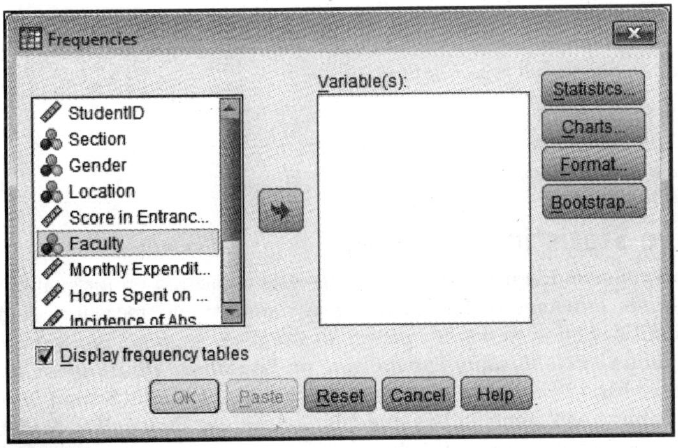

Fig.PASW–4.2

4. Click **Faculty** from the list and take it to the **Variable(s)** list box by clicking on [➡] button.
5. Keeping all other options unchanged, click **OK** to execute command. The output will be as follows:

Frequencies

Statistics

Faculty

N	Valid	120
	Missing	0

Faculty

		Frequency	Percent	Valid Percent	Cumulative Percent
Valid	Arts	34	28.3	28.3	28.3
	Commerce	57	47.5	47.5	75.8
	Science	29	24.2	24.2	100.0
	Total	120	100.0	100.0	

You see the title **Frequencies**, followed by two tables – **Statistics** and **Faculty**. The variable **Faculty**, for which the frequencies are calculated, is displayed below the title of the **Statistics** table.

The **Statistics** table shows that there are no missing values. This means that we have information about the faculty of graduation for all students.

The **Faculty** table shows that out of 120 students in our dataset, 34 students are from Arts, 57 from Commerce and 29 from Science faculty.

We can select more than one variable by holding **Ctrl** key on the keyboard and clicking the desired variables for obtaining the frequencies of more than one variable simultaneously.

Note

The variable labels and value labels will appear in the output.

Command Syntax for Frequencies

```
DATASET ACTIVATE DataSet1.
FREQUENCIES VARIABLES=Faculty
  /ORDER=ANALYSIS.
```

4.2.2 Descriptive Statistics

Descriptive Statistics command is used to describe the data measured on interval or ratio scale. **Descriptive Statistics** command uses measures of central tendency – mean; and measures of dispersion – maximum, minimum and standard deviation to discern pattern in the data. Suppose, we want to know the patterns of, **Score in Entrance Examination, Monthly Expenditure on Education, Hours spent on Reading, Incidence of Absence, Percentage of Marks Scored in First Year, Percentage of Marks Scored in Second Year, Beginning Salary** and **Annual Income of Parents** of the students, we can use **Descriptive Statistics** command. Since all these variables are measured on ratio scale, we can find maximum, minimum, range, mean and standard deviation of these variables. To obtain this:

1. Click **Analyse, Descriptive Statistics** and **Descriptives** (Fig.PASW–4.1) to get the dialogue box shown in Fig.PASW–4.3:

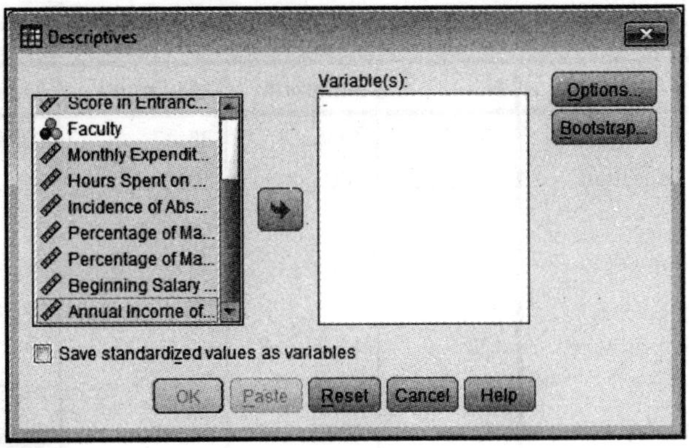

Fig.PASW–4.3

2. Select the variables Score in Entrance Examination, Monthly Expenditure on Education, Hours spent on Reading, Incidence of Absence, Percentage of Marks Scored in First Year, Percentage of Marks Scored in Second Year, Beginning Salary and Annual Income of Parents (by holding shift key and clicking on each of these variables) and move them into the Variable(s) list box by clicking on ➡ button.

3. Click the **Options** button to get the dialogue box shown in Fig.PASW–4.4:

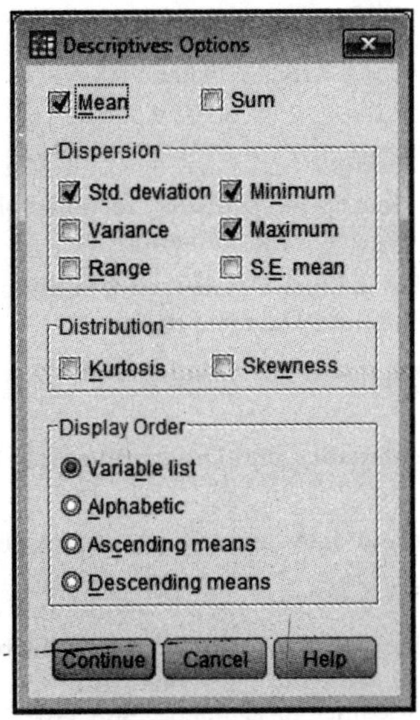

Fig.PASW–4.4

4. Select the desired statistics by clicking the appropriate check boxes. **Minimum, Maximum, Mean** and **Std. Deviation** are selected by default. Here, we shall keep the default selection of statistics.

5. **Display order** allows us to choose the order / sequence in which the variables will be displayed. Keeping the default value for **Display Order**, click the **Continue** button to go back to the previous dialogue box; click the **OK** button to execute the command. Following output shall be displayed in the Output Viewer Window:

Descriptives

Descriptive Statistics

	N	Minimum	Maximum	Mean	Std. Deviation
Score in Entrance Examination	120	45	85	60.08	7.834
Monthly Expenditure on Education	120	100	1000	511.25	177.987
Hours Spent on Reading	120	2	9	5.76	2.230
Incidence of Absence during Year	120	1	30	14.74	8.283
Percentage of Marks in First Year	120	40	89	57.98	7.603
Percentage of Marks in Second Year	120	40	85	58.57	6.796
Beginning Salary	120	6500	20000	11954.17	3084.248
Annual Income of Parents	120	150000	680000	347500.00	118812.401
Valid N (listwise)	120				

You see the title **Descriptives** followed by the **Descriptive Statistics** table. The **Descriptive Statistics** table is self-explanatory. Each row displays the measures of central tendency and dispersion for each of the variables. For example, the first row shows **number of observations (N), maximum value, minimum value, mean and standard deviation** for the variable **Score in Entrance Examination**. You may have fewer or more statistics depending on your selection in the **Options** menu.

Command Syntax for Descriptive Statistics

```
DATASET ACTIVATE DataSet1.
DESCRIPTIVES VARIABLES=Ent_Score ExpEdu HrRead Absence PerCentFirstYear PerCentSecYear
  BegSalary
    Parent_Income
  /STATISTICS=MEAN STDDEV MIN MAX.
```

It is possible to compute groupwise descriptive statistics, for example, the descriptive statistics of male and female can be obtained separately by using spit file command:

1. As discussed in chapter-2 (section 2.13), we will split the file gender-wise, to do this, click **Data** from command menu and then **Split File** from **Data** sub-menu.
2. Select **Organize output by groups** and move **Gender** from the variable list to the **Groups Based on** list; and click the **OK** button.
3. Now, click **Analyze, Descriptive Statistics,** and **Descriptives** (Fig.PASW–4.1). Select the desired variable(s) and **Options**.
4. Your output will comprise two sets of data summaries – one for **Females** and another for **Males**.

4.2.3 Explore

Explore command is used to examine the normality of data which is crucial while choosing appropriate statistical technique for the purpose of, drawing inferences from the sample. Apart from values and relative positions of mean, median and mode; values of skewness and kurtosis, normality can be examined with the help of Kolmogorov-Smirnov and Shappiro-Wilk's statistics. Graphically, normality can be examined using stem-and-leaf plot as well as Q-Q plots. **Explore** command of **Descriptive Statistics** (Fig.PASW–4.1) generates the Kolmogorov-Smirnov and Shappiro-Wilk's statistics; the stem-and-leaf plot and Q-Q plot for examining the normality of sampling distribution. Explore operates through **Examine** command. Let's examine the normality of **Percentage of Marks Scored in First Year**. The procedure for executing **Examine** command is as follows:

1. Click **Analyse, Descriptive Statistics** and **Explore** (Fig.PASW–4.1). A dialogue box as shown in Fig.PASW–4.5 will appear:

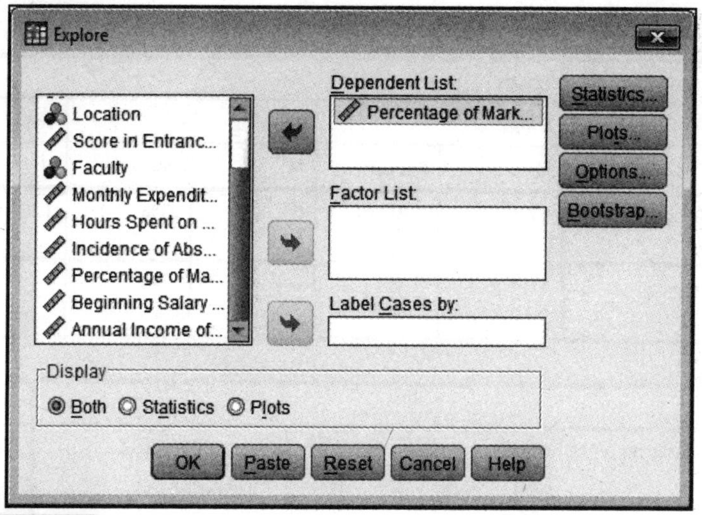

Fig.PASW–4.5

2. Select Percentage of Marks Scored in First Year and move it into the Dependent List list box.
3. Click the Plots button and to get the dialogue box shown below in Fig.PASW–4.6:

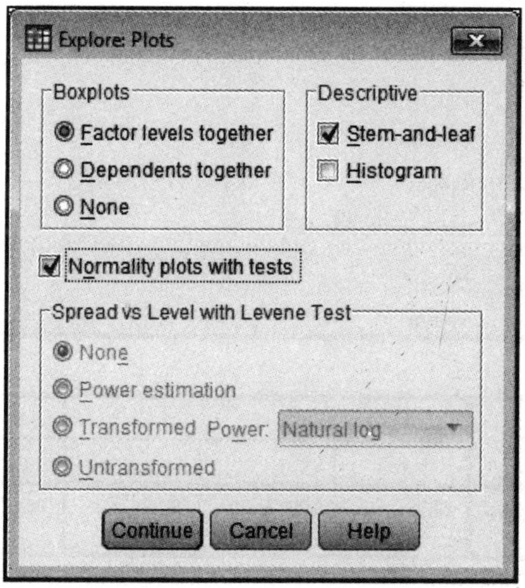

Fig.PASW–4.6

4. Click the **Normality plots with tests** check box. Keep default values for all other options.
5. Click **Continue** to go back to previous dialogue box, click **OK** to execute command. The output shall be displayed as follows:

Explore

Case Processing Summary

	Cases					
	Valid		Missing		Total	
	N	Percent	N	Percent	N	Percent
Percentage of Marks in First Year	120	100.0%	0	.0%	120	100.0%

Descriptives

			Statistic	Std. Error
Percentage of Marks in First Year	Mean		57.98	.694
	95% Confidence Interval for Mean	Lower Bound	56.61	
		Upper Bound	59.36	
	5% Trimmed Mean		58.02	
	Median		57.50	
	Variance		57.798	
	Std. Deviation		7.603	
	Minimum		40	
	Maximum		89	
	Range		49	
	Interquartile Range		8	
	Skewness		.344	.221
	Kurtosis		1.482	.438

Tests of Normality

	Kolmogorov-Smirnov[a]			Shapiro-Wilk		
	Statistic	Df	Sig.	Statistic	Df	Sig.
Percentage of Marks in First Year	.087	120	.026	.966	120	.004

a. Lilliefors Significance Correction

Percentage of Marks in First Year

Percentage of Marks in First Year Stem-and-Leaf Plot

Frequency	Stem & Leaf
3.00 Extremes	(=<40)
3.00	4. 555
4.00	4. 6667
2.00	4. 99
8.00	5. 00000011
8.00	5. 22222233
22.00	5. 4444444445555555555555
10.00	5. 6666667777
10.00	5. 8999999999
14.00	6. 00000000000001
8.00	6. 22222223
10.00	6. 4555555555
1.00	6. 7
13.00	6. 8888999999999
3.00	7. 000
1.00 Extremes	(>=89)

Stem width: 10

Each leaf: 1 case(s)

Normal Q-Q Plot of Percentage of Marks in First Year

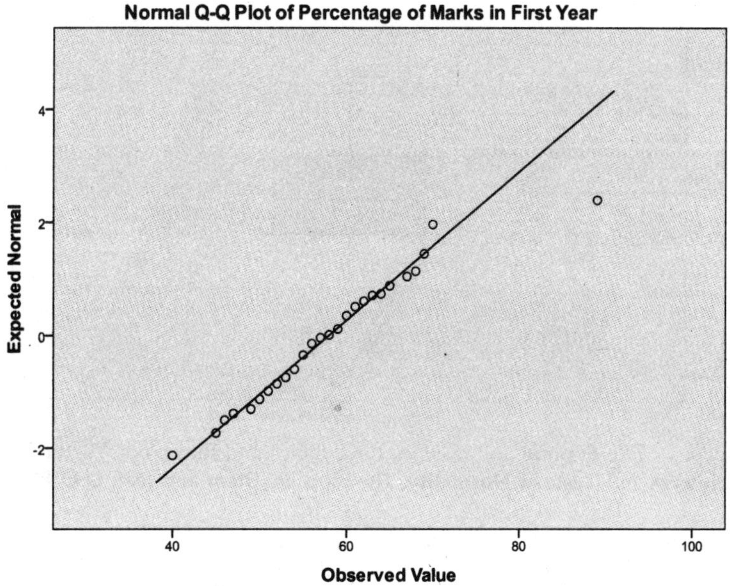

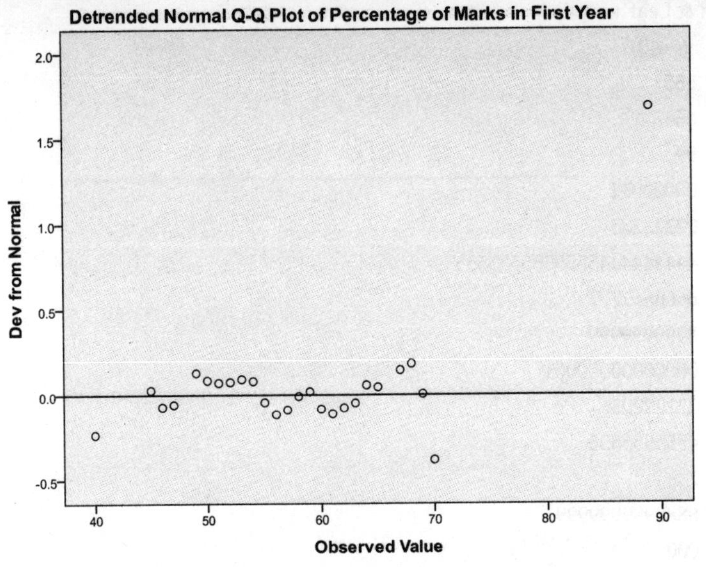

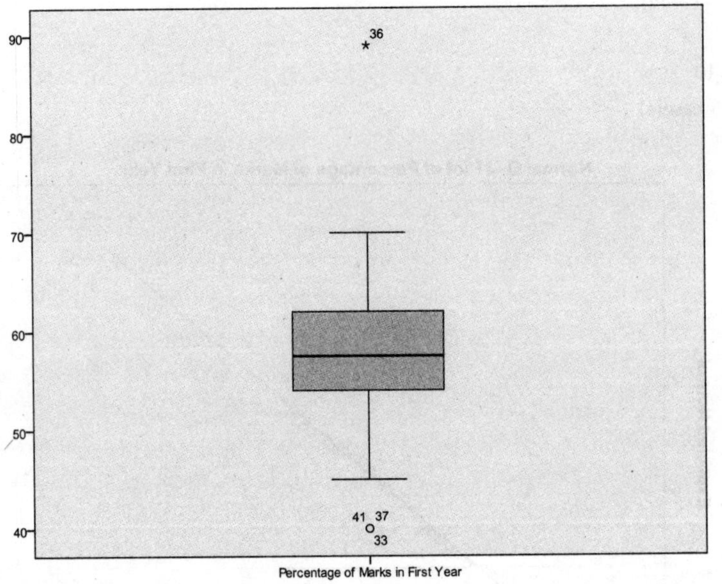

The output comprises a title **Explore**, followed by three tables and four plots. The tables are: **Case Processing Summary, Descriptives** and **Tests of Normality**. The plots are **Stem-and-leaf, Q-Q Plot, Detrended Q-Q Plot** and the **Box Plot**.

The **Case Processing Summary** table shows the number of cases analysed, number of missing values and total number of cases. In our example, there are no missing values.

The **Descriptives** table gives information about various summary measures like mean, median, variance, standard deviation, minimum, maximum, range, interquartile range, skewness and kurtosis. This table contains a statistic called 5% Trimmed Mean. This is useful when there are outliers (extreme values) in the sample.

Please note, mean is not an appropriate measure of central tendency when there are outliers in the sample; whereas median is. However, if we want to use mean in such a situation, it is advisable to remove outliers before calculating the mean. Five Percent Trimmed Mean excludes top 5% as well as bottom 5% observations (which are likely to be outliers) before calculating the mean. The mean calculated by excluding these observations is likely to be more close to the population mean.

The **Tests of Normality** table presents two statistics: Kolmogrov-Smirnov and Shapiro-Wilk.

Note

If sample size is greater than 100, one should use Kolmogorov-Smirnov statistic to examine normality otherwise, use the Shapiro-Wilk statistic.

The null and alternative hypothesis for both – Kolmogorov-Smirnov and Shapiro-Wilk test are:

- **H_0:** The sampling distribution is normal.
- **H_1:** The sampling distribution is not normal.

If the significance level is less than 0.05, null hypothesis is rejected and sampling distribution is not normal. Here, since the sample size is 120 we should interpret the normality of distribution using Kolmogorov-Smirnov's test. As the significance level of Kolmogorov-Smirnov test is less than 0.05, we interpret that the distribution for **Percentage of Marks Scored in First Year** is not normal.

The **Stem-and-Leaf plot**, Q-Q Plot and Detrended Q-Q plot gives an idea whether the variable is normally distributed or not. The **Stem-and-Leaf plot** is displayed with the variable **Percentage of Marks Score in First Year** as its title. The Stem-and-Leaf plot is a horizontal representation of histograms. Look at the stem-and-leaf plot it shows the distribution is close to normal.

The line in the **Q-Q Plot** is generated by joining the points of expected values of each observation. Therefore, if the actual data points lie exactly on the line, then the distribution is normal. Here, most of the data-points lie close to the line but not exactly on the line and therefore, the distribution of **Percentage of Marks Scored in First Year** variable is close to normal (though not perfectly normal).

The **Detrended Q-Q Plot** shows the extent of deviation of data points from the expected values. In our example, since most of the data points are clustered around the horizontal (detrended) line, we can assume that the distribution of **Percentage of Marks Scored in First Year** is close to normal.

Box Plot gives an idea about the variance of the variable. Closely examining the Box plot, we seethat there are two outliers, shown by two dots. The position of the median line is slightly away from the centre of the box, which again indicates that the distribution is slightly skewed. The detailed explanation of Box plot is given in chapter 5 (section 5.5).

Explore (Examine) command can also be used to examine group wise, the normality of a variable. For example, to examine the normality of **Percentage of Marks Scored in First Year** separately for local students and commuters, just select the variable **Location** and move it into the **Factors List** box. Repeat the procedure for executing the explore command. You will get separate statistics and graphs for both.

Command Syntax for Explore / Examine

```
DATASET ACTIVATE DataSet1.
EXAMINE VARIABLES=PerCentFirstYear
  /PLOT BOXPLOT STEMLEAF NPPLOT
  /COMPARE GROUPS
  /STATISTICS DESCRIPTIVES
  /CINTERVAL 95
  /MISSING LISTWISE
  /NOTOTAL.
```

4.2.4 Crosstabs

Crosstabs (an abbreviation of Crosstabulation) command is used to get information on the intersection of two or more categorical variables. We have discussed (Section 4.2.1) that frequencies show the numbers of cases in each level of a categorical variable but do not provide information on intersection of two variables. For example, frequencies can give the number of students from each faculty and the number of male and female students but, not the number of male and female students from each faculty. Due to the fact that the Crosstabs command provides information about the intersection of two variables, this command is beneficial to investigate such kind of information. The number of male and female students in each – arts, commerce and science faculty is an example of crosstabulation. The Crosstabs procedure is as follows:

1. Click **Analyze** from command menu and then **Descriptive Statistics** and **Crosstabs** (Fig.PASW–4.1). A dialogue box as shown below in Fig.PASW–4.7 appears on the screen:

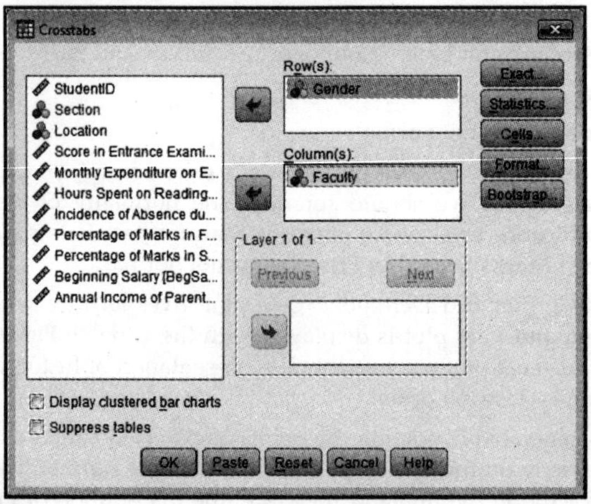

Fig.PASW–4.7

2. Select **Gender** and move it to the **Rows** list box. Select **Faculty** and move it to the **Columns** list box.
3. Click the **Cells** button to get the dialogue box as shown below in Fig.PASW–4.8:

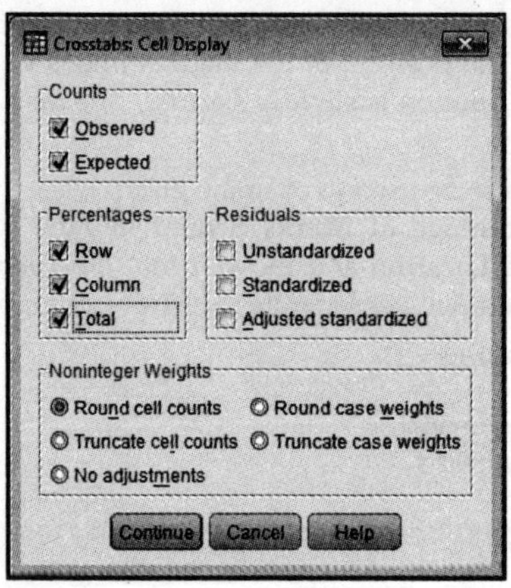

Fig.PASW–4.8

4. This allows you to add additional values to your table. **Observed** count is selected by default. Click the check boxes to select **Expected** in the **Counts** frame; and the **Row**, **Column**, and **Total** in the **Percentages** frame.

5. Click the **Continue** button to go to the previous dialogue box and then click the **OK** button to execute the command. Following output is displayed:

Crosstabs

Case Processing Summary

	Cases					
	Valid		Missing		Total	
	N	Percent	N	Percent	N	Percent
Gender * Faculty	120	100.0%	0	.0%	120	100.0%

Gender * Faculty Crosstabulation

			Faculty			Total
			Arts	Commerce	Science	
Gender	Male	Count	18	31	17	66
		Expected Count	18.7	31.4	16.0	66.0
		% within Gender	27.3%	47.0%	25.8%	100.0%
		% within Faculty	52.9%	54.4%	58.6%	55.0%
		% of Total	15.0%	25.8%	14.2%	55.0%
	Female	Count	16	26	12	54
		Expected Count	15.3	25.7	13.1	54.0
		% within Gender	29.6%	48.1%	22.2%	100.0%
		% within Faculty	47.1%	45.6%	41.4%	45.0%
		% of Total	13.3%	21.7%	10.0%	45.0%
Total		Count	34	57	29	120
		Expected Count	34.0	57.0	29.0	120.0
		% within Gender	28.3%	47.5%	24.2%	100.0%
		% within Faculty	100.0%	100.0%	100.0%	100.0%
		% of Total	28.3%	47.5%	24.2%	100.0%

The output will display a heading **Crosstabs** followed by two tables – **Case Processing Summary** and **Gender * Faculty Crosstabulation**.

The **Case Processing Summary** table shows that there are no missing values. All 120 observations were used for performing the crosstabulation.

The **Gender * Faculty Crosstabulation** table reveals that, there are three rows and four columns. The row variable has two categories: Males and Females. The first two rows represent frequency (count) and percentages of Males and Females in each Faculty (column variable category). The third row represents the total of row statistics for each Faculty. The column variable has three categories: Arts, Commerce and Science faculty. The first three columns represent the count and percentages of students in each faculty; the fourth column represents the totals of column statistics. This **Gender* Faculty crosstabulation** table can be interpreted as follows:

- There are 18 males in Arts, 31 in Commerce and 17 in Science faculty. The last column shows that out of 120 students, 66 (18+31+17) are males. Similarly, there are 16 females in Arts, 26 in Commerce and 12 in Science faculty. There are totally 54 (16+26+12) females out of 120 students.
- The **expected count** is obtained either from theory or from empirical evidences. In a crosstabulation like this, expected count is given by:

$$\textbf{Expected Count} = \frac{\sum_{i=1}^{m1} rci \sum_{j=1}^{m2} ccj}{n}$$

Where, rc = row count and cc=column count,

m1 = number of rows and m2=number of columns

n = total number of respondents (sample size).

The expected count of males in Arts is 18.7, that in Commerce is 31.4 and in Science faculty it is 16. The expected count of females in Arts is 15.3, 5.6 in Commerce and 13 in Science faculty.

- **Percentage (%) Within Gender** represents percentage of males from Arts, Commerce and Science faculty; and percentage of females from Arts, Commerce and Science faculty. In our example, out of 66 males, 27.3 % are from Arts, 47% from Commerce and 25.8% from Science faculty. Out of 54 females, 29.6% are from Arts, 48.1% from Commerce and 22.2% from Science faculty.
- **Percentage (%) Within Faculty** represents the percentage of males and percentage of females in Arts, Commerce and Science faculty. In our example, out of 34 students coming from Arts, 52.9% are males and 47.1% are females. Similarly, out of 57 students from Commerce, 54.4% are males and 45.6% are females and out of 29 students from Science faculty, 58.6% are males and 41.4% are females.
- **Percentage (%) of Total** shows that out of 120 students, 15% males come from Arts, 25.8% from Commerce and 14.2% from Science faculty. Similarly, out of 120 students, 13.3% are from Arts, 21.7 % from Commerce and 10% from Science faculty.

Command Syntax for Crosstabs

```
DATASET ACTIVATE DataSet1.
CROSSTABS
  /TABLES=Gender BY Faculty
  /FORMAT=AVALUE TABLES
  /CELLS=COUNT EXPECTED ROW COLUMN TOTAL
  /COUNT ROUND CELL.
```

The crosstabulation statistics offer numerous remarkable observations about the data. In the above table, you may try to find an association, if any, between Gender and Faculty as the expected values and, the actual counts are different from each other. The chapter on Non-parametric statistics (chapter 14, Section 14.1) discusses how to examine this relationship using inferential statistics.

Summary

In this chapter we learnt:

- Types of Measurement Scales
- Summary Measures
  - Frequencies
  - Descriptive Statistics
  - Explore
  - Crosstabs

Chapter 5

Describing Data Graphically

In this Chapter:

Summarizing the information from collected data is vital for discerning the pattern and examining relationships. The descriptive statistics provide useful information for discovering patterns. The whole idea of organizing raw data is to present it in a concise way for quicker understanding.

It is important to understand the pattern in data, once they are collected. It can be done by constructing appropriate graphs or charts. A quick glance at the graph elucidates the point much more easily than does a page filled with words and numbers. The selection of graph depends on the scale on which the data are measured and on what you want to demonstrate. In this chapter, uses of different graphs like line, pie, bar, histogram, box plot, scatter diagram, Q-Q plot and P-P plot, and the Predictive Analytic Software (PASW) procedure to create them are explained.

5.1 Line Chart

Line Charts are used to show the pattern of changes over a period of time, called trend. For example, to observe the pattern of, change in height of a child, closing prices of stocks, GDP of a country. Line charts are used to observe these patterns. To understand the procedure for constructing a line chart, open a new dataset.

Note

Remember to close the students.sav dataset. PASW will allow you to keep more than one datasets open at a time but it is recommended to keep only one dataset open to avoid confusion.

Create three variables – **Year, Final Consumption Expenditure** and **GDP**. Go to the Variable View Window and type **0** (zero) in the **Decimals** column for Year variable. Go back to the Data Editor Window and enter the data given in table 5.1:

Table 5.1: Data for Line Chart

Year	Final Consumption Expenditure ('000 Crore)	GDP ('000 Crore)	Year	Final Consumption Expenditure ('000 Crore)	GDP ('000 Crore)
1995	27.20	34.70	2001	37.40	48.40
1996	29.20	37.30	2002	38.00	50.20
1997	30.30	39.00	2003	40.40	54.40
1998	32.30	41.30	2004	42.70	59.00
1999	34.70	44.20	2005	45.80	64.40
2000	35.30	46.00			

Save this file as **gdp.sav**.

The procedure to create the line graph is as follows:

1. Click **Graphs** from command menu as shown in Fig.PASW–5.1:

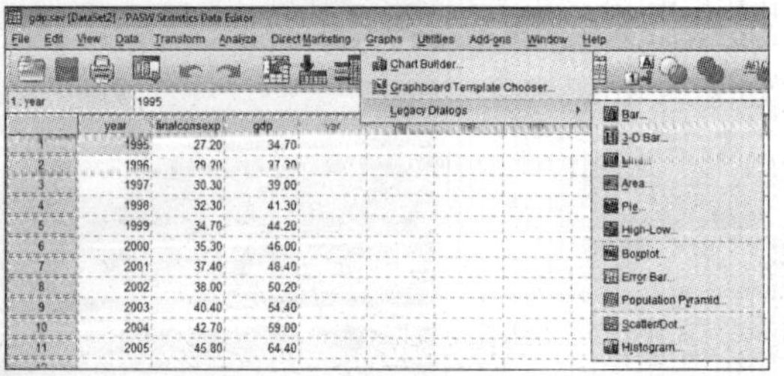

Fig.PASW–5.1

2. Click **Legacy Dialogues** and then **Line** to get the dialogue box as shown in Fig.PASW–5.2:

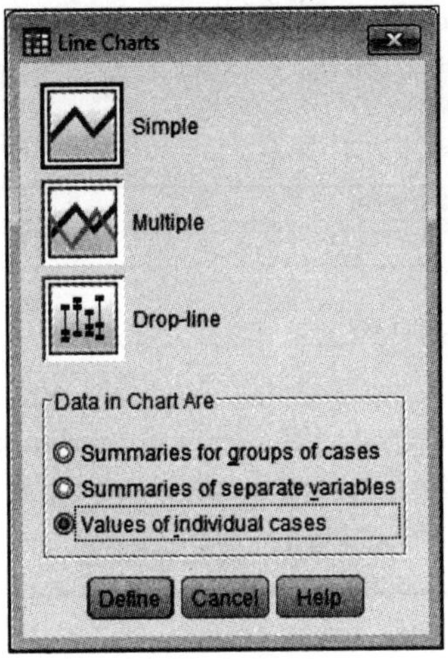

Fig.PASW–5.2

3. Select **Values of individual cases** and click **Define** to get the dialogue box shown in Fig.PASW–5.3:

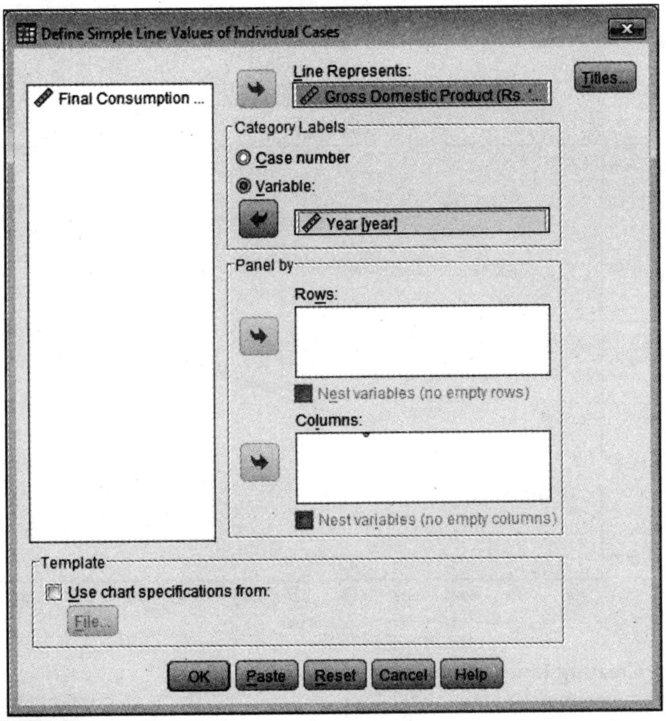

Fig.PASW–5.3

4. Select **GDP** and move it to the **Line Represents** box.
5. Click **Variable** radio button to activate the **Variable** text box. Select **Year** and move it to the **Variable** box.

6. Click **Titles** to get the dialogue box shown in Fig.PASW–5.4:

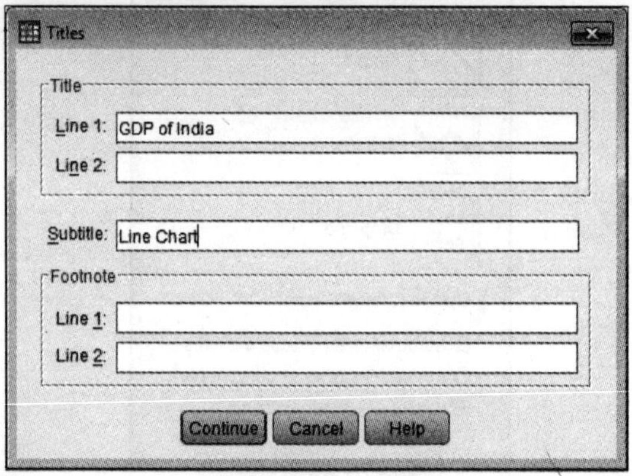

Fig.PASW–5.4

In the **Title** frame, type **GDP of India** in **Line 1** text box.

7. Type **Line Chart** in **Subtitle** text box.
8. Click **Continue** to go back to the previous dialogue box and then click **OK** to execute the command. A line chart will be displayed in the Output Viewer Window as shown below:

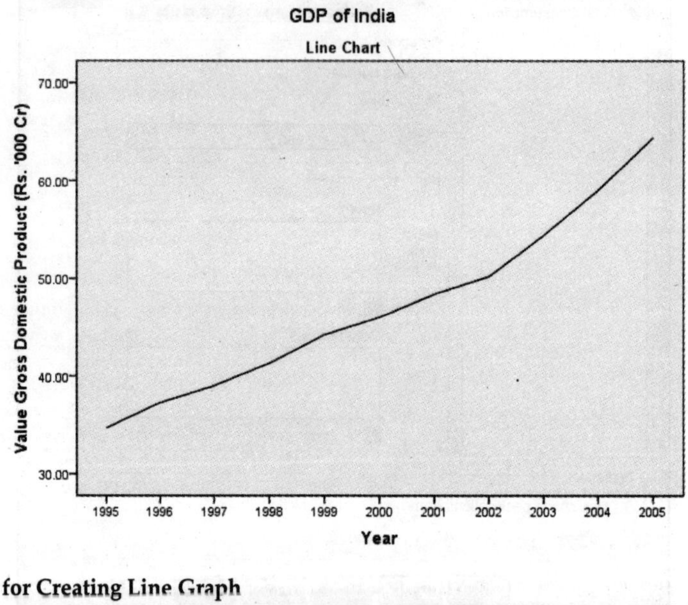

Command Syntax for Creating Line Graph

```
DATASET ACTIVATE DataSet2.
GRAPH
  /LINE(SIMPLE)=VALUE(gdp) BY year
  /TITLE='GDP of India'
  /SUBTITLE='Line Chart'.
```

You may format the graph by simply double-clicking on it in the Output Viewer Window. On double-clicking the graph, a **Chart Editor** window will open as shown in Fig.PASW–5.5:

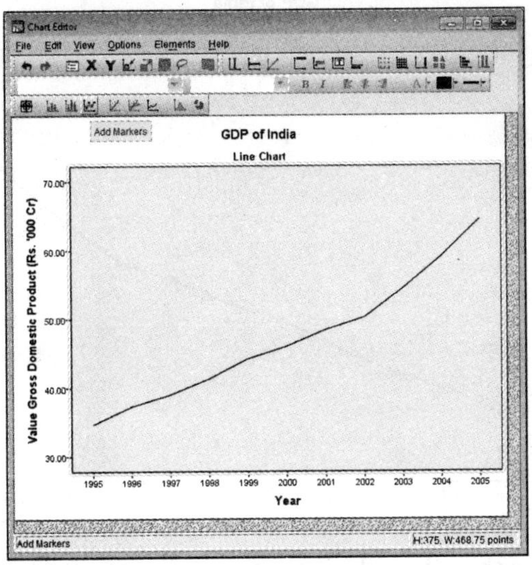

Fig.PASW–5.5

You may use any of the tools displayed on the toolbars below the menu to modify the background, colour, titles and other attributes of the chart. For example, you may click **Add Markers** icon shown to add markers to the line chart. Clicking **Add Markers** will open a dialogue box as shown in Fig.PASW–5.6:

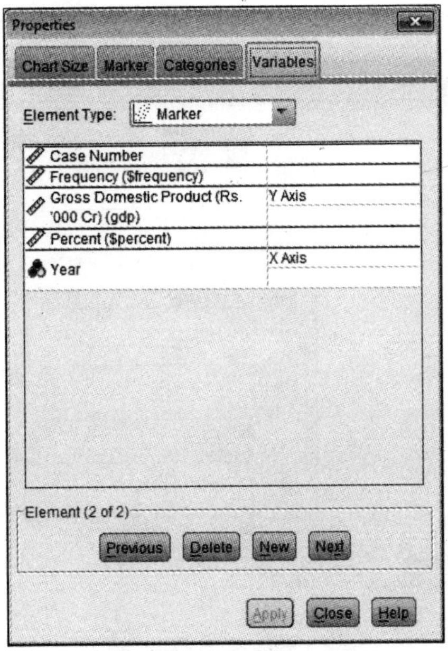

Fig.PASW–5.6

Without making any changes in the window, click **Close** button to close **Properties** dialogue box. Now, close the Chart Editor Window to see the markers on the line as shown below:

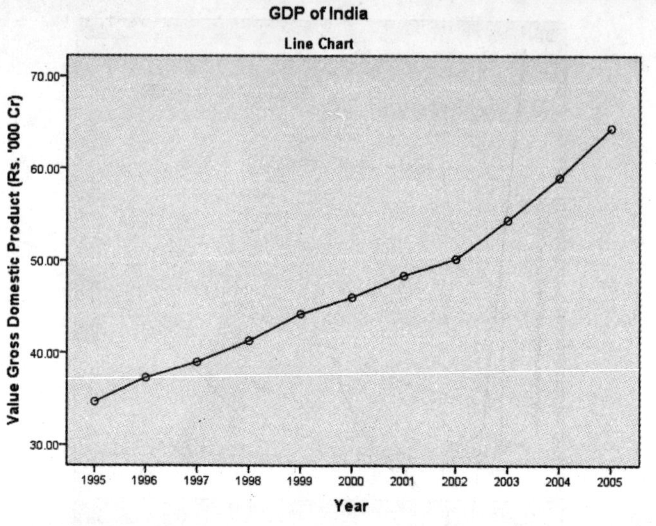

Multiple Line Chart is used to show the pattern of change in two or more variables over a period of time. We shall use the data on **Final Consumption Expenditure** and **GDP of India** for the time period 1995 to 2005 from **gdp.sav**. The procedure for obtaining Multiple Line Chart is as follows:

1. Open file gdp.sav.
2. Click Graphs, Legacy Dialogues and Line. You will get the dialogue box shown in Fig.PASW–5.2.
3. Select Multiple, Values of individual cases and click Define to get the dialogue box as shown in Fig.PASW–5.7:

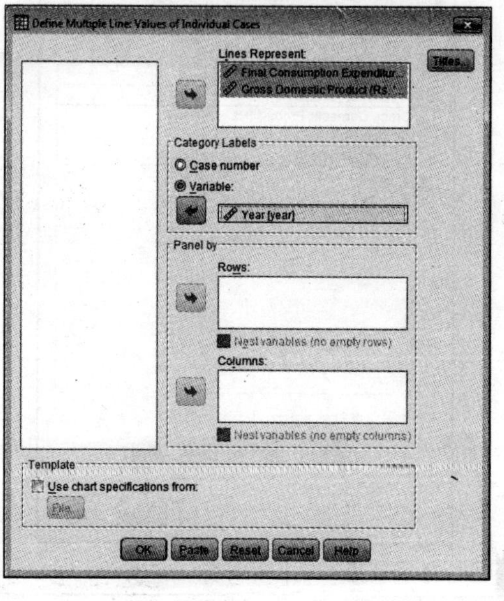

Fig.PASW–5.7

4. Select **Final Consumption Expenditure** and **GDP** together (by holding shift key) and move these variables in the **Lines Represent** box.
5. Click **Variable** radio button in the **Category Labels** frame and move **Year** to the text box.
6. Click **Title** to get the dialogue box shown in Fig.PASW–5.4.

   In **Titles** frame, type **Final Consumption Expenditure and GDP of India** in **Line 1**.
7. Type **Multiple Line Chart** in **Subtitle**.
8. Click **Continue** to go to the previous dialogue box and **OK** to execute the command. The output will appear in the Viewer Window as shown below:

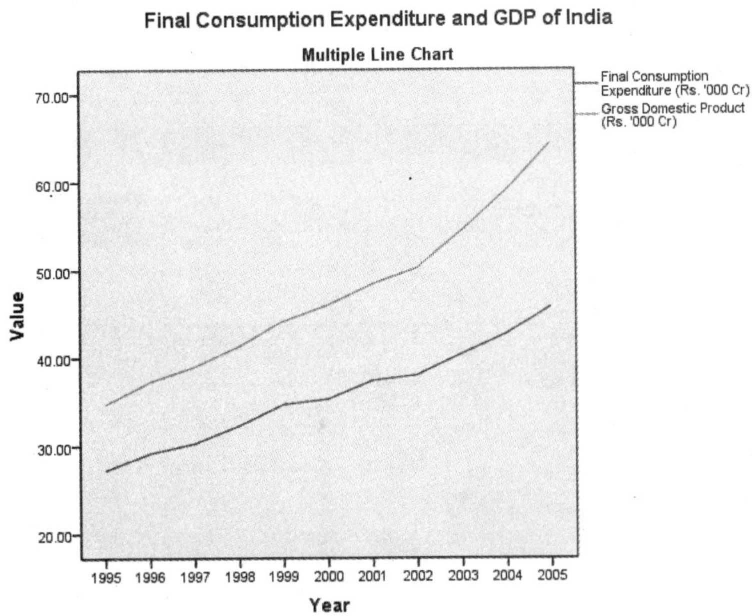

Command Syntax for Multiple Line Chart

```
GRAPH
  /LINE(MULTIPLE)=VALUE(finalconsexp gdp) BY year
  /TITLE='Final Consumption Expenditure and GDP of India'
  /SUBTITLE='Multiple Line Graph'.
```

You may double-click the graph for plotting data points, as shown in the simple line chart. You may also change the colour, scale etc. from the Chart Editor Window. Formatting of graphs is presented in detail in section 5.10.

5.2 Pie Chart

Pie charts are used to graphically display percentages of cases in each category of a variable. They can also illustrate the relative percentages of levels of a variable by graphically displaying the percentage of total cases at each level of the variable. For example, you could display the percentages of students from Arts, Commerce and Science using a bar chart. To obtain a pie chart do as follows:

1. Open students.sav.
2. Click **Graphs from command menu and Legacy Dialogues** and **Pie** from Graphs menu to get the dialogue box shown in Fig.PASW–5.8:

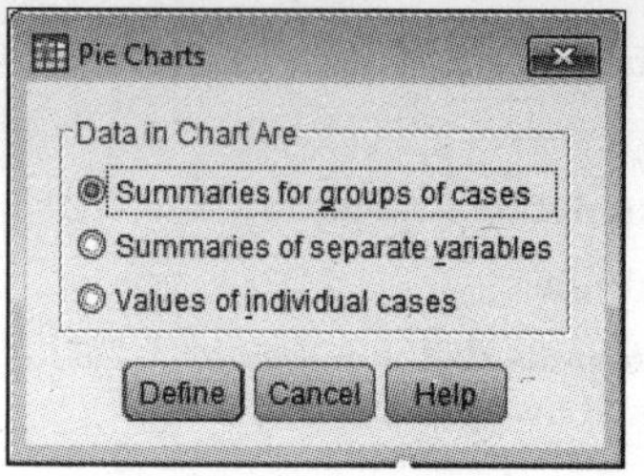

Fig.PASW–5.8

3. Select **Summaries of groups of cases** and click **Define** button to get a dialogue box shown in Fig.PASW 5.9:

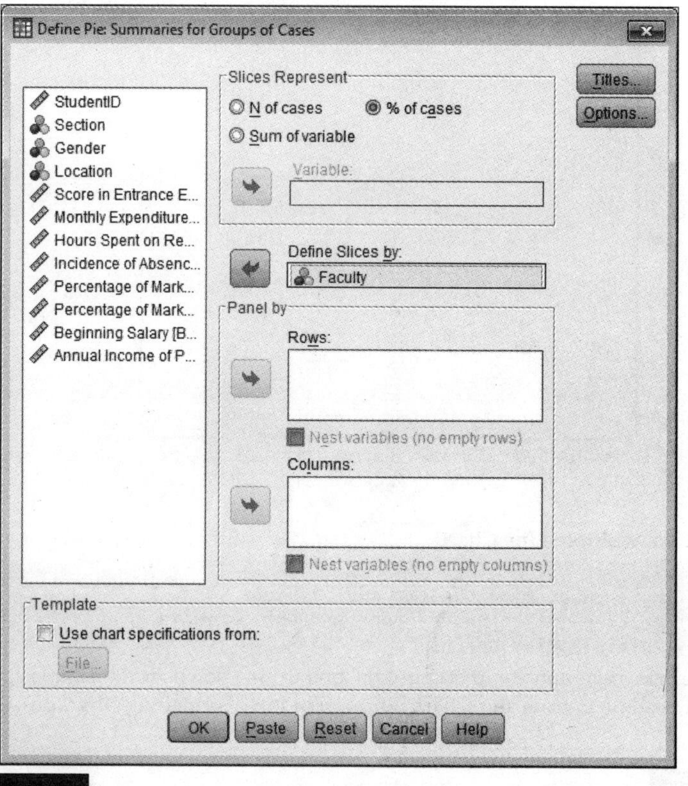

Fig.PASW–5.9

4. Select % of cases in Slices Represent box.
5. Select **Faculty** and move it into the **Define Slices by** text box.
6. Click Titles and type Faculty in Graduation in Line 1 of Title frame and Pie Chart in Subtitle.
7. Click **Continue** to return to previous dialogue box and then click **OK** to execute command. A chart appears in the Output Viewer Window as shown below:

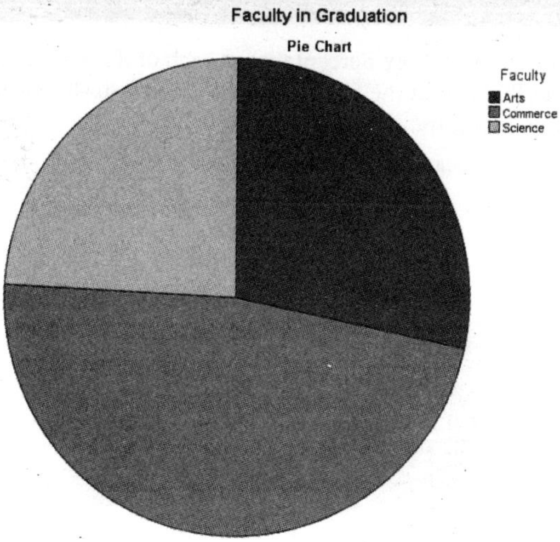

Command Syntax for Pie Chart

```
DATASET ACTIVATE DataSet1.
GRAPH
  /PIE=PCT BY Faculty
  /TITLE='Faculty in Graduation'
  /SUBTITLE='Pie Chart'.
```

Double-clicking the chart in the Output Viewer Window will open the Chart Editor Window as shown in Fig.PASW–5.10:

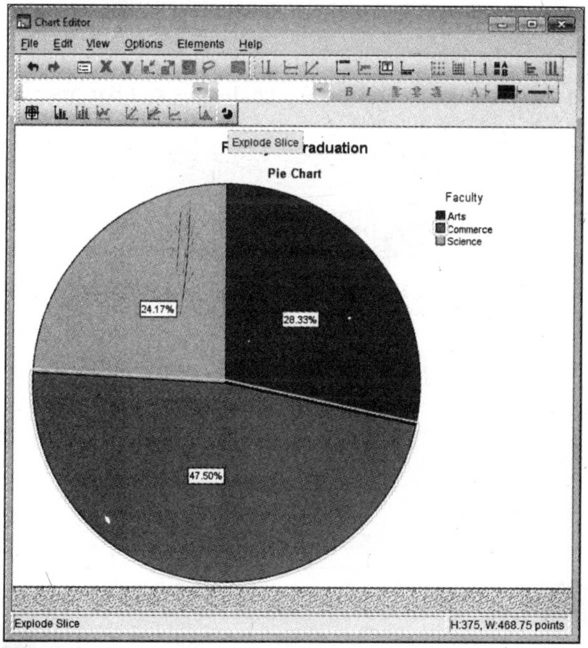

Fig.PASW–5.10

You may click on **Show Data Labels** icon to show percentages in each of the slice. You may also select a slice by clicking on it and then use **Explode Pie** icon in the Chart Editor Window to show a slice separately. The graph will now look as shown in the following figure:

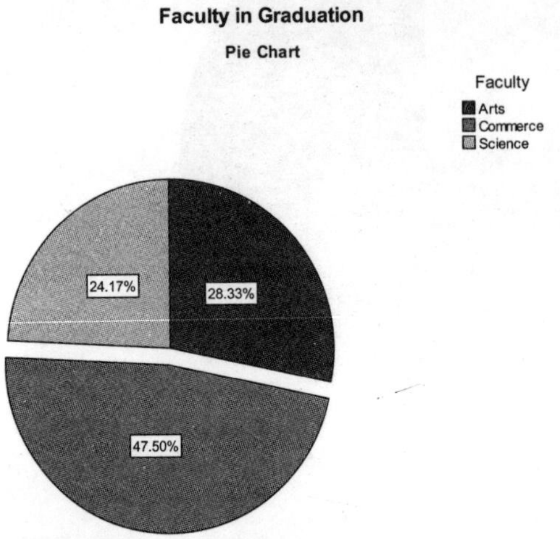

You may make other modifications by clicking appropriate icons and changing properties in the Chart Editor Window as discussed in section 5.10.

5.3 Bar Chart

Bar graphs are used to graphically display the frequency of each level of a variable. For example, you can display the number of students from Arts, Commerce and Science using a bar chart. To obtain a bar chart,

1. Click **Graphs** from the command menu and **Legacy Dialogues** and **Bar** from the **Graph** menu. A dialogue box as shown in Fig.PASW–5.11 will appear:

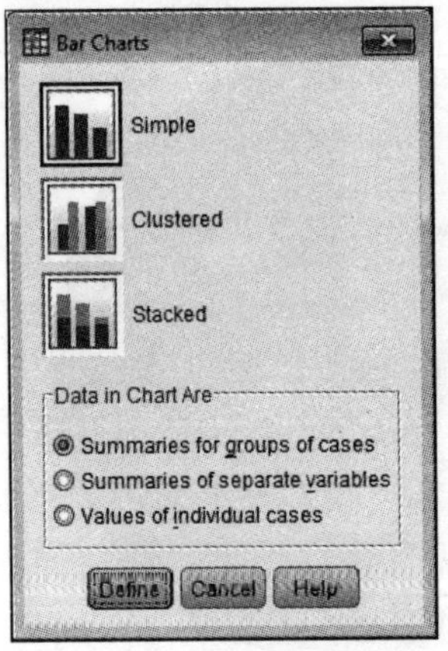

Fig.PASW–5.11

The default options are **Simple** and **Summaries for groups of cases**. Keeping the default options unchanged, click the **Define** button to get the dialogue box shown in Fig.PASW–5.12:

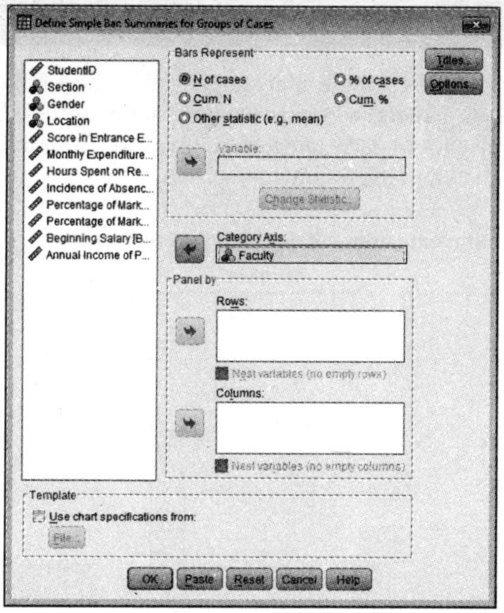

Fig.PASW–5.12

2. Select **Faculty** and move it to the **Category Axis** text box. Keep all other options unchanged.
3. Click on **Titles** button and type **Students from Different Graduation Faculties** in **Title 1** text box of Title frame; and **Bar Chart** in **Subtitle** text box.
4. Click **Continue** and then **OK** to execute the command. The chart will appear in Viewer Window as shown below:

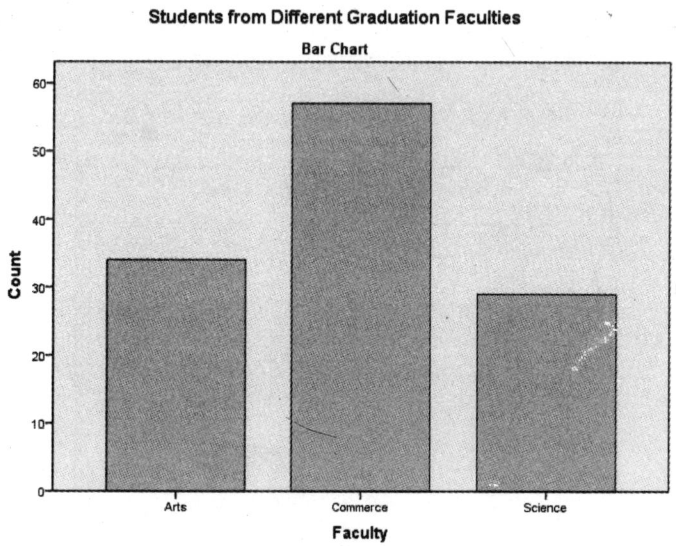

Command Syntax for Bar Charts

```
GRAPH
  /BAR(SIMPLE)=COUNT BY Faculty
  /TITLE='Students from Different Graduation Faculties'
  /SUBTITLE='Bar Chart'.
```

Similar to other charts, you may double-click the chart to go to the Chart Editor Window for formatting it. For example, you may click **Show Data Labels,** without changing anything the **Properties** dialogue box, click the **Close** button to display the frequencies of each category on the bar. Close the Chart Editor Window. The data labels will appear on the bars as shown in the following figure:

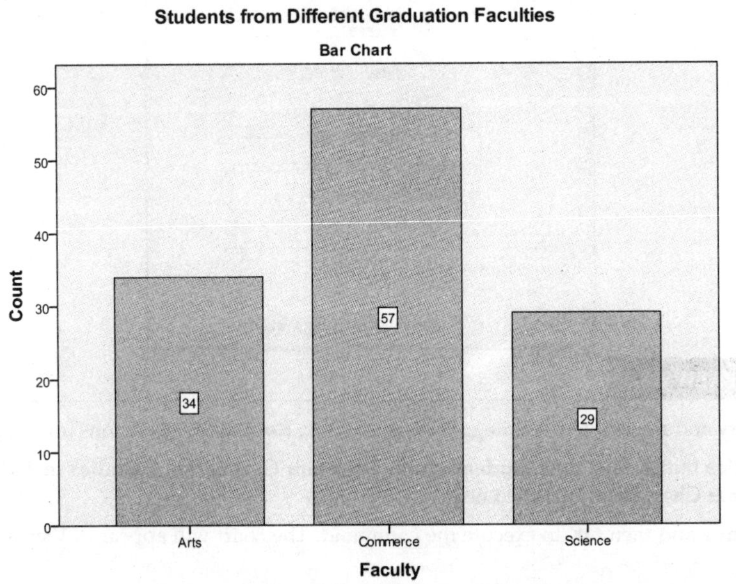

You may change the **Font Size** by clicking on the size drop down as shown in Fig.PASW–5.13:

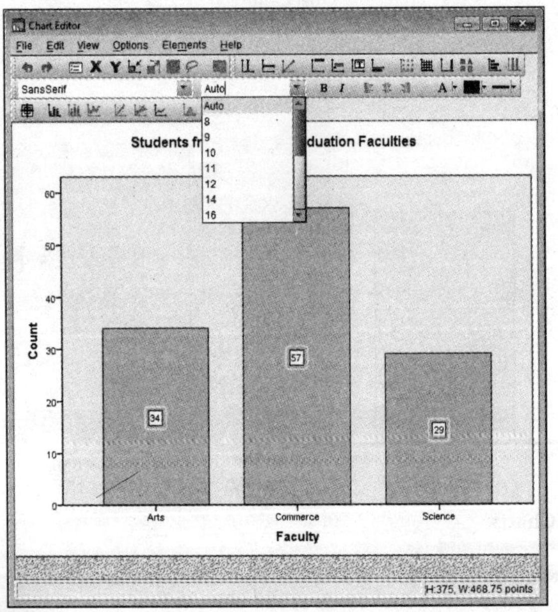

Fig.PASW–5.13

The other two types of bar graphs are used in situations where you want to graph frequencies for more than one variable. For example, you want to show number of girls and boys students separately, in each graduation faculty, so you could choose either the **Clustered** or **Stacked** options in the above dialogue box. The **Clustered** option groups together bars representing levels of a category. The procedure for clustered bar is as follows:

1. Click **Graphs** from command menu. Then, click **Legacy Dialogues** and **Bar**.
2. Select **Clustered Bar**, **Summaries for groups of cases** and click **Define**. You get the dialogue box shown in Fig.PASW–5.14:

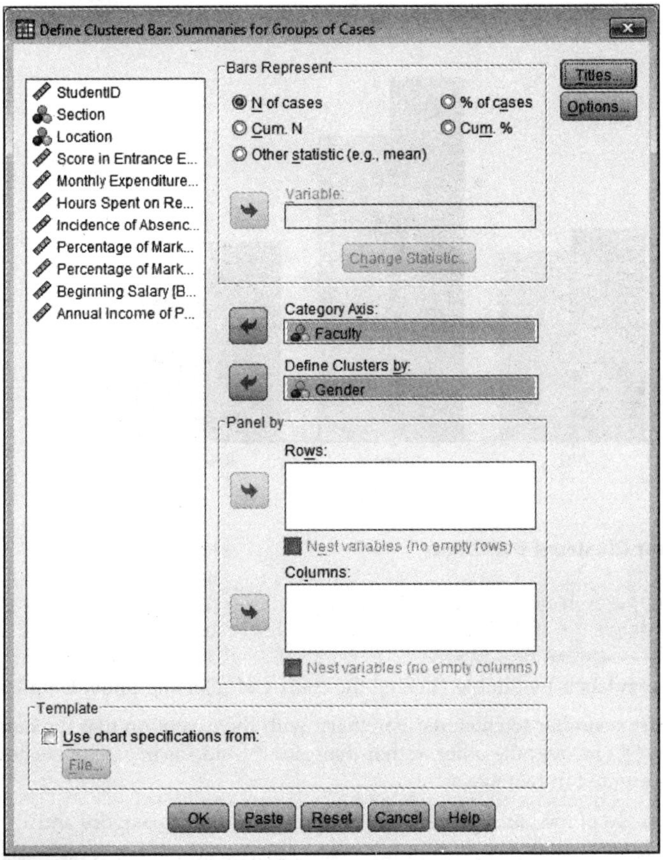

Fig.PASW–5.14

3. Select **Faculty** and move it to the **Category Axis** box.
4. Select **Gender** and move it to the **Define Clusters by** box.
5. Click on **Titles** button and type **Students from Different Graduation Faculties** in **Title 1** text box and Genderwise Classification in Title2 text box of Title frame.
6. Type **Clustered Bar Chart** in **Subtitle** text box.
7. Click **Continue** to return to previous dialogue box and then click **OK** to execute command. Following chart l appears in the Viewer Window:

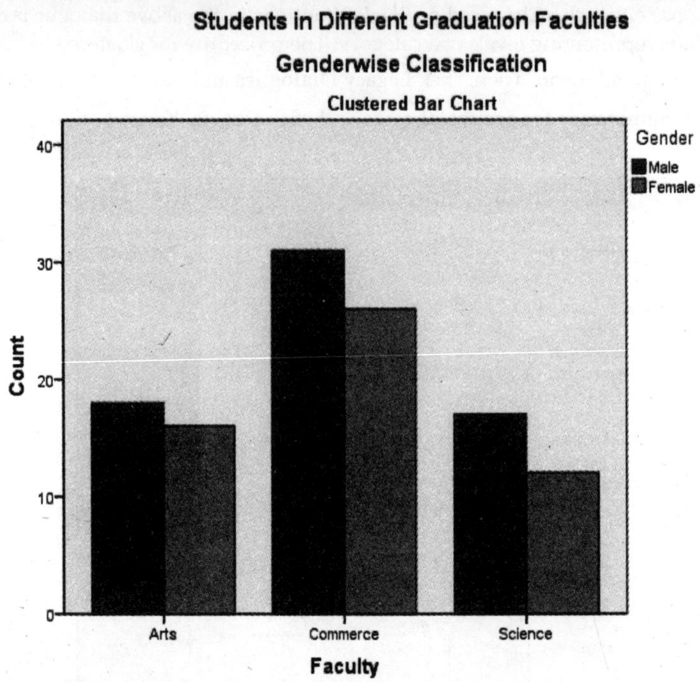

Command Syntax for Clustered Bar Charts

```
GRAPH
  /BAR(GROUPED)=COUNT BY Faculty BY Gender
  /TITLE='Students in Different Graduation Faculties' 'Genderwise Classification'
  /SUBTITLE='Clustered Bar Chart'.
```

You may give data labels by double-clicking the chart and selecting **Show Data Labels** icon.

Stacked Bar chart is similar to clustered bar chart, with the exception that the bars for each category of the variable are placed one over the other, rather than side-by-side as in case of clustered bar chart. Stacked bar charts can be presented in two ways:

- The total height of the bar represents the frequencies in each category and
- Scaled to 100 per cent: the height of the each bar-segment (levels of the variable that is used to define stacks) represents relative percentages of cases in each category. Here, the sum of percentages of the stack-variable is 100 and therefore, the total height of bars of each category is same.

The procedure for stacked bar charts is same as that of clustered bar charts. We shall use the same example to construct stacked bar charts: define **Categories** by **Faculty of Graduation** and **Stacks** by **Gender**. Follow the same procedure as followed to construct clustered bar charts.

8. Click Graphs, Legacy Dialogues and Bar. Select **Stacked** in the **Define Bar** dialogue box (Fig.PASW–5.11) to get **Define Stacked Bar: Summaries of Groups of Cases** dialogue box as shown in Fig.PASW–5.15:

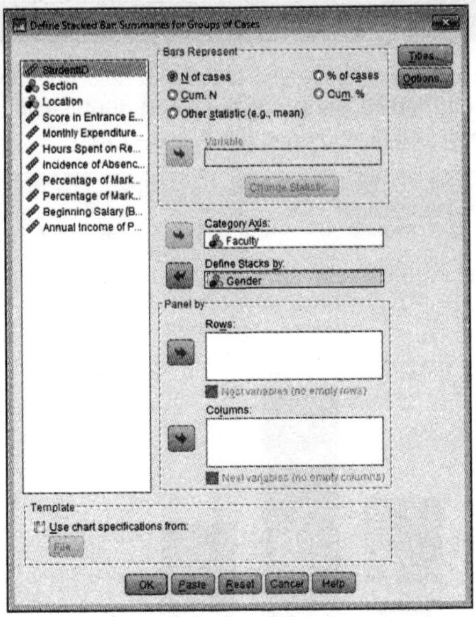

Fig.PASW–5.15

9. Select **Faculty** and move it to **Define Categories by** text box.
10. Select **Gender** and move it to the **Define Stacks by** text box.
11. Make appropriate changes in the Titles dialogue box.
12. Click **Continue** and then **OK** to get the stacked bar chart as shown below:

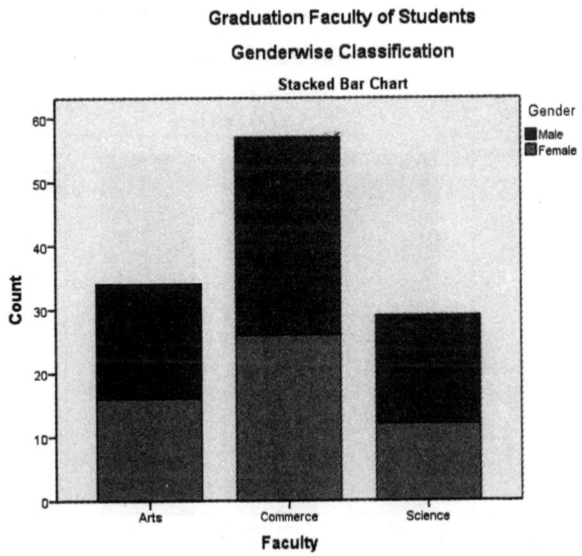

Command Syntax for Stacked Bar Charts

```
GRAPH
  /BAR(STACK)=COUNT BY Faculty BY Gender
  /TITLE='Graduation Faculty of Students' 'Genderwise Classification'
  /SUBTITLE='Stacked Bar Chart'.
```

You may give data labels by double-clicking the chart and selecting Show Data Labels icon. However, to construct a stacked bar chart that depicts percentage of cases, double-click this bar chart in the Output Viewer Window to get the Chart Editor Window shown in Fig.PASW–5.16:

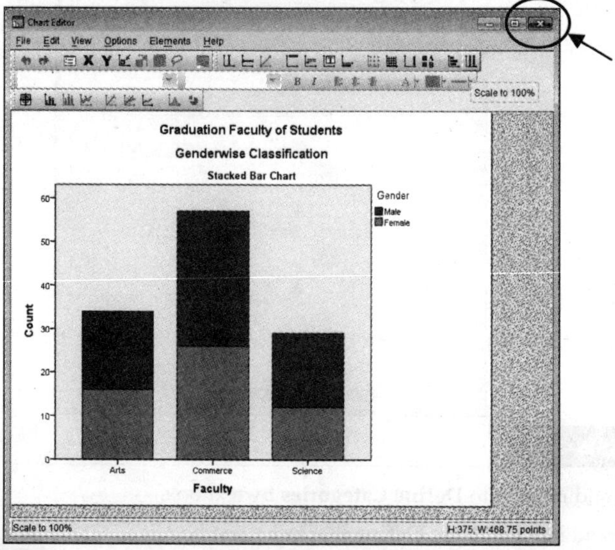

Fig.PASW–5.16

Click the icon marked with a red circle. This icon is used to transform the stacked bar chart by scaling it to 100 per cent. The scaled to 100 % stacked bar chart is shown in the following figure:

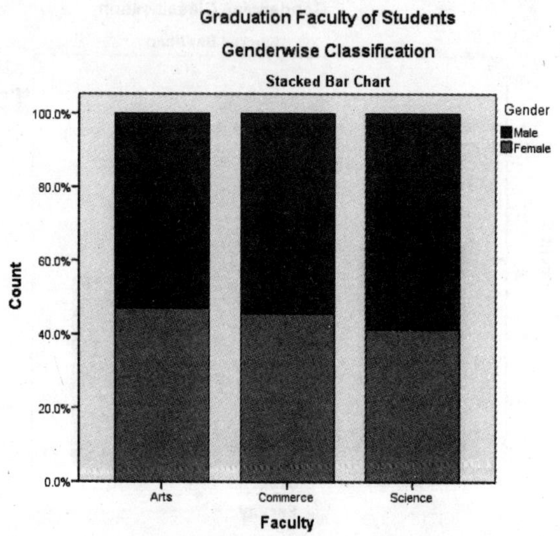

This representation of bar chart is useful for representing the relative proportions of each level of the stacked variable. In our example, it helps us in comparing the proportion of girls and boys in each faculty of graduation.

These charts can be formatted and add value labels can be added once again by clicking the appropriate icons in the Chart Editor Window (refer section 5.10 for formatting details).

5.4 Histogram and the Standard Normal Curve

Histogram, along with the standard normal curve, is used to examine the normality of data. It is a variant of bar chart where the Y-axis variable is measured on interval or ratio scale. For example, to examine the normality of the variable Percentage Marks scored in First Year, we can use histograms. The procedure for constructing a histogram is as follows:

1. Click **Graphs**, **Legacy Dialogues** and **Histogram** (Fig.PASW–5.1) to get the dialogue box shown in Fig.PASW–5.17:

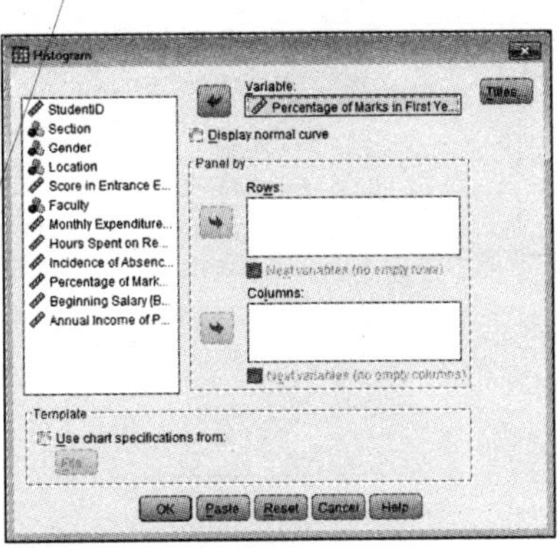

Fig.PASW–5.17

2. Select Percentage of Marks scored in First Year and move it to the Variable text box.

   You may give appropriate titles in the Titles dialogue box by clicking the Titles button.

3. Click Continue to return to previous dialogue box and then OK to execute command. The graph is displayed in the Output Viewer Window as shown below:

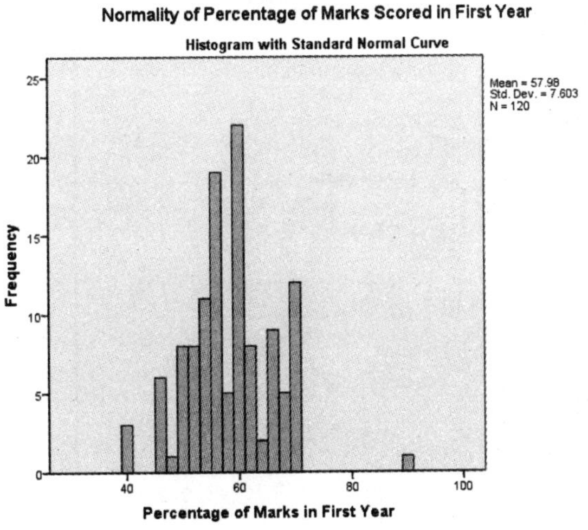

Command Syntax for Histogram

```
GRAPH
  /HISTOGRAM=PerCentFirstYear
  /TITLE='Normality of Percentage of Marks Scored in First Year'
  /SUBTITLE='Histogram with Standard Normal Curve'.
```

The diagram shows that the data is not normally distributed; to examine whether the distribution is normal or not, we can examine by superimposing a standard normal curve on this chart. To do this, double-click the chart to get the Chart Editor Window as shown in Fig.PASW–5.18:

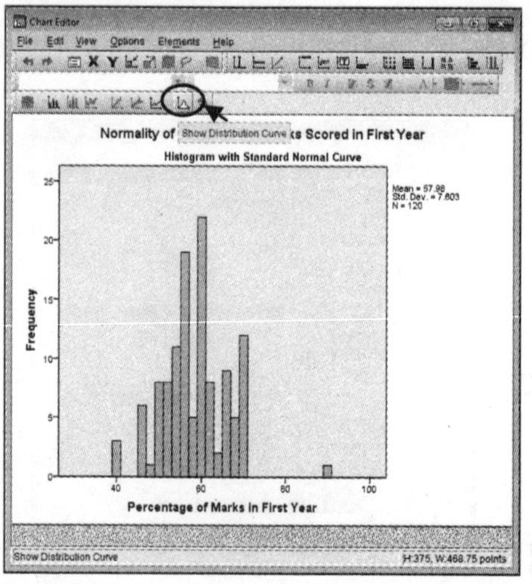

Fig.PASW–5.18

Click the **Show Distribution Curve** icon shown in Fig.PASW–5.18. This will open a **Properties** dialogue box as shown in Fig.PASW–5.19:

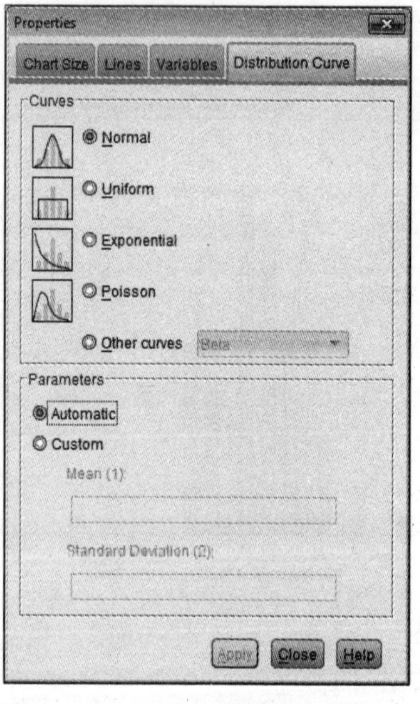

Fig.PASW–5.19

In the **Curves** frame, Normal is selected by default. Keeping this selection unchanged, click **Close** button to close the dialogue box. Close the Chart Editor Window. A curve is displayed over the histogram as shown below:

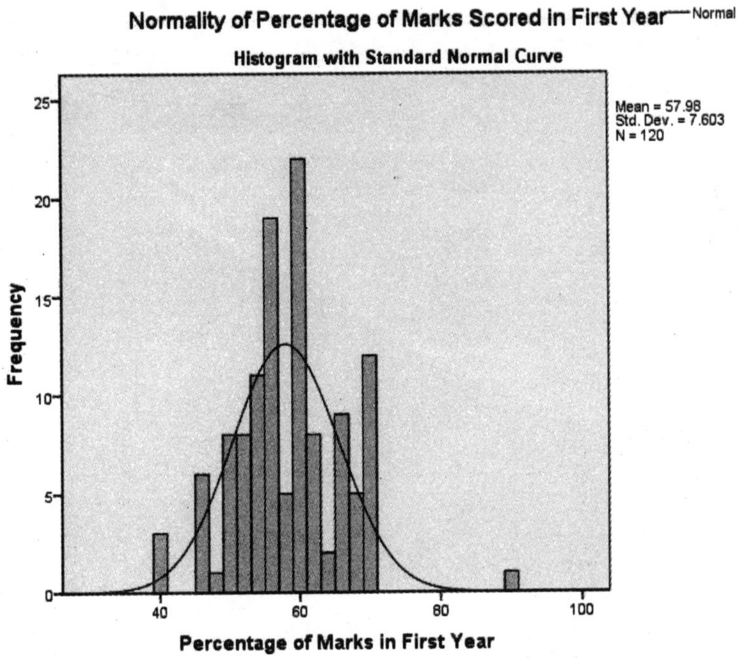

Alternatively, the standard normal curve can be generated along with the histogram if Display Normal Curve is checked in the Histogram dialogue box (Fig.PASW–5.17). Since the distribution does not fit the standard normal curve, we can say that the distribution is not normal.

5.5 Box Plot

Box plot is used to examine variance in of the variable and is another tool to examine normality. For example, we want the box plot for the variable **Percentage of Marks Scored in First Year**. To obtain box plots:

1. Click **Graphs** from the command menu and then click **Legacy Dialogues** and **Boxplot** from the **Graphs** menu. A dialogue box as shown in Fig.PASW–5.20 will be displayed on the screen:

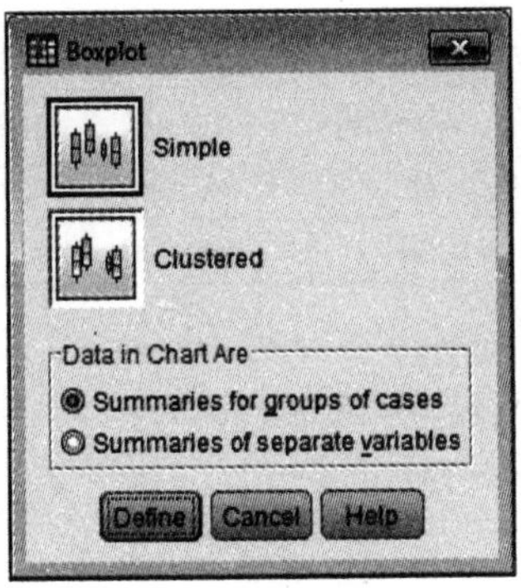

Fig.PASW–5.20

The default selections are **Simple** and **Summaries for groups of cases** in this dialogue box. Keeping those options unchanged, click the **Define** button to get the dialogue box shown in Fig.PASW–5.21:

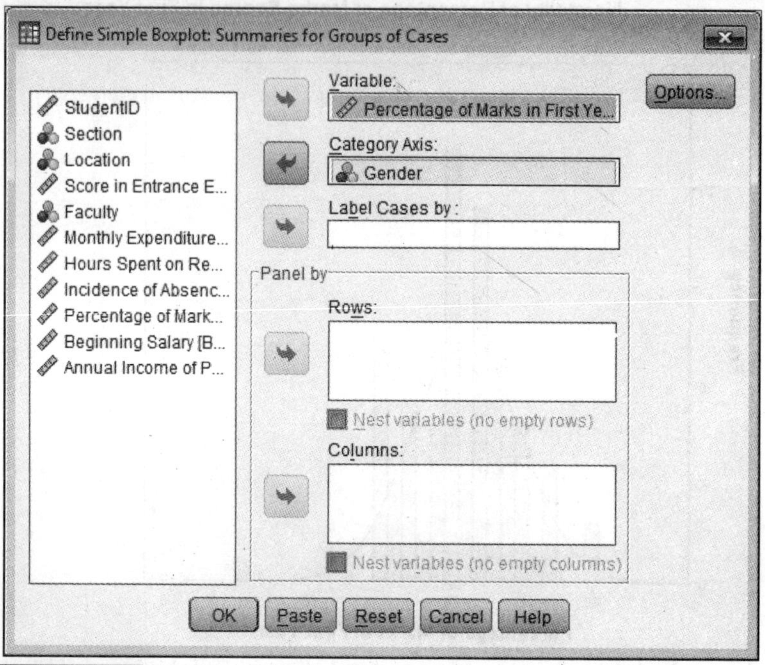

Fig.PASW–5.21

2. Select Percentage of Marks scored in First Year and move it to the Variables text box and Gender to the Category Axis.
3. Click the OK button to execute the command. The Boxplot is displayed in the Output Viewer Window as shown below (The boxplot can be read as shown by indicators – blue coloured boxes – in the diagram):

Explore

Gender

Case Processing Summary							
	Gender	Cases					
		Valid		Missing		Total	
		N	Percent	N	Percent	N	Percent
Percentage of Marks in First Year	Male	66	100.0%	0	.0%	66	100.0%
	Female	54	100.0%	0	.0%	54	100.0%

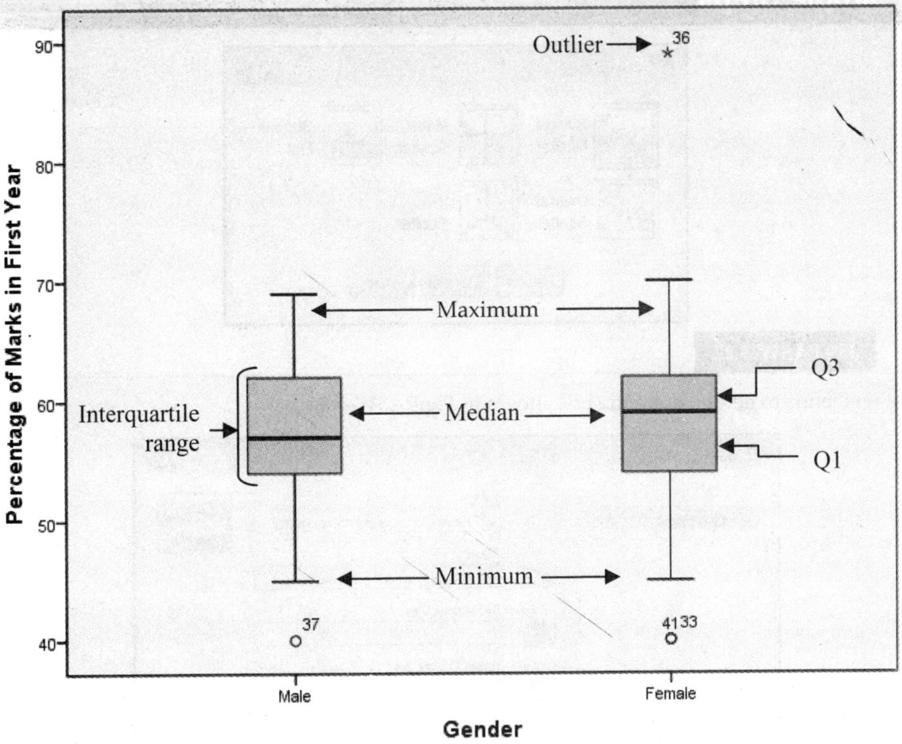

Command Syntax for Box Plots

```
EXAMINE VARIABLES=PerCentFirstYear BY Gender
  /PLOT=BOXPLOT
  /STATISTICS=NONE
  /NOTOTAL.
```

The boxplot shows that the variances of Male and Female are unequal. Moreover, from the position of median, we can say that the distribution for males is negatively skewed and that for females is positively skewed. The discussion on median and its relative position is presented in chapter-4.

5.6 Scatter Diagram

Scatter diagram is used to visually examine the relationship between two variables. It is recommended to examine the scatter plot before performing correlations between two variables. Scatter plot will reveal the nature of relationship between two variables, if it exists. For example, we try to examine the relationship between **GDP of India** and **Final Consumption Expenditure**. The procedure for obtaining scatter plot is as follows:

1. Open **gdp.sav** (created for line chart).
2. Click **Graphs** from the command menu. From the **Graphs** menu, click **Legacy Dialogues** and **Scatter** in sequence. You will get a dialogue box as shown in Fig.PASW–5.22:

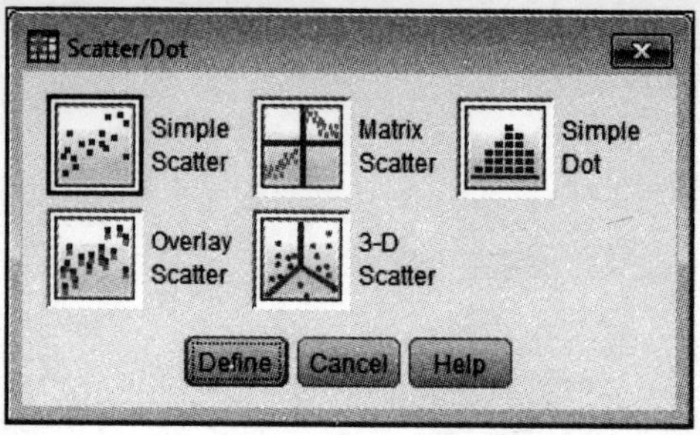

Fig.PASW–5.22

3. Click on Define to get the dialogue box shown in Fig.PASW–5.23:

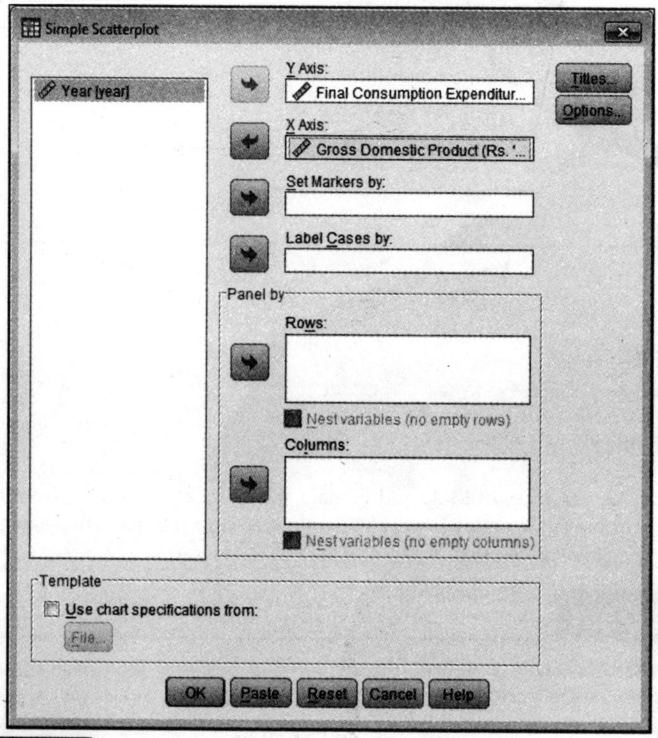

Fig.PASW–5.23

4. Select **Final Consumption Expenditure** and move it to the **Y-axis** textbox.
5. Select **GDP** and move it into **X-axis** textbox.
6. Click the Titles button and type Relationship between GDP of India and Final Consumption Expenditure in India in Title 1 and Scatter Plot in Subtitle.
7. Click **Continue** to go to previous dialogue box and then click **OK** to execute command. The output appears in the Output Viewer Window as shown below:

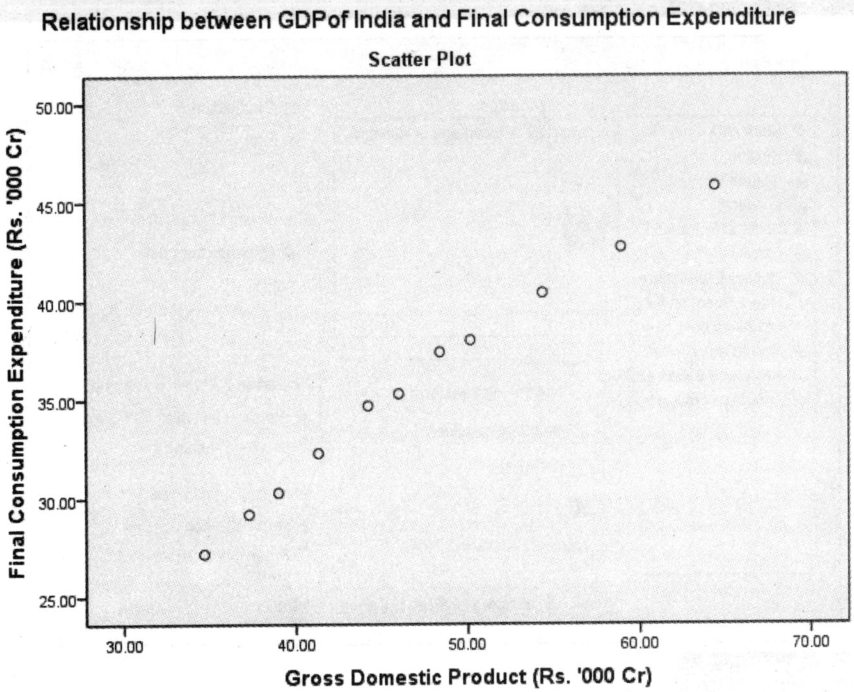

Command Syntax for Scatter Plot

```
DATASET ACTIVATE DataSet2.
GRAPH
  /SCATTERPLOT(BIVAR)=gdp WITH finalconsexp
  /MISSING=LISTWISE
  /TITLE='Relationship between GDPof India and Final Consumption Expenditure'
  /SUBTITLE='Scatter Plot'.
```

The scatter diagram shows that as the **GDP** increases, the **Final Consumption Expenditure** also increases, that is, there is a direct relationship between **GDP** and **Final Consumption Expenditure**. This can be verified using Pearson Correlation (discussed in chapter 12).

5.7 P-P Plot

P-P plots are used to graphically examine the sample distribution. Normally for performing parametric tests on a variable, it is necessary to examine the normality of distribution. P-P plots can be obtained by following procedure:

1. Open students.sav.
2. Click Analyse from the command menu. Click Descriptive Statistics and P-P plots from the Analyze menu to get the dialogue box shown in Fig.PASW–5.24:

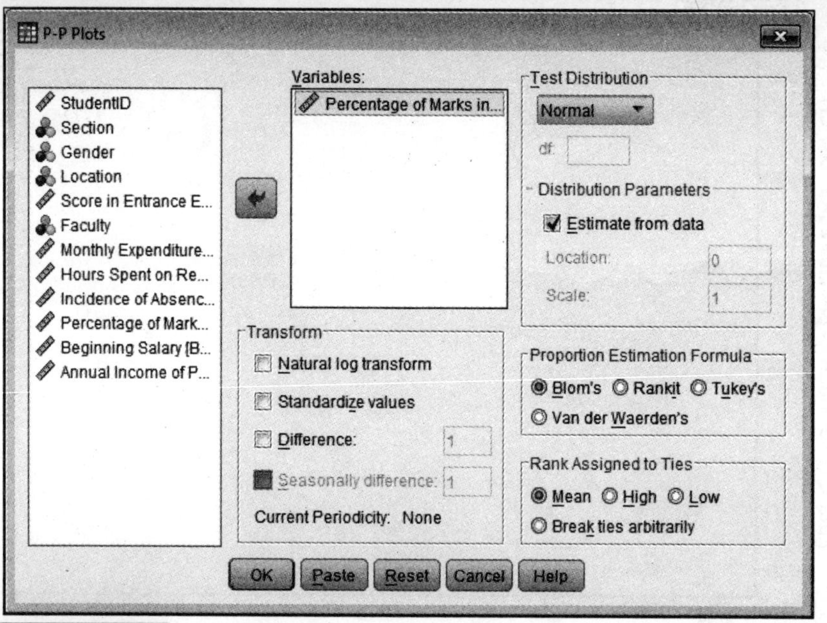

Fig.PASW–5.24

3. Select the variable for which you want to examine normality. Here, we will select **Percentage of Marks Scored in First Year** and move it into the **Variables list** box.

   Keeping all other options unchanged, click **OK** button to execute command. Following chart appears in the Output Viewer window:

PPlot

Model Description		
Model Name		**MOD_1**
Series or Sequence	1	Percentage of Marks in First Year
Transformation		None
Non-Seasonal Differencing		0
Seasonal Differencing		0
Length of Seasonal Period		No periodicity
Standardization		Not applied
Distribution	Type	Normal
	Location	Estimated
	Scale	Estimated
Fractional Rank Estimation Method		Blom's
Rank Assigned to Ties		Mean rank of tied values
Applying the model specifications from MOD_1		

Case Processing Summary		
		Percentage of Marks in First Year
Series or Sequence Length		120
Number of Missing Values in the Plot	User-Missing	0
	System-Missing	0
The cases are unweighted.		

Estimated Distribution Parameters		
		Percentage of Marks in First Year
Normal Distribution	Location	57.98
	Scale	7.603
The cases are unweighted.		

Percentage of Marks in First Year

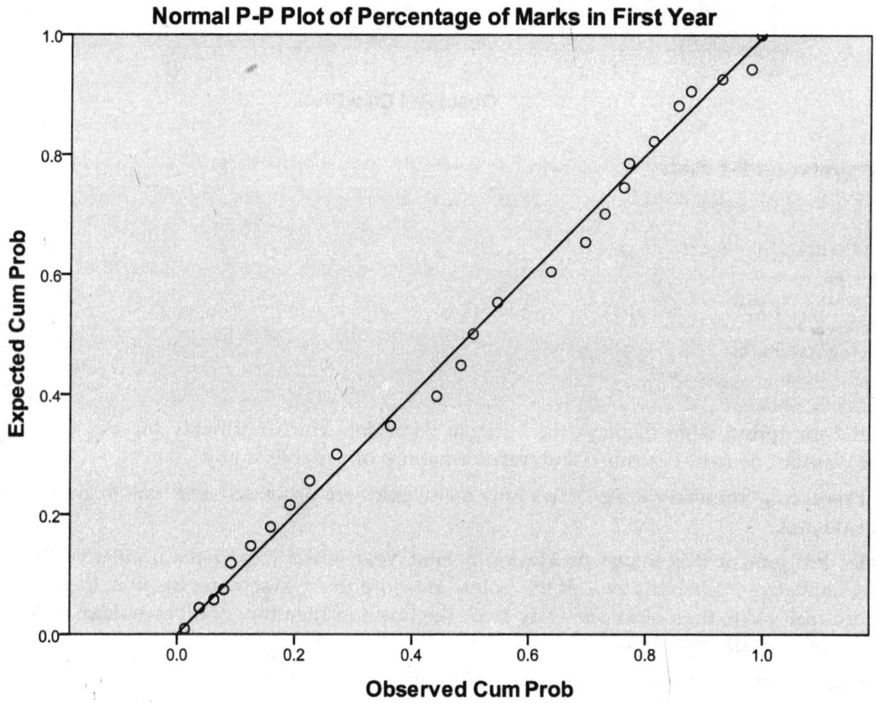

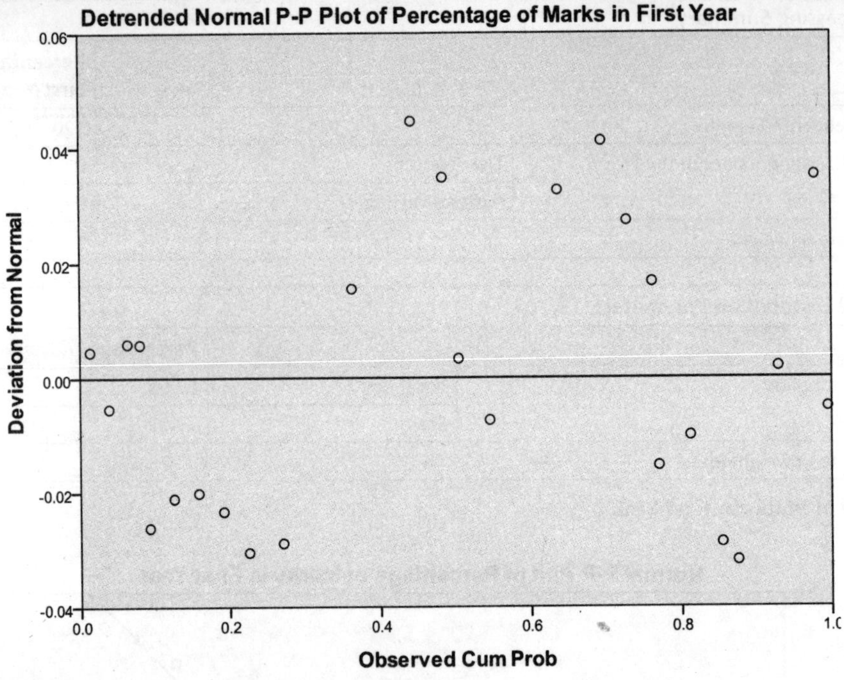

Command Syntax for P-P Plots

```
DATASET ACTIVATE DataSet1.
PPLOT
  /VARIABLES=PerCentFirstYear
  /NOLOG
  /NOSTANDARDIZE
  /TYPE=P-P
  /FRACTION=BLOM
  /TIES=MEAN
  /DIST=NORMAL.
```

The **Model Description** table displays the variable name for which normality (or any other distribution is tested), the distribution to be examined and transformations of variable, if any.

The **Case Processing Summary** table shows how many cases are processed and how many missing values are there in the dataset.

The **Normal P-P plot** of **Percentage of Marks in First Year** is the Expected Cumulative Probability versus Observed Cumulative Probability plot. If the points are close to or, exactly on the line, then the distribution is said to be normal. Here, the points are away from the line and therefore, the **Percentage of Marks Scored in First Year** is not normally distributed.

The **Detrended Normal P-P plot** of Percentage of Marks in First Year is the Deviation from Normal versus Observed Cumulative Probability plot. If the points clutter around the horizontal line and do not form any pattern, the distribution is said to be normal. Here, the points scattered away from the line and therefore, the **Percentage of Marks Scored in First Year** is not normally distributed.

5.8 Q-Q Plot

Q-Q plots are also used to graphically examine the sample distribution. The procedure for obtaining Q-Q plots is as follows:

1. Click **Analyze** from the command menu. Click **Descriptive Statistics** and **P-P plots** from the Analyze menu to get the dialogue box shown in Fig.PASW–5.25:

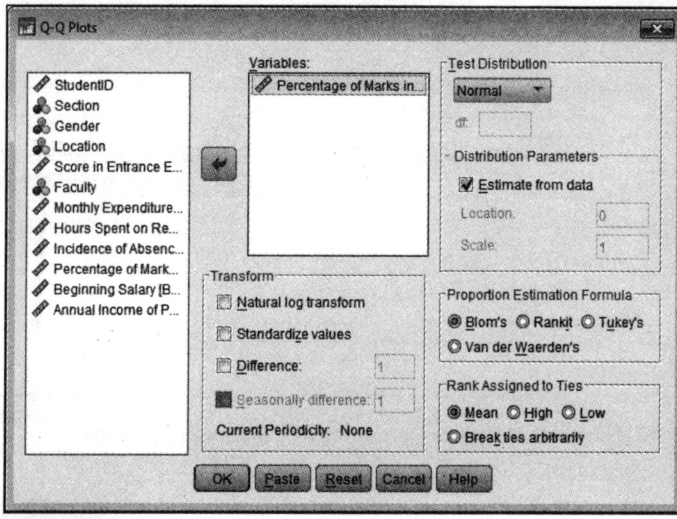

Fig.PASW–5.25

2. Select the variable for which you want to examine normality. Here, we will select **Percentage of Marks Scored in First Year** and move it into the **Variables list** box.

   Keeping all other options unchanged, click **OK** button to execute command. Following chart appears in the Output Viewer window:

P-P Plot

Model Description		
Model Name		**MOD_2**
Series or Sequence	1	Percentage of Marks in First Year
Transformation		None
Non-Seasonal Differencing		0
Seasonal Differencing		0
Length of Seasonal Period		No periodicity
Standardization		Not applied
Distribution	Type	Normal
	Location	estimated
	Scale	estimated
Fractional Rank Estimation Method		Blom's
Rank Assigned to Ties		Mean rank of tied values
Applying the model specifications from MOD_2		

Case Processing Summary		
		Percentage of Marks in First Year
Series or Sequence Length		120
Number of Missing Values in the Plot	User-Missing	0
	System-Missing	0
The cases are unweighted.		

Estimated Distribution Parameters		
		Percentage of Marks in First Year
Normal Distribution	Location	57.98
	Scale	7.603
The cases are unweighted.		

Percentage of Marks in First Year

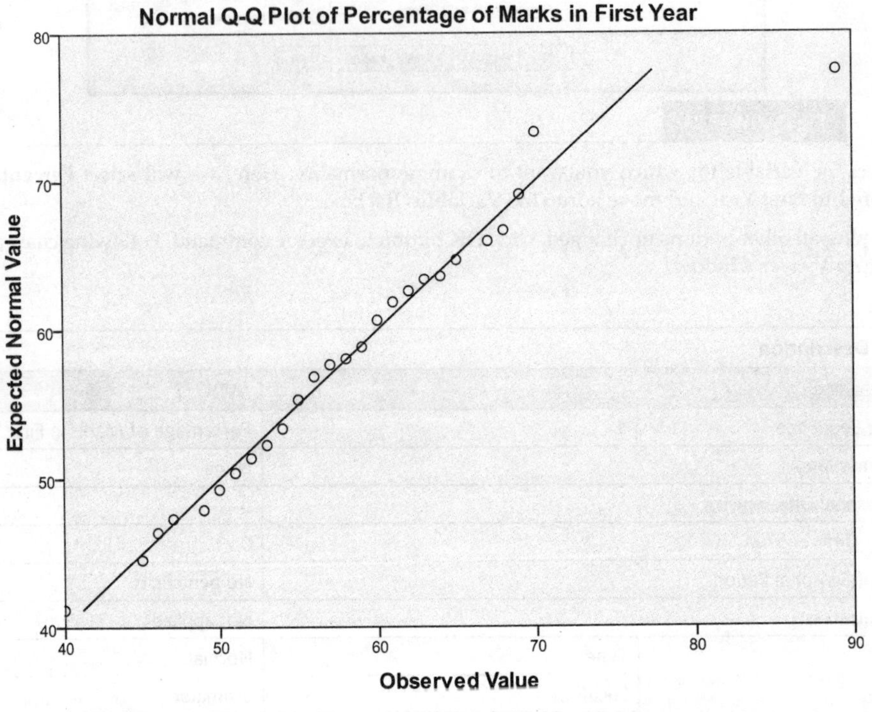

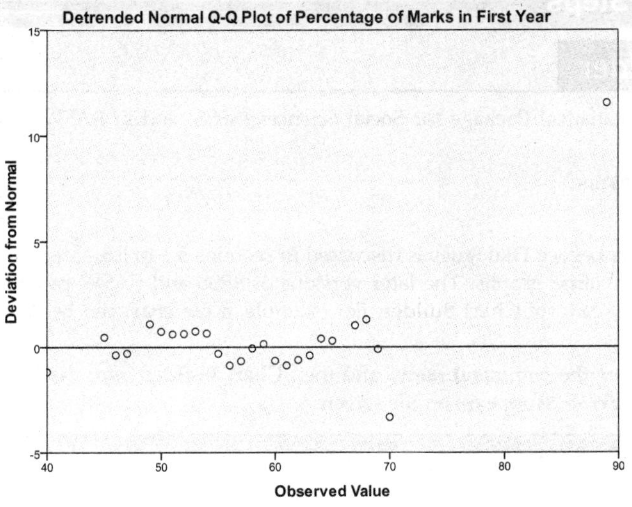

Command Syntax for Q-Q Plot

```
PPLOT
  /VARIABLES=PerCentFirstYear
  /NOLOG
  /NOSTANDARDIZE
  /TYPE=Q-Q
  /FRACTION=BLOM
  /TIES=MEAN
  /DIST=NORMAL.
```

The **Model Description** table displays the variable name for which normality (or any other distribution is tested), the distribution to be examined and transformations of variable, if any.

The **Case Processing Summary** table shows how many cases are processed and how many missing values are there in the dataset.

The **Normal Q-Q plot** of **Percentage of Marks Scored in First Year** displays the Expected Value versus Observed Values. If the points are close to or exactly on the line, then the distribution is said to be normal. Here, the points are away from the line and therefore, the **Percentage of Marks Scored in First Year** is not normally distributed.

The **Detrended Normal Q-Q plot** of **Percentage of Marks Scored in First Year** is the Deviation from Normal versus Observed Value. If the points clutter around the horizontal line and do not form any pattern, the distribution is said to be normal. Here, the points though are cluttered around the horizontal line, are not perfectly randomly distributed around the horizontal line and therefore, the **Percentage of Marks Scored in First Year** is not normally distributed.

Note that:

- Other distributions like Beta, Binomial, Poisson etc. distributions can be examined using P-P plot and Q-Q plots.
- The differences between P-P plot and Q-Q Plot are that:
  - Unlike P-P plot, Q-Q plot does not require the location and scale of the parameters of the theoretical cumulative distribution function be specified and therefore:
    - The linearity of a point on Q-Q scale is not affected by changes in location and scale.
    - The reference line in P-P plot is always y=x where as in Q-Q plot, the reference line depends on location and scale.

5.9 Chart Builder

In later versions of Statistical Package for Social Sciences (SPSS) and in PASW, two options are available for creating graphs:

- Legacy Dialogues and
- Chart Builder.

Creating graphs using Legacy Dialogues is discussed in sections 5.1 to 5.8. In earlier versions of SPSS, this was the only method of creating graphs. The later versions of SPSS and PASW provide drag and drop facility to create graphs with the help of Chart Builder. For example, a pie chart can be created using Chart Builder as follows:

1. Click **Graphs** from the command menu and then **Chart Builder** from the **Graphs** menu. A dialogue box shown in Fig.PASW–5.26 appears on the screen:

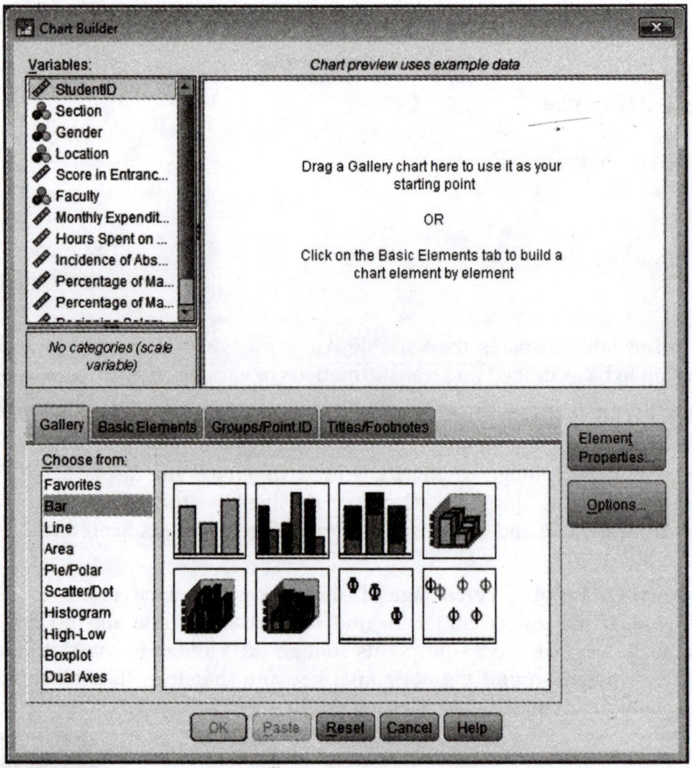

Fig.PASW–5.26

Bar is the default selection. In our example, we want to create a simple bar chart and therefore, we will drag the simple bar chart (the first bar chart in the gallery) and drop it on the chart builder area. This will bring up an **Element Properties** dialogue box as shown in Fig.PASW–5.27:

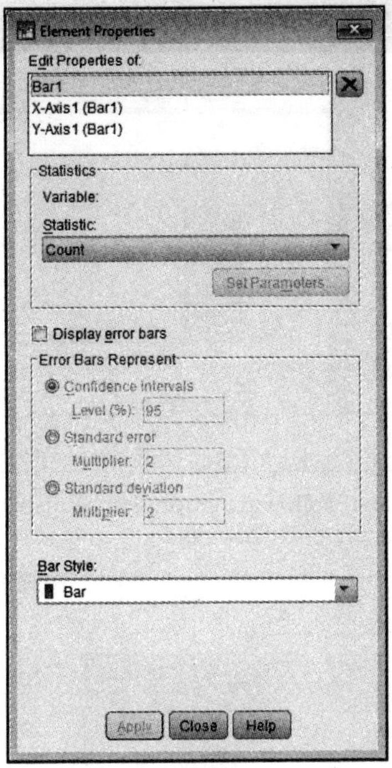

Fig.PASW–5.27

The chart builder area will now look as shown in Fig.PASW–5.28:

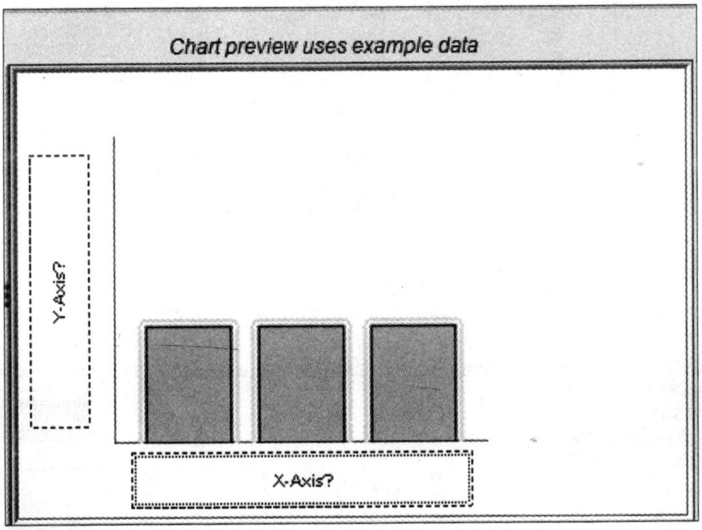

Fig.PASW–5.28

2. Drag **Faculty** and drop it on the **X-axis**. Since we have selected **Count** in the **Statistic** frame in the **Element Properties** dialogue box (Fig.PASW–5.27), **Count** will appear on the **Y-axis** as shown in Fig.PASW–5.29:

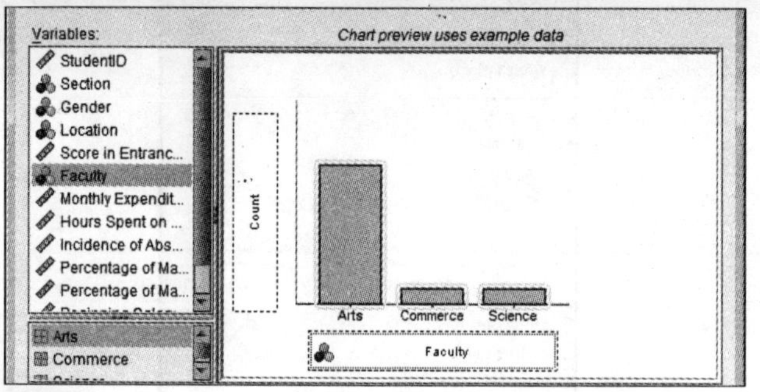

Fig.PASW–5.29

3. Click **OK** to execute the command. Following graph will be displayed in the Output Viewer window. This is similar to the one created using Legacy Dialogues.

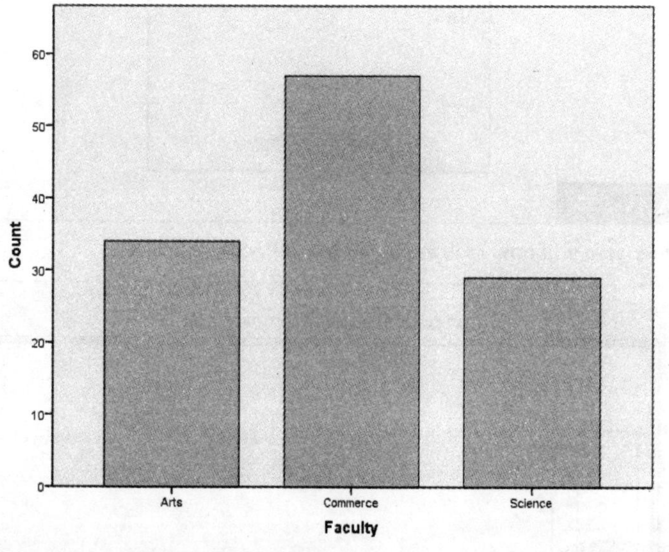

Command Syntax for Bar Chart using Chart Builder

```
* Chart Builder.
GGRAPH
  /GRAPHDATASET NAME="graphdataset" VARIABLES=Faculty COUNT()[name="COUNT"]
  MISSING=LISTWISE
    REPORTMISSING=NO
  /GRAPHSPEC SOURCE=INLINE.
BEGIN GPL
  SOURCE: s=userSource(id("graphdataset"))
  DATA: Faculty=col(source(s), name("Faculty"), unit.category())
  DATA: COUNT=col(source(s), name("COUNT"))
  GUIDE: axis(dim(1), label("Faculty"))
  GUIDE: axis(dim(2), label("Count"))
  SCALE: cat(dim(1), include("1", "2", "3"))
  SCALE: linear(dim(2), include(0))
  ELEMENT: interval(position(Faculty*COUNT), shape.interior(shape.square))
END GPL.
```

This bar chart can be formatted as per requirements.

Unlike Legacy dialogues, the chart builder graphs are sensitive to measurement scale. If the data is measured on nominal scale and the chart requires the data to be ratio scale, chart builder will not allow the user to select that variable for creating a graph.

In earlier versions of SPSS, Interactive charts were available from the Graphs menu. SPSS 16 onwards, Interactive Charts are a part of Legacy Dialogues.

5.10 Formatting Charts

Double-clicking the chart, for example the bar chart that we created just now, will open a Chart Editor Window as shown in Fig.PASW–5.30:

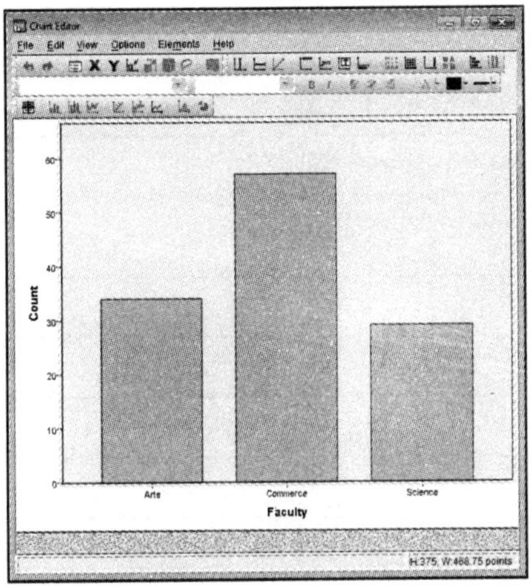

Fig.PASW–5.30

The formatting tool bar appears just below the command menu and is shown in Fig.PASW–5.31:

Fig.PASW–5.31

The use of each of these toolbar icons is given in the table 5.2:

Table 5.2: Formatting Icons and their Uses

Icon	Use	Icon	Use
	Undo		Show Derived Axis
	Redo		Show Legend
	Properties Window		Transpose a Chart Coordinate System
	Select theX-axis		Scale to 100%
	Select theX-axis		Font

Table 5.2: Formatting Icons and their Uses

Icon	Use	Icon	Use
	Rescale Chart		Font Size
	Scale to Data		Bold, Italic (any one or both can be selected)
	Rotating 3-D Chart		Align Left / Center / Right
	Lasso Select Mode		Text Color, Fill Color, Line and Border Color
	Go to Case		Data Label Mode
	Add a reference line to X-axis		Show Data Labels
	Add a reference line to X-axis		Show Error Bars
	Add a reference line from equation		Add Markers
	Insert a title		Add Fit Line at Total
	Insert an annotation		Add Fit Line at Subgroups
	Insert a text box		Add Interpolation Line
	Insert a footnote		Show Distribution Curve
	Bin Element		Explode / Collapse Slice
	Show Grid Lines		

The tool which is not applicable on a particular type of graph will remain disabled. For example, **Show Distribution Curve** is not applicable to any of the graphs except histogram. So, for all other charts, this option will remain disabled.

Summary

In this chapter we learnt:

- Line Chart
- Pie Chart
- Bar Chart
- Histogram
- Box Plot
- Scatter Diagram
- P-P Plot
- Q-Q Plot
- Chart Builder
- Formatting Charts

Chapter 6

One Sample t-Test

In this Chapter:

The one-sample t-test determines whether the observed mean is different from a population mean (or a set value).

The hypothesis testing procedure for a sample mean depends on whether the population variance σ^2 is known. When the population variance is unknown, assuming that population is normal, the test statistic follows the student's t-distribution with n-1 degrees of freedom.

This chapter and several others are concerned with statistical hypothesis testing. In this chapter:

1. We begin by defining what we mean by statistical hypothesis and statistical hypothesis testing. We shall also discuss steps in hypothesis testing.
2. Then we describe the procedure for conducting test of hypothesis for means and interpreting the results.

6.1 Hypothesis Testing

A hypothesis is a statement about population. Data is used to verify the reasonableness of the statement. So, a statistical hypothesis is a claim or assertion about an unknown population parameter.

For Example, a bulb manufacturing company claims that the average life of bulbs manufactured by them is 3000 hours. To test such claims statistically, sample data are collected and analysed. On the basis of sample findings the hypothesized value of the population parameter is either rejected or accepted.

The hypothesis that population parameter is equal to the claim of the company is referred to as the null hypothesis. A null hypothesis is identified by the symbol H_0. In our example:

- **H_0:** μ=3000

The sample statistic is used to make inference about the average life of a bulb.

The second hypothesis is simply the opposite of null hypothesis, and is called the scientific or alternative hypothesis (H_1). For our example, average life of bulb is not equal to 3000 hours as claimed by the manufacturer.

- **H_1:** $\mu \neq 3000$

This hypothesis does not specify whether the life of the bulb will be higher or lower. This type of hypothesis is known as non-directional (two-tailed) hypothesis. If we specify that the average life of the bulb is lower than (or higher than) that claimed by the manufacture, it is called directional hypothesis (one-tailed).

6.1.1 Steps in Hypothesis Testing

1. Specify the null and alternative hypothesis.
2. Select the level of significance, α.
3. Select an appropriate test statistic.
4. Formulate a decision rule.
5. Make a decision regarding null hypothesis based on sample evidence.
6. Interpret your findings.

6.1.2 Assumptions of Hypothesis Testing

Hypothesis tests are based on a set of assumptions. Test produces justifiable conclusion, if the set of assumptions are satisfied. If assumptions are violated, hypothesis test may be comprised and conclusions can be misleading.

- **Normal Sampling Distribution:** Distribution of a sample means is required to be normal. Only then, the hypothesis test using relevant distribution can be performed.
- **Random Sampling:** It is assumed that respondents (subjects or units of study) are selected at random. Generalizations from the sample to population can be done in a meaningful way only if samples are selected randomly and are representative of the population.

- **Independent Observations:** Since the values in the sample are the main requirement for almost all hypothesis tests, the values must comprise of independent observation. The important concern is that each observation is not influenced by other observation. Mostly, the requirement for independent observations can be satisfied by random sample.

6.2 Testing for Population Mean

When sample is less than 30 and population standard deviation is not known, t-distribution is used instead of standard normal distribution. The dataset for our example of bulb life as claimed by the manufacturer is shown in the following table:

Users	Bulblife	Users	Bulblife
1	2789	6	2600
2	2800	7	2895
3	2300	8	3175
4	3100	9	2500
5	2750	10	2400

The procedure for conducting one-sample t-test is given below:

1. Enter data given in the table above in the data editor and save it as **bulbs.sav**.
2. Click **Analyze** from command menu as shown in Fig.PASW–6.1.
3. Click **Compare Means** and **One-Sample t-Test** from the **Analyze** menu (Fig.PASW–6.1). A dialogue box appears as shown in Fig.PASW–6.2:

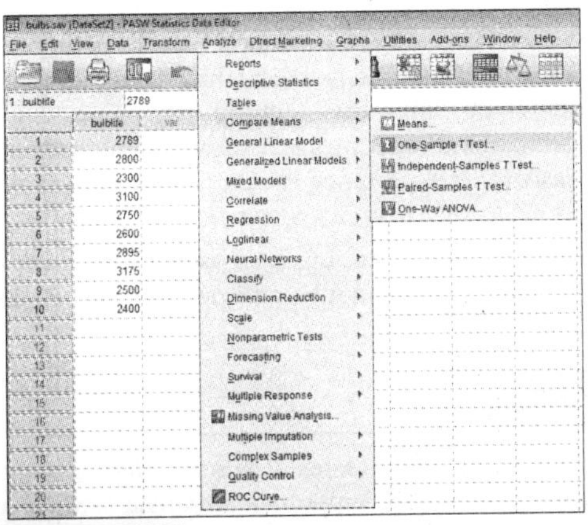

Fig.PASW–6.1

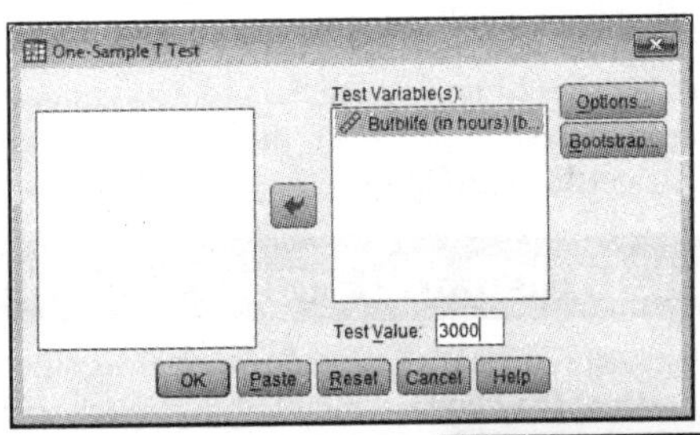

Fig.PASW–6.2

4. Select the variable **Bulb-Life (in hours)** and move it in the **Test Variable(s)** box.
5. Type the hypothesized population mean value (in our example, **3000**) in the **Test Value** box.
6. Click **OK** button to execute command. Following output will appear in the Output Viewer Window:

T-Test

One-Sample Statistics				
	N	Mean	Std. Deviation	Std. Error Mean
Bulblife (in hours)	10	2730.90	285.681	90.340

One-Sample Test						
	Test Value = 3000					
	T	df	Sig. (2-tailed)	Mean Difference	95% Confidence Interval of the Difference	
					Lower	Upper
Bulblife (in hours)	-2.979	9	.015	-269.100	-473.46	-64.74

Command Syntax for One Sample t-Test

```
T-TEST
  /TESTVAL=3000
  /MISSING=ANALYSIS
  /VARIABLES=bulblife
  /CRITERIA=CI(.95).
```

You will see the title **T-Test** followed by two tables – **One Sample Statistics** and **One Sample Test**. The **One Sample Statistics** table gives summary measures (also called the descriptive statistics) for the variable **Bulblife (in hours)**. The second table – **One Sample Test** gives the **t**-statistic along with its associated **2-tailed significance** level (also called the p –value).

An obtained p-value shows a theoretical risk of Type – I error. Researchers usually want p to be less than 0.05. A Type – I error occurs when the null hypothesis H_0 is true and the researcher rejects it.

The t-test is a robust test. It does not lose power when the assumption of normality is violated, particularly, when the sample size is large enough. Erroneous conclusions can be drawn if the t-test is used incorrectly. If a sample size is small (less than 30) and the distribution is not normal, other non-parametric testing procedures may be considered.

The results of **One Sample Test** table show that there is a significant difference between the hypothesized mean and the sample mean, since t-statistic is -2.979 and its associated p-value is 0.015 which is less than 0.05. The interpretation of a statistically significant result should be made cautiously. A study may show a statistically significant result when there is really no effect in the population. Sometimes statistically significant outcomes arise but, due to sampling error or; it could arise due to researcher expectancy effects. Confounding variable, as well as human participation may influence the outcome.

Researcher should review the data to prevent any possible error. Data cleaning is advisable before undertaking statistical analysis. Remember, that extreme or unusual observations cannot be arbitrarily altered or discarded to report pertinent findings.

6.3 Statistical and Practical Significance

The discussion on statistical and practical significance will be useful here. A result that is statistically significant (high t value) may be too small to have much importance in real world. Suppose, a researcher finds that a new drug, treating blood pressure brings down the blood pressure by 5 units (measured in terms of mmHg).Though these findings are statistically significant, they may not be, practically significant.

Summary

In this chapter we learnt:

- Hypothesis testing.
- Steps in hypothesis testing.
- Assumptions of hypothesis testing.
- Testing for population mean.
- Statistical and practical significance.

Chapter 7

Independent Sample t-Test

In this Chapter:

Two basic experimental designs are employed to study differences in two groups. Independent group design involves experiments using two conditions. In this design, subjects are randomly selected from the subject population and then randomly assigned to either experimental or control condition. For example, the differences in productivity, employment and use of high-yielding variety (HYV) between irrigated farms and non-irrigated farms can be studied using Independent Sample t-test. Independent Sample t-test can also be used to study the gender differences in performance, IQ level and physical characteristics. One can study the differences in the average life of bulbs of two companies (for example, Bajaj and Surya) using Independent Sample t-test.

The other design is the repeated measures design which is also referred to as before-after or panel design. Here, a single sample is measured at two different points in time.

In this chapter we shall discuss assumptions of Independent Sample t-test, procedure for undertaking Independent Sample t-test and interpretation of the findings.

7.1 Assumptions of Independent Sample t-Test

The assumptions for undertaking Independent Sample t-test are as follows:

- Dependent variable is measured in ratio or interval scale.
- Sample mean is normally distributed.
- Respondents are selected randomly.
- Respondents of both the groups are not related, that is, independent samples.
- Variances of both the groups are equal.

We shall examine whether there is any difference in Percentage of Marks Scored by local students and commuting students. Independent Sample t-test is chosen as the respondents of two different groups are independent of each other (local and commuters). Moreover, the variable Percentage of Marks Scored in First Year is a ratio data. If the scores on dependent variable are ordinal, a non-parametric Wilcoxon Rank Sum test or Mann-Whitney can be used.

The null and alternative hypothesis for examining difference in Percentage of Marks Scored in First Year of local and commuting students are:

- **H_0:** There is no difference in Percentage of Marks Scored by local students and students who commute ($\mu_l=\mu_c$).
- **H_1:** The Percentage of Marks Scored by local students and students who commute are different ($\mu_l \neq \mu_c$).

7.2 Procedure for Testing for Differences in Means between Groups

In order to perform independent sample t-test, following procedure is undertaken:

1. Open the file **students.sav**.
2. Click on **Analyze** from the command menu as shown in Fig.PASW–7.1:

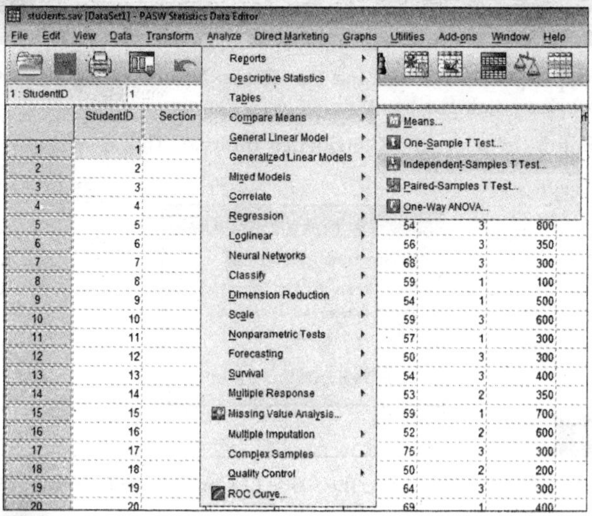

Fig.PASW–7.1

3. Select **Compare means** and **Independent Sample T-test** from the **Analyze** menu to get the dialogue box shown in Fig.PASW–7.2:

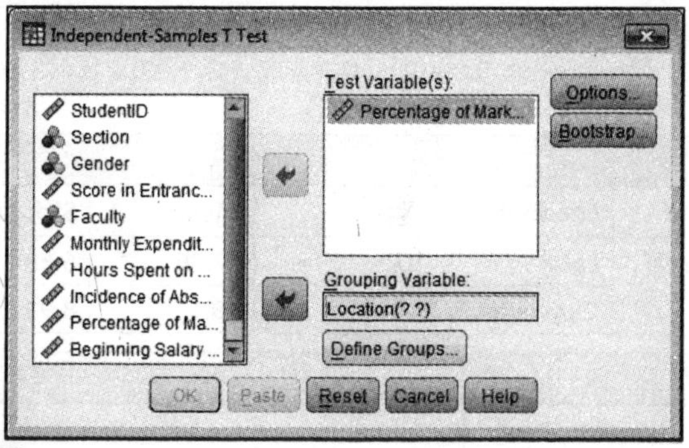

Fig.PASW–7.2

4. The **Test Variable** is **Percentage of Marks Scored in First Year** and the groups to be compared are local and commuting students. So **Location** is the **Grouping Variable**.

   To define these two groups – local and commuting students, click on **Define Groups** button to get the dialogue shown in Fig.PASW–7.3:

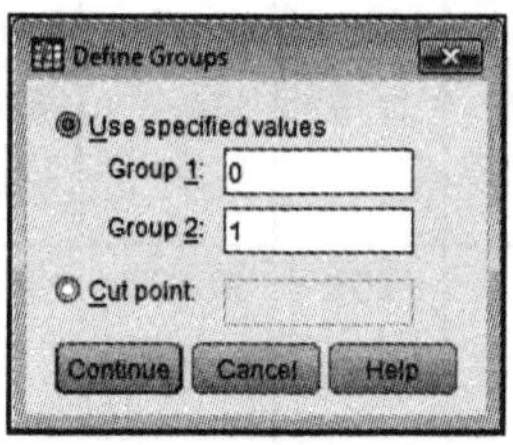

Fig.PASW–7.3

5. Assign code **0** to **Group 1** (local students) and **1** to **Group 2** (commuting Students) and click the **Continue** button to return to previous dialogue box.
6. Click the **Options** button to select the **Confidence Interval**. This displays a dialogue box as shown in Fig.PASW–7.4:

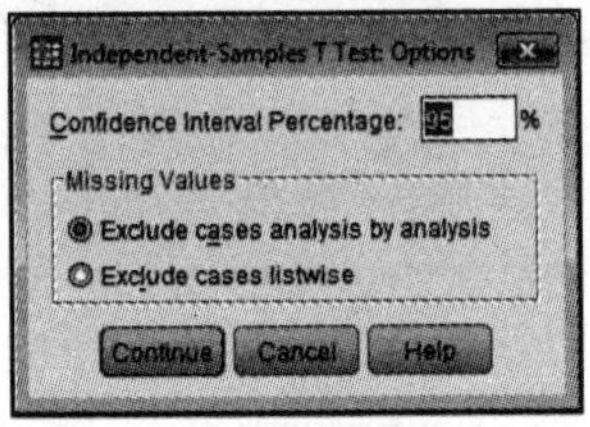

Fig.PASW–7.4

7. Since the chosen value of α is 0.05, we keep the value of **Confidence Interval** of **95%**.
8. Click **Continue** and then **OK** button to execute the command. Following results in the form of two tables – Group Statistics and Independent Samples Test will appear in the Output Viewer window:

Command Syntax for Independent Samples t-Test

```
T-TEST GROUPS=Location(0 1)
  /MISSING=ANALYSIS
  /VARIABLES=PerCentFirstYear
  /CRITERIA=CI(.95).
```

T-Test

Group Statistics					
	Location	N	Mean	Std. Deviation	Std. Error Mean
Percentage of Marks in First Year	Local	72	57.86	6.634	.782
	Commuter	48	58.17	8.933	1.289

Independent Samples Test										
		Levene's Test for Equality of Variances		t-test for Equality of Means						
									95% Confidence Interval of the Difference	
		F	Sig.	t	df	Sig. (2-tailed)	Mean Difference	Std. Error Difference	Lower	Upper
Percentage of Marks in First Year	Equal variances assumed	3.235	.075	-.215	118	.830	-.306	1.422	-3.122	2.511
	Equal variances not assumed			-.203	80.692	.840	-.306	1.508	-3.306	2.695

You see the title **T-Test** followed by two tables – **Group Statistics** and **Independent Samples Test**. The **Group Statistics** table displays the summary measures (N, mean, Std. Deviation, std. Error Mean) of the variable (score) selected, for the independent sample t-test for both the groups – commuters as well as local students. **Independent Samples Test** table presents the statistics that are critical to the research question. This table contains two sets of analysis:

The first assumes equal variances and the second does not. The Levene's test decides which version of the t-test to report. If the Levene's test shows no significant violations of assumption, you should report the "equal variances assumed" version of the t-test. This t ratio refers to Students't, where as "equal variances not assumed" version of t-ratio refers to Welch t. To assess whether the variances of two groups are equal or not, we are required to utilize the significance level linked with the value beneath the Levene's Test for Equality of Variances title. The null and alternative hypotheses for Levene's Test for Equality of Variances are as follows:

- **H_0:** Variances of two groups are equal.
- **H_1:** Variances of two groups are unequal.

In our example, we fail to reject the null hypothesis, since the F-value is 3.235 and its associated significance value is .075 (>0.05. Please note that here, the Box Plots discussed in Chapter – 3 helps in visually examining the differences in variances of two groups.

The t-value is –0.215 and associated significance value is .830, therefore we do not reject the null hypothesis for equality of means. In common parlance, there is no statistically significant difference in the Percentage of Marks Scored by local students and students who commute.

7.3 Interpretation of Null Results

When study reveals a non-significant result, it is not correct to conclude that we accept null hypothesis – H_0. For a non-significant result, there could be many explanations. A significance test may yield non-significant results even when the null hypothesis is correct. For instance when the effect size is very small, non-significant result may arise or,it can be caused due to a sampling error; the measure of dependent variable may not be reliable or it is not sensitive to explanatory variable all these can be reasons for non-significant results. You should remember that, result of a single study is not conclusive proof of the null hypothesis.

7.4 Effect Size

Effect size (ES) is a name given to an index that measures the magnitude of an independent variable. Unlike significance tests, this index is independent of sample size. That, an effect is statistically significant does not inevitably imply that the effect has any "practical significance". As the sizes of the sample surge, the possibility to discover small mean differences between statistically significant advances 1. Effect size measures help to clarify the meaning of significant or nonsignificant effects. It is useful in comparison across studies to have, an effect size index that is independent of sample size and also independent of unit of measurement.

There is a wide array of formulas used to measure ES.

In general, ES can be measured in two ways:

- As the standardized difference between two means, or
- As the connection between the personal scores on the dependent variable and independent variable arrangement. This association is referred as "Effect Size". The effect size affiliation can be calculated straightaway as the point-biserial link between the continuous dependent variable and the dichotomous independent variable. The point-biserial is unique instance of the Pearson product-moment bond that is applied when one of the variables is dichotomous. You can calculate the ES relation with the help of the CORR procedure in Predictive Analytic Software (PASW).

For independent samples t-test, Cohen's *d* is calculated as follows:

$$d = \frac{M_1 - M_2}{S_p}$$

Where S_p is calculated by taking square root of the value of S_p^2. The difference in numerator reflects the influence of independent variable. The standard deviation in the denominator indicates the effects of confounding or extraneous variables. In our example the value of Cohen's *d* would be – 0.039.

A t-ratio can also be converted into a point biserial correlation. The value of point biserial ranges from 0 to 1. The value 0 indicates on relationship. Point biserial is calculated as follows:

$$r_{pb} = \sqrt{\frac{t^2}{t^2 + df}}$$

The value of point biserial will be 0.0197 in our example.

Alternative measure of Effect size index is the eta squared (η^2) coefficient. It measures proportion of variation in dependent variable explained by independent variable. It can be calculated from the *t* ratio:

$$\eta^2 = \sqrt{\frac{t^2}{t^2 + df}}$$

The value of η^2 can range from 0 to 1. A related statistic omega squared provides more conservative estimate of the proportion of variance in dependent variable that may be associated with independent variable.

Summary

In this chapter we learnt:

- Assumptions for independent sample t-test.
- Procedure for testing differences in means between groups.
- Interpretation of null Results.
- Effect size.

Chapter 8

Paired Samples t-Test

In this Chapter:

Paired Samples t-test examines the difference in means of the dependent samples. Out of the two basic experimental designs, one design is employed to study differences between two groups. The other design is used to compare each respondent with self, at another point in time for example, comparing performance of students before and after vacations, sales before and after advertisement etc. These examples represent situations in which events are closely matched. Therefore, paired samples t-test is also called dependent samples t-test. Two samples are said to be dependent if each member of one sample relates to the member of the other sample. In that case, the assumption of independent samples is violated and therefore, independent sample t-test will be inappropriate. Thus, in this situation, paired sample t-test is more desirable. Therefore, paired Samples t-test is also known as dependent sample t-test, matched-sample t-test, related sample t-test or repeated measures t-test. In this chapter, we shall discuss the assumptions of paired samples t-test, the procedure for undertaking paired samples t-test and interpreting the findings.

8.1 Assumptions of Paired Samples t-Test

The assumptions of paired samples t-test are same as those of independent samples t-test except that in paired samples t-test, the samples are not independent.

- Dependent variable is measured on ratio or interval scale.
- Sample mean is normally distributed.
- Respondents are selected randomly.

We shall discuss now, how paired-sample t-test is conducted in PASW. In our sample dataset, the information related to marks scored in first test and second test are given. Let's examine whether the performance of students have improved or not.

The null and alternative hypothesis for examining the difference in scores of local and commuting students are:

- **H_0:** There is no difference between Percentage of Marks Scored in First Year and Percentage of Marks Scored in Second Year.
- **H_1:** There is difference between Percentage of Marks Scored in First Year and Percentage of Marks Scored in Second Year.

8.2 Procedure for Paired Sample t-test

1. Open the file – **students.sav**.
2. Click **Analyze** from command menu as shown in Fig.PASW–8.1:

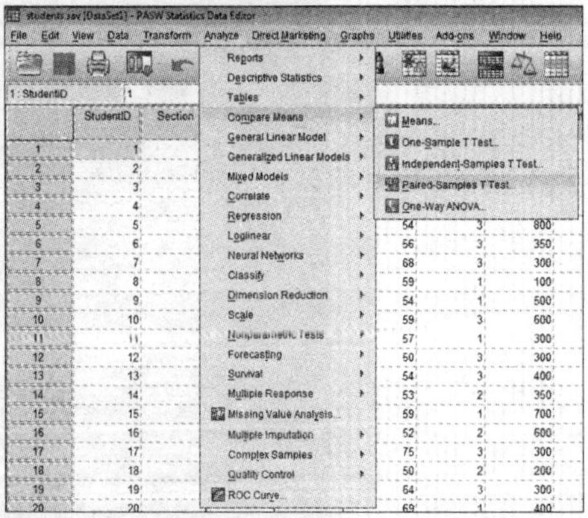

Fig.PASW–8.1

3. Click **Compare Means** and **Paired-Samples t-test** from Analyze menu (Fig.PASW–8.1) to get the following dialogue box shown in Fig.PASW–8.2:

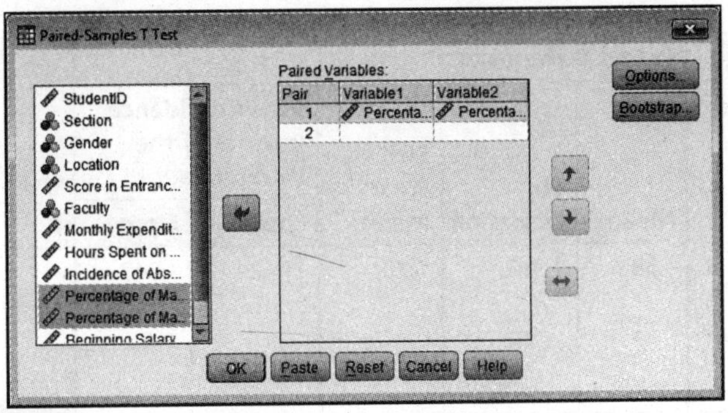

Fig.PASW–8.2

4. Select two variables – **Percentage of Marks in First Year** and **Percentage of Marks in Second Year** and shift them to **Paired Variables** list box by clicking the right arrow button in the centre.

5. Click **Options** button to get the dialogue box shown in Fig.PASW–8.3:

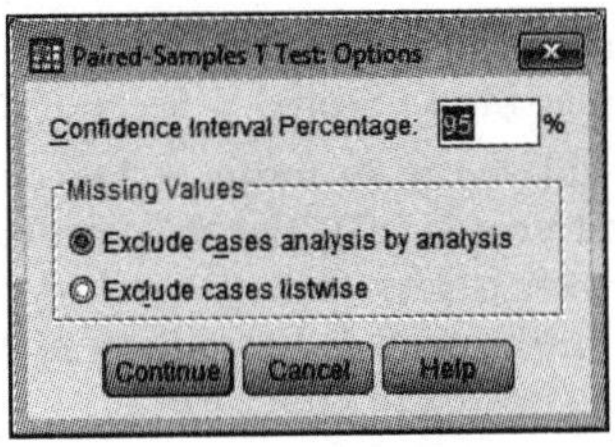

Fig.PASW–8.3

6. Keeping the default value of Confidence Interval Percentage unchanged, click Continue button to go to the previous dialogue box and then click OK to execute command. This will generate the following output in the output window:

Command Syntax for Paired Samples t-Test

```
T-TEST PAIRS=PerCentFirstYear WITH PerCentSecYear (PAIRED)
  /CRITERIA=CI(.9500)
  /MISSING=ANALYSIS.
```

T-Test

Paired Samples Statistics

		Mean	N	Std. Deviation	Std. Error Mean
Pair 1	Percentage of Marks in First Year	57.98	120	7.603	.694
	Percentage of Marks in Second Year	58.57	120	6.796	.620

Paired Samples Correlations

		N	Correlation	Sig.
Pair 1	Percentage of Marks in First Year & Percentage of Marks in Second Year	120	.920	.000

Paired Samples Test

		Paired Differences					t	df	Sig. (2-tailed)
					95% Confidence Interval of the Difference				
		Mean	Std. Deviation	Std. Error Mean	Lower	Upper			
Pair 1	Percentage of Marks in First Year - Percentage of Marks in Second Year	-.583	2.992	.273	-1.124	-.043	-2.136	119	.035

The output displays three tables – Paired Samples Statistics, Paired Samples Correlations and Paired Samples Test under the title T-Test.

Paired Samples Statistics table displays the summary measures (Mean, N, Std. Deviation, Std. Error of Mean) of selected variables for the paired t-test. The mean of the **Percentage of Marks Scored in First Year** is 57.98 and **Percentage Marks Scored in Second Year** is 58.57.

Paired Samples Correlations table provides the information related to correlation between the Percentage Marks Scored in First Year and Percentage Marks Scored in Second Year.

Paired Samples Test table gives the difference in mean of **Percentage of Marks scored in First Year** and **Percentage of Marks Scored in second year** (-.583). The table generated the value of t-statistic of -2.136 with associated significance value .035, which is less than 0.05 (chosen α value). Therefore, we reject the null hypothesis and can say that there is improvement in **Percentage of Marks Scored in Second Year** by students as compared to the **Percentage of Marks Scored in First Year.**

Summary

In this chapter we learnt:

- Assumptions for paired samples t-test.
- Procedure for paired samples t-test.
- Interpretation of results of paired samples t-test.

Chapter 9

One-Way ANOVA

In this Chapter:

One-Way Analysis of Variance (ANOVA) examines the differences between more than two independent samples. One-way ANOVA is used when you have a categorical independent variable (with two or more categories) and a normally distributed interval or ratio dependent variable. Here, the objective is to test for differences in the means of the dependent variable broken down by the levels of the independent variable. For example, comparison of the **Percentage of Marks Scored in First Year** by students belonging to three distinct educational backgrounds or, land productivity across different farm size groups etc. Changes in the dependent variable in ANOVA are presumed to be the results of changes in the independent variable.

One-Way ANOVA can be thought of as a sequence of Independent Sample t-test but in doing so, the degree of freedom is reduced. Using multiple t-test for testing the hypothesis that 'k population means are equal' is not appropriate. When more than one t-test is run, each at a specified level of significance (such as α=0.05), the type – I error rate increases. ANOVA permits us to test hypothesis of equality of k population means, while maintaining the type – I error rate at the pre-established α level, for the entire set of comparison. One-Way ANOVA efficiently compares between more than two groups, and also preserves a degree of freedom. However, if the One-Way ANOVA suggests that there is some difference in means of groups; Post Hoc Analysis provides details about the pair-wise difference in means, across groups.

Analysis of Variance can be done using any one of the following experimental designs:

- **Completely Randomized Design:** In this experimental design, there is only one independent variable with two or more levels (also called treatments or classifications) and the difference in mean scores of these two or more independent populations is examined. For two levels, we use independent sample t-test to examine the mean difference; for three or more levels, we use one-way Analysis of Variance (ANOVA).
- **Randomized Block Design:** In this experimental design, there is one independent variable with two or more levels, and a second level variable, called blocking variable, which the researcher wants to control. The **Repeated Measures Design** is a special case of randomized block design, where an individual respondent is considered to be one block level. The same sets of respondents are subjected to all levels or treatments. Here, if different sets of respondents are chosen then the individual differences would affect the mean scores. In repeated measures design, we are controlling for individual differences. Here too, if the independent variable has two levels, we use dependent / paired sample t-test for comparison of means. For three or more levels, we use Repeated Measures ANOVA. Chapter 10 discusses in detail the assumptions and method of undertaking Repeated Measures ANOVA.
- **Factorial Design:** There are two or more independent level variables in this experimental design. Every level of an independent variable is studied for each level of remaining (other) independent variables. In factorial design, the impact of two (or more) independent variables is examined simultaneously. If there are two independent variables, we use Two-way ANOVA. Chapter 11 discusses in detail the assumptions and method of undertaking Two-Way ANOVA.

In this chapter we shall focus our discussion on assumptions and procedure for undertaking One-Way ANOVA; procedure for performing Post Hoc Analysis and interpreting results.

9.1 Assumptions of One-Way ANOVA

The assumptions for undertaking one-way ANOVA are as follows:

- Dependent variable is measured in ratio or interval scale.
- Sample mean is normally distributed.
- Respondents are selected randomly.
- Respondents of all the groups are not related.
- Variances of all the groups are equal.

ANOVA is robust with respect to violations of assumptions, except in case of unequal variances with unequal sample sizes. To illustrate let's say, a researcher is interested in studying differences in the performance of three categories of **Faculties** – Arts, Commerce and Science, that is, students belonging to three distinct backgrounds.

Here, we have one dependent variable – **Percentage Marks Scored in First Year**, and the independent variable –**Faculty** that has three categories / levels.

The null and alternative hypothesis for examining the difference in **Percentage of Marks Scored in First Year** of the students coming from different **Faculties** – Arts, Commerce and Science backgrounds are:

- **H_0:** There is no difference in **Percentage of Marks Scored in First Year** of students belonging to different **Faculties**.
- **H_1:** The mean Percentage of Marks Scored in First Year by students belonging to at least one **Faculty** is different.

9.2 Procedure for Testing for Differences in Means between Groups

1. Click **Analyze** from command menu as shown in Fig.PASW–9.1:

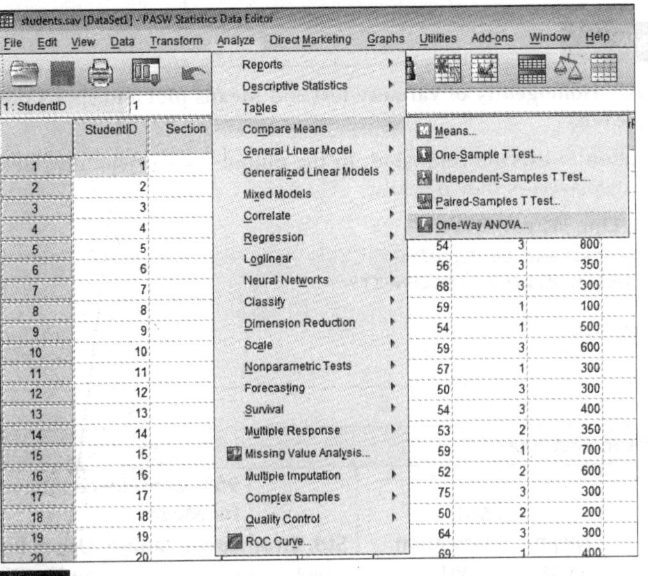

Fig.PASW–9.1

2. Click **Compare Means** from **Analyze** menu and **One-way ANOVA** from the **Compare Means** menu to get the dialogue box shown in Fig,PASW–9.2:

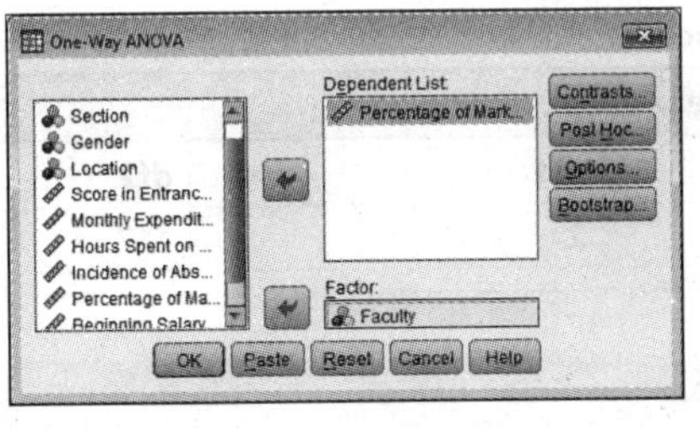

Fig.PASW–9.2

3. Select and bring the variable Percentage of Marks Scored in First Year to the Dependent List.
4. Select **Faculty** and bring it to the **Factor** text box.
5. Click **Options** button to get the dialogue box shown in Fig.PASW–9.3:

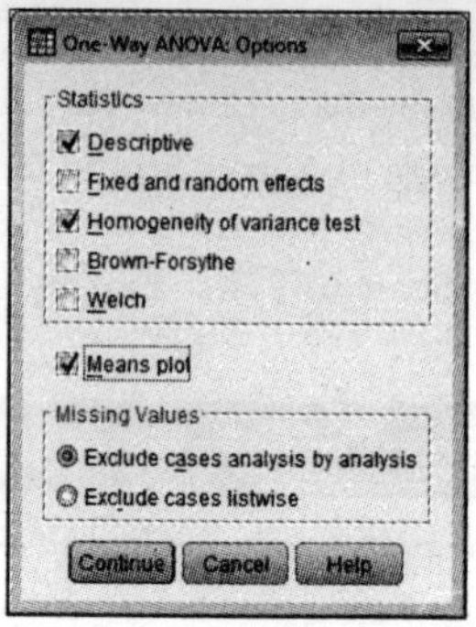

Fig.PASW–9.3

6. Select **Descriptive, Homogenity of variance test** and **Means plot** and click **Continue** button to go back to previous dialogue box.
7. Click the **OK** button to execute command. In the output viewer window, table for the descriptives and ANOVA will be displayed as shown below:

Command Syntax for One-Way ANOVA

```
ONEWAY PerCentFirstYear BY Faculty
  /STATISTICS DESCRIPTIVES HOMOGENEITY
  /PLOT MEANS
  /MISSING ANALYSIS.
```

Oneway

Descriptives

Percentage of Marks in First Year

	N	Mean	Std. Deviation	Std. Error	95% Confidence Interval for Mean		Minimum	Maximum
					Lower Bound	Upper Bound		
Arts	34	55.91	6.201	1.063	53.75	58.08	40	70
Commerce	57	59.09	7.246	.960	57.16	61.01	40	70
Science	29	58.24	9.357	1.737	54.68	61.80	40	89
Total	120	57.98	7.603	.694	56.61	59.36	40	89

Test of Homogeneity of Variances

Percentage of Marks in First Year

Levene Statistic	df1	df2	Sig.
1.682	2	117	.190

ANOVA

Percentage of Marks in First Year

	Sum of Squares	df	Mean Square	F	Sig.
Between Groups	217.360	2	108.680	1.909	.153
Within Groups	6660.607	117	56.928		
Total	6877.967	119			

Means Plots

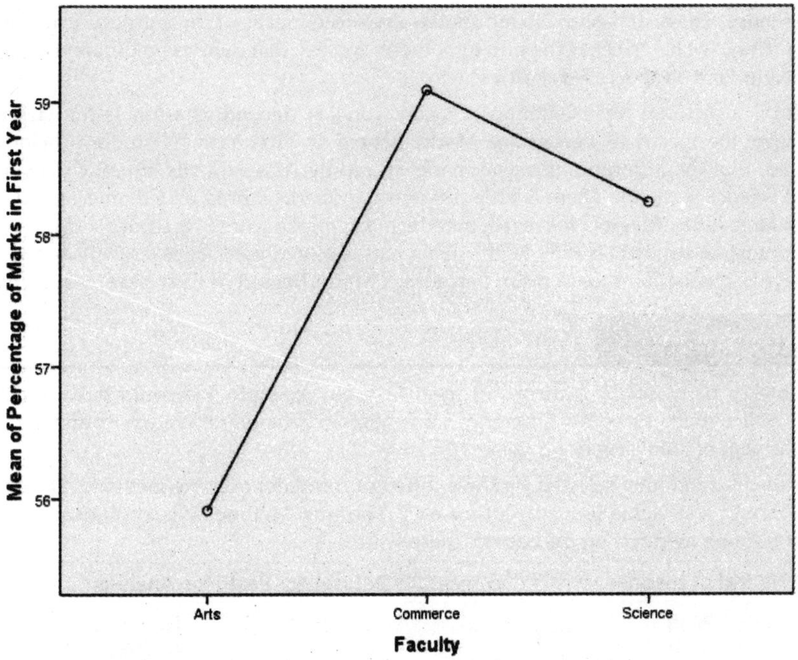

The output displays three tables – **Descriptives, Test of Homogeneity of Variances** and **ANOVA** – under the title **Oneway**, and one graph under the title **Means Plot**.

The **Descriptives** table gives information on number of cases, mean, std. deviation and confidence interval.

The **Test of Homogeneity of Variances** table reports the Levene's statistic along with its significance level. Levene's test is used to examine the equality of variance. The null and alternative hypotheses for Levene's Test for Equality of Variances are as follows:

- **H_0:** Variances of two groups are equal.
- **H_1:** Variances of two groups are unequal.

Since the F-value is 1.682 and its associated significance (0.190) is greater than 0.05, we fail to reject the null hypothesis, and say that the variances are equal for all the three groups.

ANOVA table provides information for testing hypothesis. **F**-value is used as a test of significance of differences in mean across the groups. For each, Predictive Analytic Software (PASW) reports the degrees of freedom, sum of squares and mean square (sum of squares divided by the degrees of freedom).

Between Groups sum of squares is the sum of all squared differences between the means for each group and the grand mean, multiplied by the number of observations (subjects) per group.

Within Group sum of squares is the sum of all the squared differences between each individual data point and the mean for that group.

Between Groups Degrees of Freedom (DF) can be obtained by subtracting one from number of groups.

Within Group Degrees of Freedom (DF) can be obtained by subtracting one and number of groups from number of observations (subjects / cases).

Mean Square is the sum of squares divided by the degrees of freedom.

F-value is the ratio between-groups mean square and within-group mean square. The F-ratio in this example equals 1.909, and its associated p-value (sig.) is reported as .153. It indicates probability of observed value happening by chance. The results show that difference between means of three groups (categories) of **Faculty** is non-significant. Thus, we fail to reject the null hypothesis and say that there is no difference in mean **Percentage of Marks Scored in First Year** across **Faculties**.

The **Means Plot** is a pictorial representation of mean scores of dependent variable for each group. Here, the **Means Plot** shows the means of **Percentage Marks Scored in First Year** by students belonging to different **Faculties You see** that the difference in mean marks scored by Arts students are much lower as compared to Commerce and Science students. There is little difference in marks scored by Commerce and Science students. A closer examination of the **Means Plot** reveal that the mean marks scored by students from Arts faculty is 56 % where as for Commerce students it is 59 %; the mean marks scored by Science students are 57%. Therefore, we can say that there is small difference in mean **Percentage Marks Scored in First Year** by students.

9.3 Post Hoc Analysis

Post Hoc test makes pairwise comparisons of means. In our example, we could have undertaken Post Hoc analysis, if the null hypothesis of no difference were rejected. Therefore, we try to understand the Post Hoc analysis with the help of following example:

Twenty-five students, randomly selected for three different computer training methods. The dataset of Table 9.1 gives **Marks Scored** by students (out of 100) for each **Training Method**. We try to examine the difference in effectiveness of training methods on the basis of these scores:

Table Error! No text of specified style in document..**1: Dataset for Post Hoc Analysis**

Training Method	Marks Scored	Training Method	Marks Scored	Training Method	Marks Scored
1	89	2	82	3	79
1	86	2	83	3	77
1	88	2	88	3	76
1	92	2	86	3	73
1	93	2	87	3	75
1	88	2	91	3	77
1	87	2	89	3	74
1	85	2	90	3	78
				3	74

Create a new datafile by entering the data given in table 9.1 and save it as posthoc.sav.

Note

*You have to define two variables: **Method** – this will be a categorical variable with three categories (Training Method1, Training Method2 and Training Method3) – and **Marks Scored**, which will be a scale (ratio) variable.*

In this example, we follow the procedure for undertaking Analysis of Variance, with Marks Scored as Dependent Variable and **Training Method** as Independent Variable to get the following output:

Oneway

Descriptives

Marks Scored

	N	Mean	Std. Deviation	Std. Error	95% Confidence Interval for Mean Lower Bound	95% Confidence Interval for Mean Upper Bound	Minimum	Maximum
Training Method1	8	88.50	2.777	.982	86.18	90.82	85	93
Training Method2	8	87.00	3.207	1.134	84.32	89.68	82	91
Training Method3	9	75.89	2.028	.676	74.33	77.45	73	79
Total	25	83.48	6.384	1.277	80.84	86.12	73	93

Test of Homogeneity of Variances

Marks Scored

Levene Statistic	df1	df2	Sig.
.667	2	22	.523

ANOVA

Marks Scored

	Sum of Squares	df	Mean Square	F	Sig.
Between Groups	819.351	2	409.676	56.724	.000
Within Groups	158.889	22	7.222		
Total	978.240	24			

The **F**-ratio for this example equals 56.724 and its associated p-value (sig.) is less than 0.05. Thus, the null hypothesis is rejected and we can say that there is significant difference in **Marks Scored** by students across three different **Training Methods**. Here, we shall undertake Post Hoc Analysis to make a pairwise comparison of **Training Methods** by examining the pairwise difference in **Marks Scored** by students.

9.4 Procedure for undertaking Post Hoc Analysis

1. Click **Analyze** from command menu and then **Compare Means** and **One-Way ANOVA** in sequence (Fig.PASW–9.1).
2. Select Marks Scored as Dependent variable and Training Method as Factor.
3. Click on **Post Hoc** button to get the dialogue box shown in Fig.PASW–9.4:

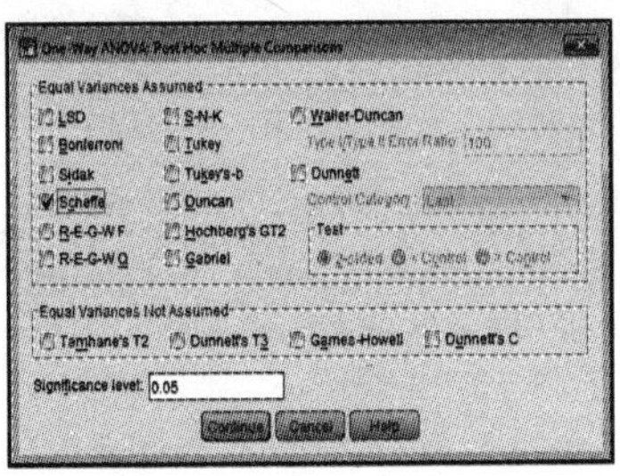

Fig.PASW–9.4

4. Select **Scheffe** and click **Continue** button to go back to previous dialogue box.
5. Click **OK** button to execute the command. You see two additional tables as shown below in the output viewer windows:

Command Syntax for One-Way ANOVA with Post Hoc Analysis

```
DATASET ACTIVATE DataSet2.
ONEWAY marks BY trainingmethod
  /STATISTICS DESCRIPTIVES HOMOGENEITY
  /PLOT MEANS
  /MISSING ANALYSIS
  /POSTHOC=SCHEFFE ALPHA(0.05).
```

Post Hoc Tests

Multiple Comparisons

Marks Scored

Scheffe

(I) Training Method	(J) Training Method	Mean Difference (I-J)	Std. Error	Sig.	95% Confidence Interval	
					Lower Bound	Upper Bound
Training Method1	Training Method2	1.500	1.344	.545	-2.03	5.03
	Training Method3	12.611*	1.306	.000	9.18	16.04
Training Method2	Training Method1	-1.500	1.344	.545	-5.03	2.03
	Training Method3	11.111*	1.306	.000	7.68	14.54
Training Method3	Training Method1	-12.611*	1.306	.000	-16.04	-9.18
	Training Method2	-11.111*	1.306	.000	-14.54	-7.68

*. The mean difference is significant at the 0.05 level.

Homogeneous Subsets

Marks Scored

Scheffe[a,b]

Training Method	N	Subset for alpha = 0.05	
		1	2
Training Method3	9	75.89	
Training Method2	8		87.00
Training Method1	8		88.50
Sig.		1.000	.533

Means for groups in homogeneous subsets are displayed.

a. Uses Harmonic Mean Sample Size = 8.308.

b. The group sizes are unequal. The harmonic mean of the group sizes is used. Type I error levels are not guaranteed.

Two more tables appear in the output viewer window just below the ANOVA table. Multiple Comparisons table is displayed under the title Post Hoc Tests and Marks Scored table is displayed under the title Homogenous Subsets.

Multiple Comparisons table shows the difference in Means and associated significance level between each pair of groups. You see from this table (first row) that the difference in mean Marks Scored by students between Training Method1 and Training Method2 is 1.5 with associated significance level of .545 (which is greater than 0.05), which means that the difference of 1.5 marks is not statistically significant. The second row shows the difference in Marks Scored by students between Training Method1 and Training Method3. The difference is 12.61 and significance level is .000 (which is less than 0.05) and therefore, we can say that the difference in Marks Scored by Training Method1 and Training Method3 is statistically significant. In the third row, Training Method2 is compared with Training Method1 and therefore the difference and significance level will be same as that of first row. In fourth row, Training Method2 is compared with Training Method3. The difference in mean marks is 11.11 and associated significance level is .000, which means that the difference in Marks Scored by students differs between Training Method2 and Training Method3.

Each comparison appears twice, as each of the methods is compared with the remaining two methods. The magnitude of difference and significance level remains the same, only the sign changes with change in the reference group. The reference group is denoted by 'I' and the other categories are denoted by 'J'.

The Homogenous Subsets table created using Scheffe's test show that Training Method1 and Training Method2 are homogenous, where as Training Method3 is a different set. Here, N represents the sample size for each group.

The **Means Plot** will be displayed just below the **Marks Scored** table. You can see the difference in means of **Marks Scored** from the **Means Plot** shown below:

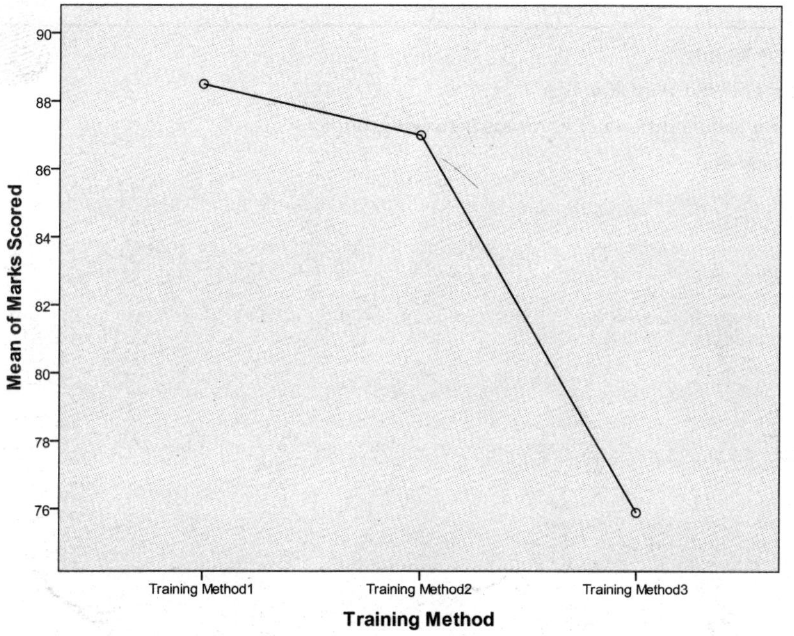

Means Plot clearly shows that the **Marks Scored** by **Training Method3** is much less than the **Marks Scored** by **Training Method1** and **Training Method2**. Thus, results of the **Means Plot** confirm the results given by the **F**-value in the **ANOVA** table.

9.5 Measure of Association

In ANOVA, when null hypothesis is rejected it shows that there are significant differences among sample means. Do note that, with larger sample sizes, these statistically significant differences may have very little practical significance.

A measure of strength of the association between the independent and dependent variables in ANOVA is the Omega squared (ω^2; these indicate the proportion of variance in the dependent variable that is explained by the levels of the independent variable. The concept is similar to the coefficient of determination (r^2). The formula for Omega squared is:

$$w2 = \frac{SS_B - (k-1)MS_W}{SS_T + MS_W}$$

Where,

SSB= Between sum of squares

MSW=Within sum of squares

SST=Total sum of squares

K= number of groups.

Omega squared provides useful information to understand the relationship between the independent and dependent variables in ANOVA. A modest Omega squared may be found even though the F-ratio in the ANOVA is very large. In such case, one should refrain from over-interpreting the significance of results.

Summary

In this chapter we learnt:

- Assumptions of One-Way ANOVA.
- Procedure for testing difference in means between groups.
- Post Hoc analysis.
- Measures of Association.

Chapter 10

One-Way Repeated Measures ANOVA

In this Chapter:

One-Way Repeated Measures ANOVA examines difference in more than two related samples. It is similar to Paired-Sample t-test except that in One-Way Repeated Measures ANOVA, the observations are taken for the same sample in more than two situations, for example the difference between ratings given by students to three different teaching methods, ratings given by senior citizens about cleanliness and security in four major gardens of the city etc. Here, the sample / respondents are same in all the given situations. One method of capturing individual differences is by repeating the sample in all the given situations. Thus, Repeated Measures design is also called Within-Subject design. In this chapter, we shall focus on assumptions of One-Way Repeated Measures ANOVA, procedure for undertaking One-Way ANOVA and interpretation of the results.

10.1 Assumptions of One-Way Repeated Measures ANOVA

The assumptions for undertaking One-Way Repeated Measures ANOVA are as follows:

- Dependent variable is measured in ratio or interval scale.
- Sample mean is normally distributed.
- Respondents are selected randomly.
- Variances of all groups are equal.

For example, we want to know the differences in Marks Scored by students who have undergone the three training programmes of Predictive Analytic Software (PASW). We chose 10 students randomly who attended the three training programmes and record their marks as shown in Table 10.1:

Table 10.1: Dataset for Repeated Measures ANOVA

Students	Training1	Training2	Training3
1	67	90	63
2	79	92	65
3	45	88	54
4	69	93	55
5	54	87	69
6	77	85	64
7	85	91	66
8	70	92	70
9	72	85	72
10	78	86	68

To examine the difference in marks scored by students in different training programmes, One-Way Repeated Measures ANOVA is undertaken. The null and alternative hypotheses are:

- **H_0:** There is no difference in marks scored by students in all the three training programmes.
- **H_1:** The marks scored by students in at least one of the three training programmes are different.

The procedure for undertaking One-Way Repeated Measures ANOVA is presented in the following section.

10.2 Procedure for Undertaking One-Way Repeated Measures ANOVA

1. Click **Analyze** from command menu as shown in Fig.PASW–10.1:

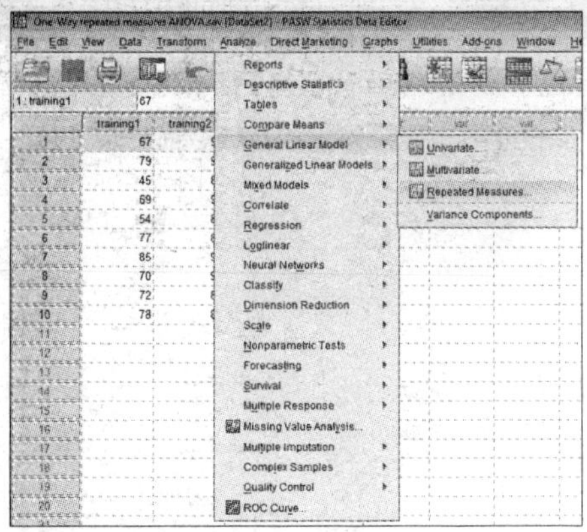

Fig.PASW–10.1

2. Select **General Linear Model** and **Repeated Measures** in sequence, as shown in Fig.PASW–10.1 to get the dialogue box shown in Fig.PASW–10.2:

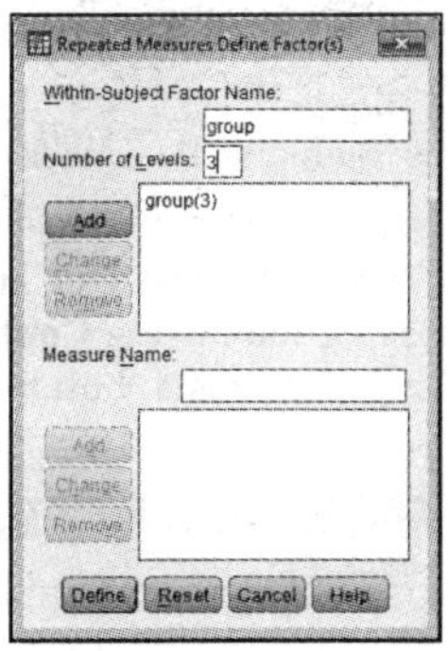

Fig.PASW–10.2

3. Type group in Within-Subject Factor Name box and 3 in Number of Levels and click Add button.
4. Click **Define** button to get the dialogue box shown in Fig.PASW–10.3:

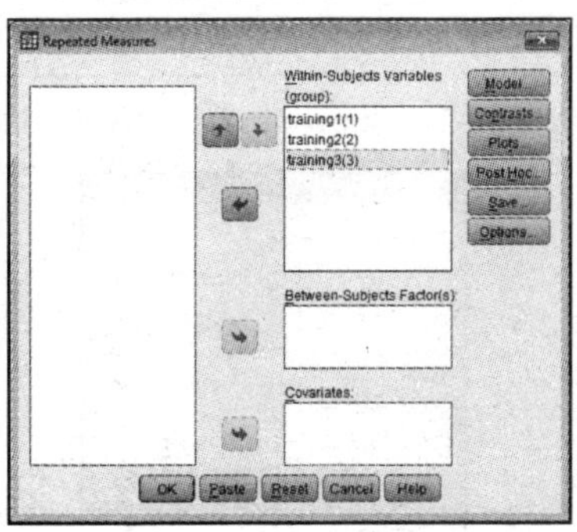

Fig.PASW–10.3

5. Initially, _?_(1), _?_(2) and _?_(3) will be listed in **Within-Subjects Variables (group)** list box. Click on **Training1** and move it into **Within-Subjects Variable** list box. Then move **Traning2** as well as **Training3** in the same list box.

6. Click **Model** button to get the dialogue box shown in Fig.PASW–10.4:

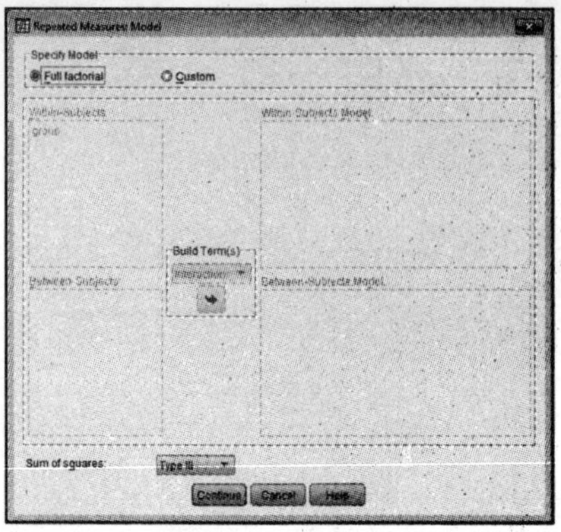

Fig.PASW–10.4

The default model is **Full Factorial** and we shall use the same but, you may specify your own design by clicking on Custom Model radio button.

7. Without making any changes in this dialogue box, click the **Continue** button to go back to previous dialogue box.

8. Click **Contrasts** button. **Contrasts** is similar to **Post Hoc** analysis and makes comparisons between two groups at a time; the only difference being that, using **Contrasts,** comparison is possible between a group and a composite of groups. Clicking **Contrasts** button will generate the dialogue box shown in Fig.PASW–10.5:

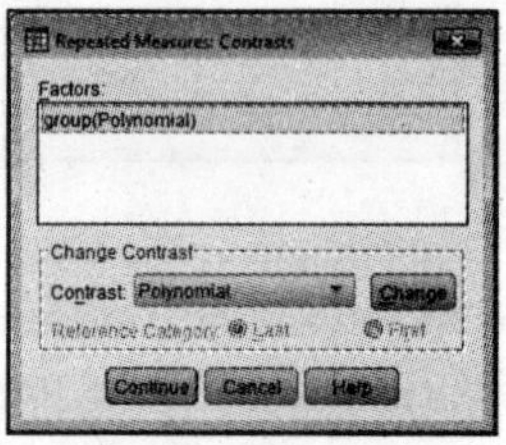

Fig.PASW–10.5

9. Click **Plots** button to get the dialogue box shown in Fig.PASW–10.6:

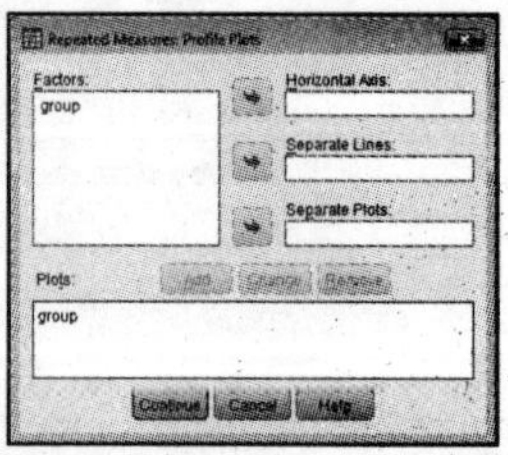

Fig.PASW–10.5

10. Select **group** and move it into **Horizontal Axis** box and click **Add** button to bring it to the plots text area.

11. Click **Continue** button to go back to previous dialogue box.

Note

Post Hoc analysis is used to make group-wise comparisons between different pairs of independent factors, if the samples are unrelated. Therefore it cannot be used here.

12. Click Save button to get the dialogue box shown in Fig.PASW–10.7:

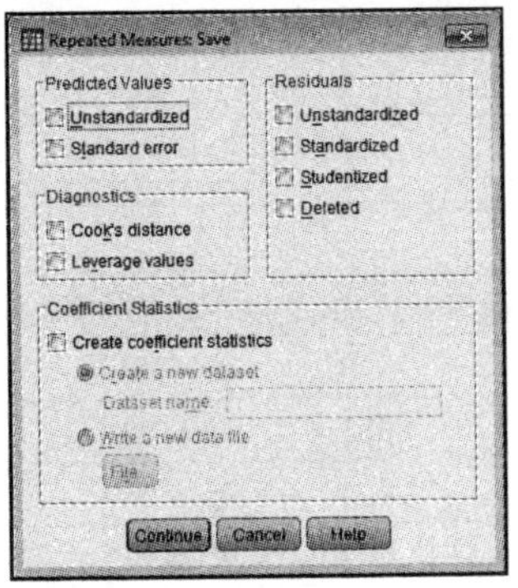

Fig.PASW–10.7

You can save **Predicted Values**, **Residuals**, **Diagnostics** and **Coefficient Statistics** by checking appropriate boxes in the dialogue box shown in Fig.PASW–10.7.

13. Click the **Continue** button to go to previous dialogue box and click **Options** button to get the dialogue box shown in Fig.PASW–10.8:

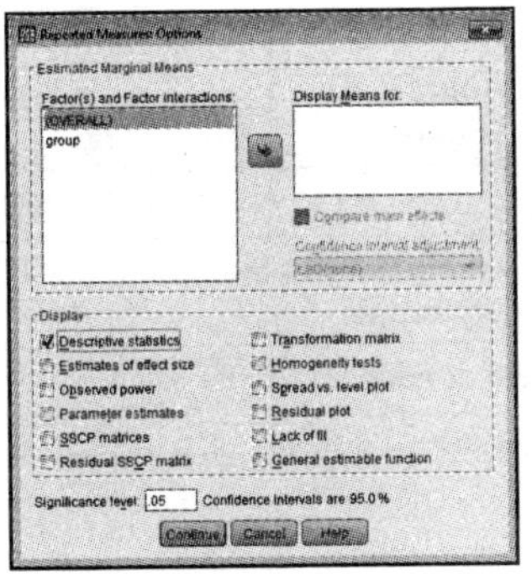

Fig.PASW–10.8

14. In the **Display** frame, check the **Descriptive statistics** option (Fig.PASW–10.8) and then click **Continue** button.

15. Click **OK** button. The output will be displayed in the output viewer window as follows:

General Linear Model

Within-Subjects Factors

Measure:MEASURE_1	
group	group
1	1
2	2
3	3

Descriptive Statistics			
	Mean	Std. Deviation	N
Training1	69.60	12.076	10
Training2	88.90	3.071	10
Training3	64.60	6.004	10

Multivariate Tests[b]

Effect		Value	F	Hypothesis df	Error df	Sig.
Group	Pillai's Trace	.919	45.605[a]	2.000	8.000	.000
	Wilks' Lambda	.081	45.605[a]	2.000	8.000	.000
	Hotelling's Trace	11.401	45.605[a]	2.000	8.000	.000
	Roy's Largest Root	11.401	45.605[a]	2.000	8.000	.000

a. Exact statistic

b. Design: Intercept
Within Subjects Design: group

Mauchly's Test of Sphericity[b]

Measure:MEASURE_1

Within Subjects Effect		Mauchly's W	Approx. Chi-Square	Df	Sig.	Epsilon[a] Greenhouse-Geisser	Huynh-Feldt	Lower-bound
dimension1	group	.768	2.112	2	.348	.812	.965	.500

Examines the null hypothesis to check, whether or not the error covariance matrix of the orthonormalized transformed dependent variables is relative to an identity matrix.

a. May be employed to adapt the degrees of freedom for the balanced tests of significance. The Tests of Within-Subjects Effects table shows the corrected test.

b. Design: Intercept
Within Subjects Design: group

Tests of Within-Subjects Effects

Measure:MEASURE_1

Source		Type III Sum of Squares	df	Mean Square	F	Sig.
group	Sphericity Assumed	3293.267	2	1646.633	30.470	.000
	Greenhouse-Geisser	3293.267	1.623	2028.774	30.470	.000
	Huynh-Feldt	3293.267	1.929	1706.869	30.470	.000
	Lower-bound	3293.267	1.000	3293.267	30.470	.000
Error(group)	Sphericity Assumed	972.733	18	54.041		
	Greenhouse-Geisser	972.733	14.610	66.582		
	Huynh-Feldt	972.733	17.365	56.018		
	Lower-bound	972.733	9.000	108.081		

Tests of Within-Subjects Contrasts

Measure:MEASURE_1

Source	Group	Type III Sum of Squares	df	Mean Square	F	Sig.
group	Linear	125.000	1	125.000	2.057	.185
	Quadratic	3168.267	1	3168.267	66.977	.000
Error(group)	Linear	547.000	9	60.778		
	Quadratic	425.733	9	47.304		

Tests of Between-Subjects Effects

Measure:MEASURE_1
Transformed Variable:Average

Source	Type III Sum of Squares	Df	Mean Square	F	Sig.
Intercept	165912.033	1	165912.033	1993.691	.000
Error	748.967	9	83.219		

Profile Plots

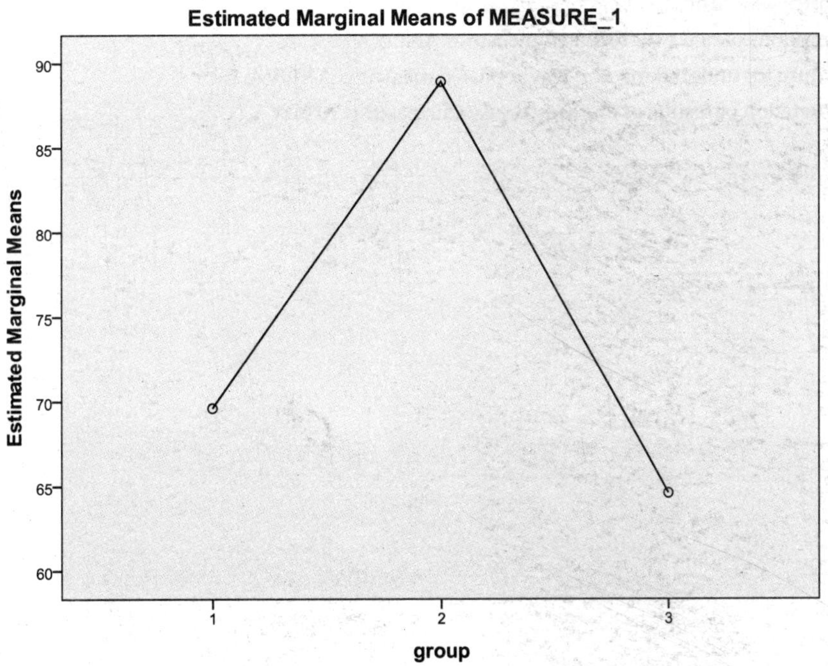

The **Within-Subject Factors (Measure: Measure_1)** table shows the codes assigned to different categories of the categorical variable.

The **Descriptive Statistics** table shows the mean marks scored, standard deviation and the sample size.

The **Multivariate Tests** table will be relevant only when there are two or more dependent variables.

The **Mauchly's Test of Sphericity** examines the following hypotheses:

- **H_0:** Variances are equal for all the categories (groups).
- **H_1:** Variance of at least one category (group) is different.

The test statistic – **Mauchly's W** – shown in the table is .768 and the associated significance is .812 (greater than 0.05). This means that we fail to reject the null hypothesis and, that the variances of all groups are equal.

Since the Mauchly's test shows that the variances of all the groups are equal, we shall see the **F**-ratio corresponding to **Sphericity Assumed** in the **Test of Within-Subject Effects** table. The **F**-ratio is 30.470 and associated significance is .000 (less than 0.05), therefore null hypothesis is rejected. Therefore, the mean **Marks Scored** by the students through different training methods are different.

The **Test of Within-Subject Contrasts** table shows that the **F**-ratio associated with **Linear** relationship between mean **Marks Scored** by students and **Training Methods** is 2.057 and associated significance is .185 (greater than 0.05), which means that we fail to reject the null hypothesis of linear relationship. The **F**-ratio corresponding to **Quadratic** relationship between mean **Marks Scored** and **Training Methods** is 66.977 and associated significance is .000 (less than 0.05), thus null hypothesis of quadratic relationship is rejected. Thus, the quadratic component of **Training Method** has an impact on the **Marks Scored**.

This is further supported by the **Profile Plots** which shows that the extent of variation in **Estimated Marginal Means** has quadratic relationship with **Training Methods**.

Summary

In this chapter we learnt:

- Assumptions of one-way repeated measures ANOVA.
- Procedure for undertaking one-way repeated measures ANOVA.
- Interpretation of results of one-way repeated measures ANOVA.

Chapter 11

Two-Way ANOVA

In this Chapter:

Two-way ANOVA examines the effect of two or more independent variables, measured on categorical scale, on the dependent variable measured on ratio scale. For example, economists interested in the effect of seed variety and farm size on productivity or employment; investigators interested in knowing the effect of dosage and gender effectiveness of drug for Migraine; psychologist interested in studying the effect of training methods and gender on performance or, an HR Manager interested in the effect of training method and age of workers on productivity. All of the above can use two-way ANOVA.

We have discussed in earlier chapters that Analysis of Variance (ANOVA) is the one-way classification procedure for testing the null hypothesis that the population means for the k levels of a single independent variable are equal. Two-way ANOVA is an extension to the one-way ANOVA. Two independent variables (factors) are simultaneously included for the analysis, hence the name two-way. In this chapter, we will confine to two factors – fixed effects model.

Two-way ANOVA takes the effect of both variables into account at the same time. It helps to study simultaneous effects of both the independent variables on the dependent variable. We can with the help of two-way ANOVA study whether the effect of one independent variable is actually being caused or, modified in some way by the other independent variable. Two-way ANOVA also shows whether there is an interaction between the two independent variables. Interaction is the expression of association between two or more independent variables. In presence of interaction effect, effect of each independent variable varies, depending on the other variable.

In this chapter, we shall discuss assumptions and procedure for undertaking of two-way ANOVA; also, interpreting the results.

11.1 Assumptions of two-way ANOVA

The assumptions for undertaking two-way ANOVA are as under:

- The population needs to be normally disseminated. It is the same population from where the samples were received. Data inside every cell of the design is supposed to be normally disseminated. Response variable that is, dependent variable, need to be normally disseminated.
- The samples should be free. Observations are independent in that, there are, no repeated objects or subjects in any factor combination.
- The disparities of the populations should be same. In other words, there should be homogeneity of variances.
- The group should have similar sample size.

When there are huge and same numbers of studies in every cell of the factorial, two-way ANOVA is considered to be vigorous with respect to the violations of the assumptions.

With the two-way ANOVA, three sets of hypotheses are associated.

There are null hypotheses for every set and they are as follows.

- The population means of the first factor are equal. This is like the one-way ANOVA for the row factor.
- The population means of the second factor are equal. This is like the one-way ANOVA for the column factor.
- There is no communication between the first and second factors. This is identical to executing an experiment for independence with contingency tables.

Let us understand two-way ANOVA with the help of an example. Many students from different educational background join coaching classes to prepare for various entrance examinations. The performance of the students depends on the kind of training they get in coaching classes and their educational background.

Suppose there are two coaching classes that prepare students for entrance test for admission into professional courses. Let's assume these students belong to Arts, Commerce and Science faculty only. **Marks Scored in Entrance Test** will be the response variable. **Coaching classes** and educational background (**Graduation**

Faculty) will be two independent variables (Factors).**Coaching classes** will have two levels and **Graduation Faculty** will have three levels. Twenty Four students are randomly selected taking coaching from different classes and have different educational background. The dataset (**two-way ANOVA.sav**) is given in Appendix – A.

The null and alternative hypotheses for two-way ANOVA will be as follows:

- **H_0:** Mean entrance score of students taking coaching from different Classes do not differ.
- **H_1:** There is difference in mean entrance score of students taking coaching from different Classes.
- **H_0:** Mean entrance score of students from different Graduation Faculty do not differ.
- **H_1:** The mean score of at least one of the Graduation Faculties is different.
- **H_0:** There is no interaction effect between Coaching Classes and Graduation Faculty.
- **H_1:** There is interaction effect between Coaching Classes and Graduation Faculty.

11.2 Procedure for Undertaking Two-Way ANOVA

1. Create the file from the data given in appendix – A (**two-way ANOVA.sav**) and save it as **two-way ANOVA.sav**.
2. Click **Analyze** from the command menu as shown in Fig.PASW–11.1:

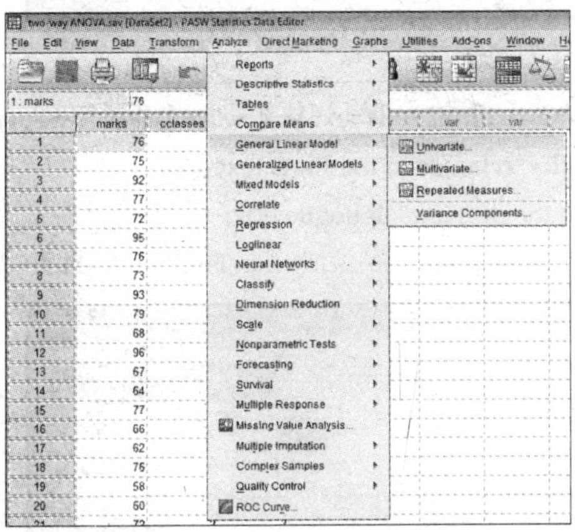

Fig.PASW–11.1

3. Click **General Linear Model** and **Univariate** as shown in Fig.PASW–11.1 to get the dialogue box shown in Fig.PASW–11.2:

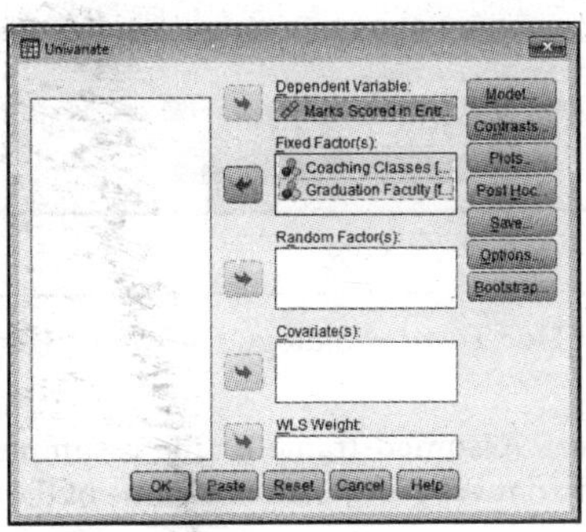

Fig.PASW–11.2

4. Select Marks Scored in Entrance Test and move it to the Dependent Variable text box.
5. Select Coaching Classes and Graduation Faculty simultaneously and bring it to Fixed Factors list box.
6. Click Plots to get the dialogue box shown in Fig.PASW–11.3:

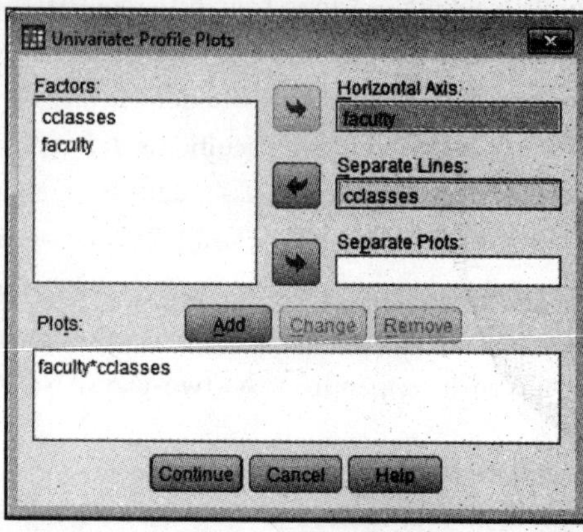

Fig.PASW–11.3

7. Select **faculty** and drag it to **Horizontal Axis** text box and **cclasses** to **Separate Lines** text box.
8. Click **Add** button to get **faculty*cclasses** in the **Plots** text area.
9. Click **Continue** to go back to the previous dialogue box.
10. Click **Post Hoc** button to get the dialogue box shown in Fig.PASW–11.4:

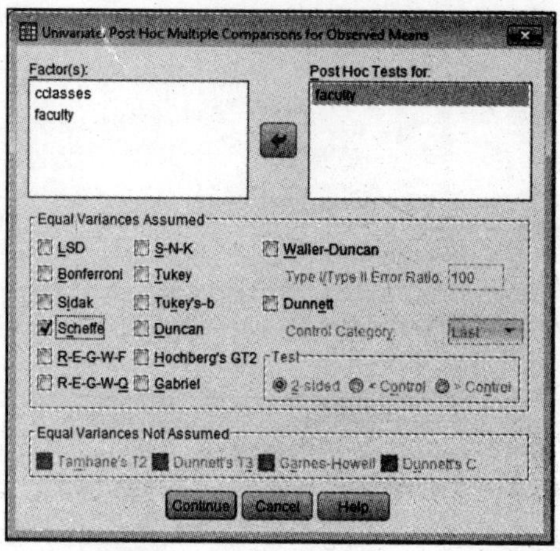

Fig.PASW–11.4

11. Select **Faculty** and drag it to **Post Hoc Test for** dialogue box. **Post Hoc** analysis for **Coaching Classes** is not relevant, as it has only two levels.
12. Select **Scheffe** in **Equal Variances Assumed** frame (If the assumption of equal variance is violated, we have to select a test from **Equal Variances Not Assumed** frame of the dialogue box).
13. Click **Continue** button to go back to the previous dialogue box.
14. Click **Options** button to get the dialogue box shown in Fig.PASW–11.5:

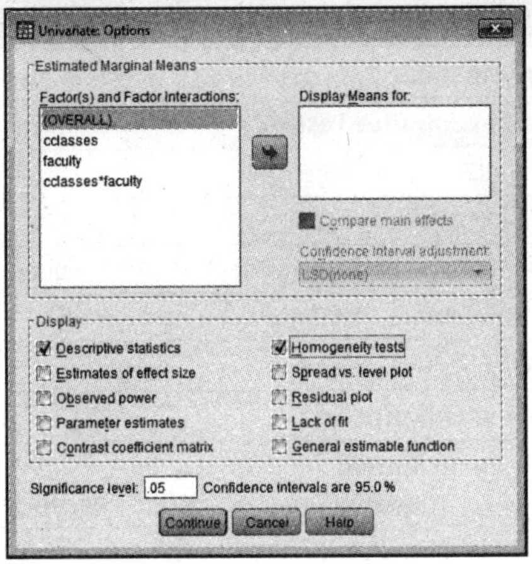

Fig.PASW–11.5

15. Select Descriptive Statistics and Homogenity Test check boxes.
16. Click **Continue** button to go back to the previous dialogue box and **OK** button to execute the command. Following output will be displayed in the output viewer window.

Univariate Analysis of Variance

Between-Subjects Factors

		Value Label	N
Coaching Classes	1	Class1	12
	2	Class2	12
Graduation Faculty	1	Arts	8
	2	Commerce	8
	3	Science	8

Descriptive Statistics

Dependent Variable:Marks Scored in Entrance Test

Coaching Classes		Graduation Faculty		Mean	Std. Deviation	N
dimension1	Class1	dimension2	Arts	77.00	1.414	4
			Commerce	72.00	2.944	4
			Science	94.00	1.826	4
			Total	81.00	10.027	12
	Class2	dimension2	Arts	63.25	4.113	4
			Commerce	61.75	1.708	4
			Science	75.75	2.630	4
			Total	66.92	7.090	12
	Total	dimension2	Arts	70.13	7.882	8
			Commerce	66.88	5.915	8
			Science	84.87	9.978	8
			Total	73.96	11.130	24

Levene's Test of Equality of Error Variances[a]			
Dependent Variable:Marks Scored in Entrance Test			
F	df1	df2	Sig.
1.492	5	18	.241
Tests the null hypothesis that the error variance of the dependent variable is equal across groups.			
Design: Intercept + cclasses + faculty + cclasses * faculty			

Tests of Between-Subjects Effects					
Dependent Variable:Marks Scored in Entrance Test					
Source	**Type III Sum of Squares**	**df**	**Mean Square**	**F**	**Sig.**
Corrected Model	2726.708[a]	5	545.342	80.296	.000
Intercept	131276.042	1	131276.042	19328.988	.000
cclasses	1190.042	1	1190.042	175.221	.000
faculty	1472.333	2	736.167	108.393	.000
cclasses * faculty	64.333	2	32.167	4.736	.022
Error	122.250	18	6.792		
Total	134125.000	24			
Corrected Total	2848.958	23			
a. R Squared = .957 (Adjusted R Squared = .945)					

Post Hoc Tests

Graduation Faculty

Multiple Comparisons								
Marks Scored in Entrance Test Scheffe								
(I) Graduation Faculty		**(J) Graduation Faculty**		**Mean Difference (I-J)**	**Std. Error**	**Sig.**	**95% Confidence Interval**	
							Lower Bound	**Upper Bound**
dimension2	Arts	dimension3	Commerce	3.25	1.303	.069	-.22	6.72
			Science	-14.75*	1.303	.000	-18.22	-11.28
	Commerce	dimension3	Arts	-3.25	1.303	.069	-6.72	.22
			Science	-18.00*	1.303	.000	-21.47	-14.53
	Science	dimension3	Arts	14.75*	1.303	.000	11.28	18.22
			Commerce	18.00*	1.303	.000	14.53	21.47
Based on observed means. The error term is Mean Square(Error) = 6.792.								
*. The mean difference is significant at the .05 level.								

Homogeneous Subsets

Marks Scored in Entrance Test				
Scheffe[a,b]				
Graduation Faculty		**N**	**Subset 1**	**Subset 2**
dimension1	Commerce	8	66.88	
	Arts	8	70.13	
	Science	8		84.87
	Sig.		.069	1.000

Means for groups in homogeneous subsets are displayed.
Based on observed means.
The error term is Mean Square(Error) = 6.792.

a. Uses Harmonic Mean Sample Size = 8.000.

b. Alpha = .05.

Profile Plots

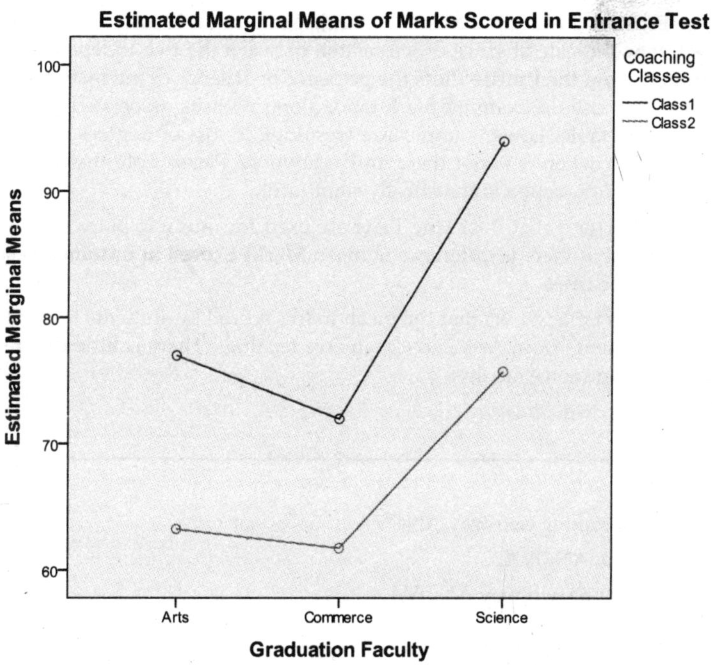

Four tables – Between-Subjects Factors, Descriptive Statistics, Levene's Test for Equality of Error Variances and Test of Between-Subjects Effects – are displayed under the title Univariate Analysis of Variance. This is followed by Multiple Comparisons table under Post Hoc title. Under the Post Hoc title another title Graduation Faculty (which is the dependent variable) also appears. Marks Scored in Entrance Test table is displayed under the Homogenous Subsets title. This is followed by the Profile Plots.

Between-Subjects Factors table gives the categorical coding for each **Fixed Factor** and the sample size in each category.

Descriptive Statistics table indicates that the **Dependent Variable** is **Marks Scored in Entrance Test**. This table gives location-wise mean, standard deviation and number of observations (sample size) in each of the category of **Graduation Faculty**.

Levene's Test for Equality of Error Variance examines whether the variance in the dependent variable is constant across the groups of not. The null and alternative hypotheses for Levene's test are:

- **H_0:** Variances are equal in all the groups.
- **H_1:** Variance in at least one group is different.

The **F**-ratio examines difference in variance across groups. The F-ratio is 1.492 and associated significance level is .241 (which is greater than 0.05).This means we fail to reject the null hypothesis and we proceed with the assumption that the error variances of all the groups are equal.

Test of Between-Subjects Effects table is the two-way ANOVA table. The **F**-ratio for **Coaching Classes** is 175.221 and the p-value is less than 0.05. The **F**-ratio for **Graduation Faculty** is 108.393 and p-value is less than 0.05. Therefore, the main effects of **Coaching Classes** and **Graduation Faculty** are significant. The **F**-ratio of **Coaching Classes by Graduation Faculty** interaction is 4.736 and associated p-value is less than 0.05. Thus, the **Coaching Classes by Graduation Faculty** interaction effect (shown as **Coaching Classes*Faculty** in the table) is also statistically insignificant and therefore, the two variables jointly affect the dependent variable. Thus, two-way (interaction) effect is significant.

However, the **Profile Plots** in our example shows absence of interaction effect. The **Profile Plot** shows the Coaching Classwise **Estimated Marginal Means** for each **Graduation Faculty**. Since the lines for both **Coaching Classes** are parallel, they indicate absence of interaction between the two independent variables. Though, one cannot judge accurately from the **Profile Plots** the presence or absence of interaction between two independent categorical variables. One should examine the **F**-ratio, along with its associated p-value given in the **Test of Between-Subjects Effects** table. Lower sample size (resulting in loss of degrees of freedom) and other factors might show an interaction when it is not there and vice versa. Please note that as per the **Test of Between-Subjects Effects** table, the interaction is statistically significant.

We had discussed in Chapter 9 that **Post Hoc** Tests are used for multiple pairwise comparisons. The table on **Post Hoc** Analysis shows that there is difference in mean **Marks Scored in Entrance Test** by students belonging to different **Graduation Faculties**.

The **Homogenous Subsets** table shows that the mean marks scored by students from Science faculty are higher than marks scored by students from Arts and Commerce faculties. There is little difference in marks scored by students from Arts and Commerce faculty.

Summary

In this chapter we learnt:

- Assumptions of undertaking two-way ANOVA.
- Procedure for two-way ANOVA.
- Interpreting the results of two-way ANOVA.

Chapter 12

Correlation

In this Chapter:

Correlation is a measure of the linear relationship between two variables. It expresses the extent to which two variables vary together, for example, Expenditure on Advertisement and Sales, Investment in Infrastructure and GDP of a country etc. Correlation coefficients reveal the magnitude and direction of the relationships. A correlation coefficient includes a range of value that exists from -1 to +1. The values, which are near to +1, signify a firm association between the variables that are being associated. The values, which are nearer to 0, signifies no or insignificant association. The kind of bonding between the variables is illustrated by the sign of a correlation coefficient. When a correlation coefficient is positive, the association, or correlation between the variables is positive. This is, because as one variable surges in value, the value of other variable also surges..

A correlation coefficient of any magnitude or sign, whatever its statistical significance does not imply causation. The coefficient does not distinguish between independent and dependent variables and treats them symmetrically.

In the given example (**students.sav**) we study the relationship between the **Percentage of Marks Scored in First Year** by the students and **Incidence of Absence**. A negative value indicates a negative linear relationship between these two variables. The test scores of the students are likely to be negatively correlated with incidence of absence because, as the number of days of missed classes increase, test scores typically decrease.

It is advisable to plot a scattergram before examining the extent of correlation numerically to get a prima facie idea whether the correlation exists between two variables or not. The procedure for plotting a scattergram is discussed in Chapter-5.

In this chapter, we shall discuss assumptions of correlations, procedure for undertaking bivariate correlation (Pearson' Coefficient), rank correlation (Spearman's Rho) and partial correlation, and interpreting the results.

12.1 Assumptions of Correlations

The assumptions for undertaking correlations are as follows:

- Data should be measured on ratio or interval scale for estimating Pearson's Correlation coefficient. (However, if the data is measured on ordinal scale, Spearman's Rho should be used and if measured on nominal scale, Biserial correlation is used.)
- Variables are normally distributed.
- Data should be available on related pairs, for every observation on X variable, there has to be a corresponding observation on Y variable of the same sample unit.
- The variance for both the variables should be equal.

To examine the relationship between Hours Spent on Reading, Percentage Marks Scored in the First Year and Incidence of Absence, the null and alternative hypotheses will be:

- **H_0:** There is no correlation between the two variables.
- **H_1:** There is correlation between two variables.

12.2 Procedure for Undertaking Correlations

In Predictive Analytic Software (PASW), you will be able to compute three types of correlations – **Bivariate Partial** and **Distances**. We will discuss the first two types of correlations in this chapter. The **Bivariate Correlation** measures the nature of relationship between two variables. **Partial Correlations** measure the association between two variables but want to iron out the effect of one or more other variables.

12.2.1 Bivariate Correlations

1. Click **Analyze** from the command menu as shown in Fig.PASW–12.1:

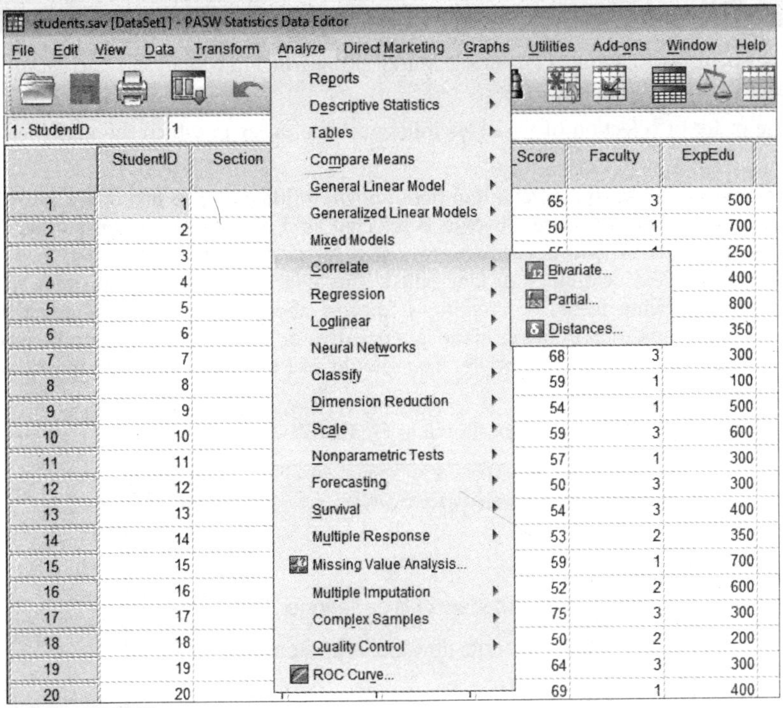

Fig.PASW–12.1

2. Click **Correlate** and **Bivariate** as shown in Fig.PASW–12.1 to get the dialogue box shown in Fig.PASW–12.2:

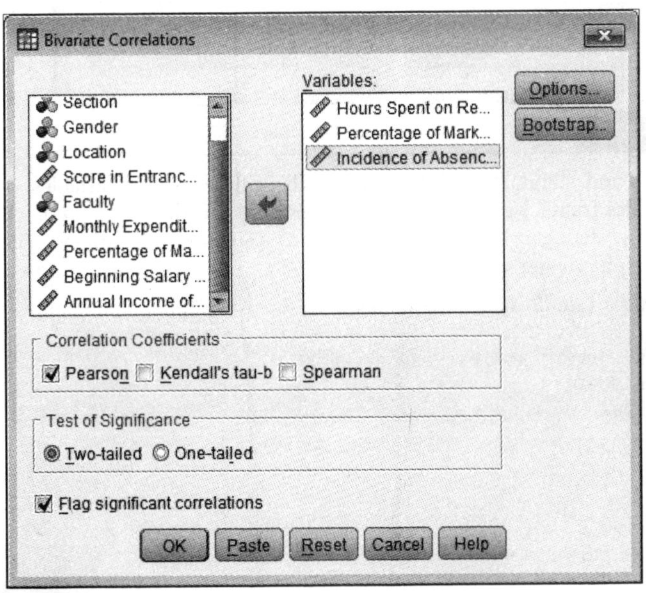

Fig.PASW–12.2

3. Select Hours Spent on Reading, Percentage Marks Scored in First Year and Incidence of Absence; and move these variables to the Variables box.

   Note that the order of selection of variables influences the order in which the variables are listed in the output.

   For our example, we will keep the default options shown in the dialogue box of Fig.PASW–12.2. Select the kind of correlation coefficient. Here, Pearson is selected as it is suitable for continuous data, while other two that is, Kendall's tau-b and Spearman are suited for ranked data. After that, from that the Test of Significance option, select Two-tailed or One-tailed. This selection is required to check whether or not the hypothesis, which is being tested, is creating a forecast about the direction of effect between the two variables; whether the prediction being made is a negative or positive relationship between the variables, and then the one-tailed test is appropriate. You should use the two-tailed test if you are not making a directional prediction.

4. Click on **Options** to get the dialogue box shown in Fig.PASW–12.3:

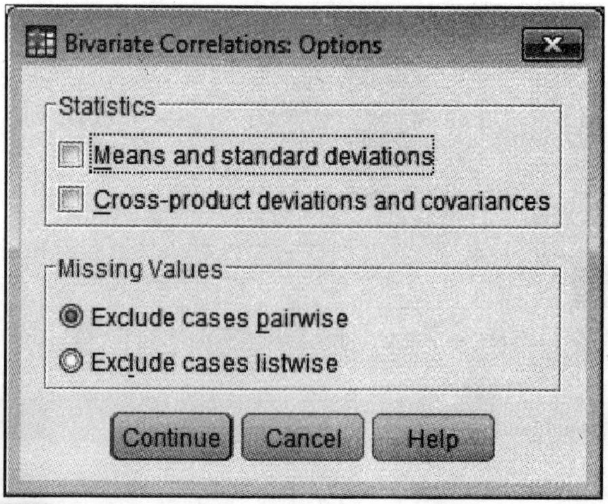

Fig.PASW–12.3

5. To find out means and standard deviations for each of the selected variables, select appropriate check boxes in the **Statistics** frame. Keeping the default values of this dialogue box, click **Continue** button to go back to the previous dialogue box and **OK** button to execute the command. Following output shall be displayed in the output viewer window:

Command Syntax for Bivariate (Pearson) Correlation

```
CORRELATIONS
  /VARIABLES=HrRead PerCentFirstYear Absence
  /PRINT=TWOTAIL NOSIG
  /MISSING=PAIRWISE.
```

Correlations

Correlations				
		Hours Spent on Reading	Percentage of Marks in First Year	Incidence of Absence during Year
Hours Spent on Reading	Pearson Correlation	1	.290**	-.279**
	Sig. (2-tailed)		.001	.002
	N	120	120	120
Percentage of Marks in First Year	Pearson Correlation	.290**	1	-.573**
	Sig. (2-tailed)	.001		.000
	N	120	120	120
Incidence of Absence during Year	Pearson Correlation	-.279**	-.573**	1
	Sig. (2-tailed)	.002	.000	
	N	120	120	120

**. Correlation is significant at the 0.01 level (2-tailed).

Under the major heading – **Correlations, a** table titled **Correlations** is displayed.

Predictive Analytic Software (PASW) produces a correlation matrix showing correlations between all possible pairs of variables and indicates the number of cases used to compute them.

Three pieces of information appear in each cell of the correlation matrix. The top most number is the value of correlation coefficient; the number below it is the two tailed p-value for the correlation; and the bottom number in the cell show the sample size.

The correlations between Hours Spent on Reading and Percentage Marks Scored in First Year; Percentage Marks Scored in First Year and Incidence of Absence, and the correlation between Incidence of Absence and Hours Spent on Reading appears in correlation matrix. The results of correlation reveal that:

- There is a linear positive correlation between **Hours Spent on Reading** and **Percentage Marks Scored in First Year.** The correlation coefficient is .290 and is statistically significant as the p-value is less than 0,05.
- **Incidence of Absence** and **Percentage of Marks Scored in First Year** are negatively correlated, the correlation coefficient is -.573 and it is statistically significant ($p < .05$).
- There is a negative correlation between **Hours Spent on Reading** and **Incidence of Absence**. The correlation coefficient is -.279 and it is statistically significant ($p<0.05$)

Each correlation appears twice in the square matrix, as the upper-right triangle is a mirror image of the lower left triangle.

12.2.2 Rank Correlations

The Spearman's rho correlation is an ordinal measure. It is a widely used non-parametric technique. Rho correlates ranks between two ordered variables. In the presence of extreme values or outliers, rank correlations are often used. Moreover, if the sample does not follow a normal distribution, Spearman's rho is used. However, this measure is very sensitive to tied ranks and too many ties distort the coefficient size.

The procedure for finding rank correlations is just the same as finding correlations; however, select **Spearman** in the **Correlations Coefficients** frame in the dialogue box shown Fig.PASW–12.2 and click **OK** button to execute command. Following output in will be displayed in the Output Viewer Window:

Command Syntax for Rank (Spearman) Correlation

```
NONPAR CORR
  /VARIABLES=HrRead PerCentFirstYear Absence
  /PRINT=SPEARMAN TWOTAIL NOSIG
  /MISSING=PAIRWISE.
```

Nonparametric Correlations

Correlations

			Hours Spent on Reading	Percentage of Marks in First Year	Incidence of Absence during Year
Spearman's rho	Hours Spent on Reading	Correlation Coefficient	1.000	.283**	-.278**
		Sig. (2-tailed)	.	.002	.002
		N	120	120	120
	Percentage of Marks in First Year	Correlation Coefficient	.283**	1.000	-.580**
		Sig. (2-tailed)	.002	.	.000
		N	120	120	120
	Incidence of Absence during Year	Correlation Coefficient	-.278**	-.580**	1.000
		Sig. (2-tailed)	.002	.000	.
		N	120	120	120

**. Correlation is significant at the 0.01 level (2-tailed).

Correlations table is displayed under the heading **Nonparametric Correlations**. The non-parametric correlations are interpreted in the same way as Pearson's Correlation. The results of non-parametric correlation reveal that:

- There is a positive and statistically significant correlation between **Hours Spent in Reading** and **Percentage of Marks Scored in First Year**. The correlation coefficient is .283 and p-value is less than 0.05.
- There is a negative correlation between **Incidence of Absence** and **Percentage of Marks Scored in First Year**. The correlation coefficient is -.580 and it is statistically significant ($p<0.05$).
- There is a negative correlation between **Incidence of Absence** and **Hours Spent in Reading**. The correlation coefficient is -.278 and it is statistically significant ($p<0.05$).

12.2.3 Partial Correlations

The second type of correlation listed under the **Correlate** sub-menu is the partial correlation, which measures an association between two variables with the effects of one or more other variables factored out. To obtain a partial correlation:

1. Click Analyze from command menu and then **Correlate** and **Partial** as shown in Fig.PASW–12.1 to get the dialogue box shown in Fig.PASW–12.4:

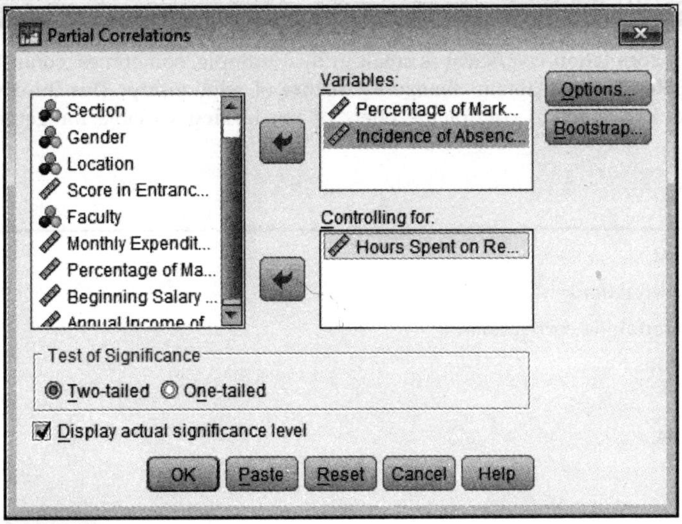

Fig.PASW–12.4

2. Select the variables we want to correlate and the variable which we want to control then move them to the respective boxes. In this example, we are correlating **Percentage of Marks Scored in First Year** with **Incidence of Absence** while controlling for **Hours Spent on Reading**. Thus, we have a measure of the association between **Percentage of Marks Scored in First Year** with **Incidence of Absence**, while removing the association between **Hours Spent on Reading** and the two variables we are correlating.

3. Click **OK** button to obtain the following output in the Output Viewer Window:

Command Syntax for Partial Correlations

```
PARTIAL CORR
  /VARIABLES=PerCentFirstYear Absence BY HrRead
  /SIGNIFICANCE=TWOTAIL
  /MISSING=LISTWISE.
```

Partial Corr

Correlations

Control Variables			Percentage of Marks in First Year	Incidence of Absence during Year
Hours Spent on Reading	Percentage of Marks in First Year	Correlation	1.000	-.535
		Significance (2-tailed)	.	.000
		Df	0	117
	Incidence of Absence during Year	Correlation	-.535	1.000
		Significance (2-tailed)	.000	.
		Df	117	0

Under the heading **Partial Corr**, a **Correlations** table is displayed. Notice that the correlation coefficient of **Incidence of Absence and Percentage of Marks Scored in First Year** has changed. That is because we have controlled for **Hours Spent on Reading**.

Though the change in correlation coefficient is small in this example, sometimes, controlling a third variable like **Hours Spent on Reading** can totally change the nature of relationship. This third variable is called the lurking variable. It is important to control the effect of the lurking variable for getting more meaningful relationship.

Summary

In this chapter we learnt:

- Assumptions of correlations.
- Procedure for undertaking correlations.
- Bivariate correlations.
- Rank correlations.
- Partial correlations.

Chapter 13

Multiple Regression

In this Chapter:

Regression analysis is one of the most widely used statistical techniques and has many applications in business, economics and other social sciences. It refers to the statistical technique of modeling relationship between variables.

One important objective of regression analysis is to arrive at a mathematical relationship which can be used to predict values for one variable, based on the values for the remaining variables, called the independent variables.

Correlation coefficients and scatter plots provide some broad idea about the relationships among variables and may suffice for some purpose. But often, researcher is interested in modeling the relationship for prediction purposes. Regression analysis cannot be interpreted as a procedure for establishing cause-and-effect relationship between variables. It can only indicate how or, to what extent variables are associated with each other. Any conclusions about cause-and-effect must come from theory or judgment of the individual analyst.

Regression analysis with only one independent variable is called simple linear regression; with two or more independent variables, it is called multiple regression analysis.

The bivariate linear regression may be specified as:

$Y=\beta_0 + \beta_1 x_1$, where

The value of the dependent variable Y is a linear function of the independent variable X. The intercept β_0 is the value for the linear function when it crosses the Y axis. The slope β_1 is the change in Y for a unit change in X.

Multiple regressions help to know the relative importance of a number of independent (explanatory) variables when they are used to predict dependent variable.

The dependent (predicted) variable is required to be measured on a continuous ratio scale. The independent (explanatory) variables can be continuous, categorical or a combination of two.

The least squares method is widely used to estimate the regression equation. This method minimizes the sum of squared deviations between the observed values and the estimated values of the dependent variable.

In our given example, we can take the **Percentage of Marks Scored in the First Year** as a dependent variable and **Incidence of Absence** as an independent variable. We shall discuss the procedure for doing multiple regression analysis by including two additional variables – **Expenditure on Education** and **Hours Spent on Reading** in the regression equation.

In this chapter we shall discuss the assumptions of linear regression, the procedure for undertaking linear regression and interpreting the results.

13.1 Assumptions of Linear Regression

The assumptions of Linear Regression are:

- Disturbance (error) term (u_i) and explanatory variables (x_i) are unrelated, that is, $cov(u_i x_i)=0$.
- Variance of error term is constant.
- Successive error terms are not related.
- The mean of error terms is zero.

The null and alternative hypotheses for linear regression are:

- **H_0:** $\beta_i = 0$
- **H_1:** $\beta_i \neq 0$

13.2 Procedure for undertaking Linear Regression

1. Click **Analyze** from the command menu as shown in Fig.PASW–13.1:

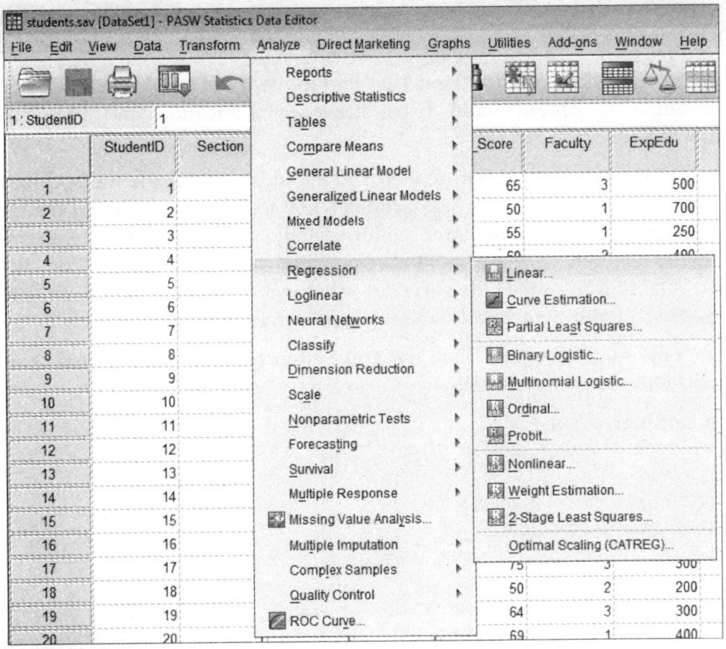

Fig.PASW–13.1

2. Click **Regression** and **Linear** as shown in Fig.PASW–13.1 to get the dialogue box shown in Fig.PASW–13.2:

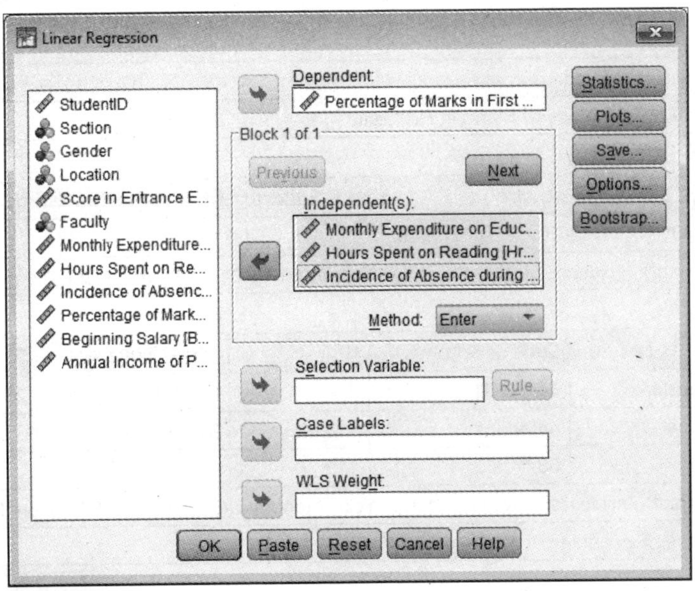

Fig.PASW–13.2

3. Select Percentage of Marks Scored in First Year and move it to Dependent text box. Select Hours Spent on Reading, Incidence of Absence and Expenditure on Education and bring these variables to the Independent(s) list box.

   Note that before you run a regression model, you should consider the method for selecting or excluding variables in that model. The Method box facilitates you to select from one of the five methods- **Stepwise, Remove, Backward, Forward, and Enter**. Unfortunately, we cannot offer a comprehensive discussion of the characteristics of each of these methods here, but you have options for choosing the method for removing and retaining the predictor variables in your regression equation. In this example, we will use the default method – **Enter**, which is a standard approach in regression models.

4. Keeping other options unchanged, click the **OK** button to execute command. Following output will be displayed in the Output Viewer Window:

Command Syntax for Regression

```
REGRESSION
  /MISSING LISTWISE
  /STATISTICS COEFF OUTS R ANOVA
  /CRITERIA=PIN(.05) POUT(.10)
  /NOORIGIN
  /DEPENDENT PerCentFirstYear
  /METHOD=ENTER ExpEdu HrRead Absence.
```

Regression

Variables Entered/Removed[b]

Model	Variables Entered	Variables Removed	Method
1	Incidence of Absence during Year, Monthly Expenditure on Education, Hours Spent on Reading[a]	.	Enter

a. All requested variables entered.

b. Dependent Variable: Percentage of Marks in First Year

Model Summary

Model	R	R Square	Adjusted R Square	Std. Error of the Estimate
1	.600[a]	.360	.343	6.162

a. Predictors: (Constant), Incidence of Absence during Year, Monthly Expenditure on Education, Hours Spent on Reading

ANOVA[b]

Model		Sum of Squares	df	Mean Square	F	Sig.
1	Regression	2473.601	3	824.534	21.716	.000[a]
	Residual	4404.365	116	37.969		
	Total	6877.967	119			

a. Predictors: (Constant), Incidence of Absence during Year, Monthly Expenditure on Education, Hours Spent on Reading

b. Dependent Variable: Percentage of Marks in First Year

Coefficients[a]						
Model		Unstandardized Coefficients		Standardized Coefficients		
		B	Std. Error	Beta	t	Sig.
1	(Constant)	60.029	2.644		22.702	.000
	Monthly Expenditure on Education	.005	.003	.116	1.558	.122
	Hours Spent on Reading	.4 57	.264	.134	1.731	.086
	Incidence of Absence during Year	-.489	.071	-.533	-6.888	.000
a. Dependent Variable: Percentage of Marks in First Year						

Under the title **Regression**, four tables – **Variables Entered and Removed, Model Summary, ANOVA** and **Coefficients** – will be displayed. The detailed explanation for each of these tables is as follows:

Variables Entered and Removed table:

- **Model:** PASW facilitates you to assign numerous models in one regression command. This discloses the number of models being assigned. If there is more than one model, information related to it will also be displayed here.
- **Variables Entered:** PASW facilitates you to insert variables into a regression in blocks. In addition PASW facilitates a procedural regression. Therefore, the variables, which are inserted into the current regression, need to be remembered. Depending upon the method (stepwise or any other) used for estimation, list of independent variables included in the estimation procedure will be displayed here.
- **Variables Removed:** This column provides a list of variables that were deleted from the current regression. Generally, this column remains vacant until a procedural regression is executed.

Model Summary table:

- **Method:** This column tells you the method that the Predictive Analytic Software (PASW) used to run the regression. Enter implies that every independent variable was inserted in normal style. The other options for estimation procedure are stepwise, remove, backward and forward. If you did a stepwise regression, the entry in this column would tell you that.
- **Model:** PASW facilitates you to assign numerous models in one regression command. This discloses the number of models being assigned.
- **R:** R is the link between the examined and supposed value of a dependent variable. In addition, R is the square root of R-Squared.
- **R-Square:** R-Square shows the percentage of the total variation of dependent variable – **Percentage of Marks Scored in First Year** – that can be explained by the independent variable(s) – **Expenditure on Education, Incidence of Absence** and **Hours spent on Reading**. R-Square is also called the coefficient of determination in two-variable case and it is known as multiple coefficient of determination in case when more than two variables are included in model. R-square tells how well the sample regression line fits the data.

  In this particular example the value of R-square is .360, which means that about 36 per cent variations in the dependent variable – **Percentage of Marks Scored in First Year** is explained jointly by all the independent variables – **Expenditure on Education, Incidence of Absence** and **Hours spent on Reading.**
- **Adjusted R-square:** When additional independent variables are included in the model, each variable will explain some of the variance in the dependent variable. Additional explanatory variables will not reduce R square.

In case of multiple regression, the adjusted R-square attempts to yield a more realistic picture of the fit of regression value to estimate the R-squared for the population. The value of R-square is .360, while the value of Adjusted R-square is .343.

- **Std. Error of the Estimate:** The standard error of the estimate, also called the root mean square error, is the standard deviation of the error term, and is the square root of the Mean Square Residual (or Error).

ANOVA table:

- **Model:** PASW facilitates you to assign numerous models in one regression command. This discloses the number of models being assigned.

  This is the source of variance – Regression, Residual and Total. The Total variance is partitioned into variance which can be explained, by the regression model (independent variables). The Residual model, which is also known as Error, does not describe the variance. Note, the Sums of Squares for the Regression and Residual add up to the Total, reflecting the fact that the Total is partitioned into Regression and Residual variance. For example, the total of regression sum of squares (2473.601) and residual sum of square (4404.365) is 6877.967.

- **Sum of Squares:** These are the Sum of Squares associated with the three sources of variance – Total, Model and Residual. R-square is obtained from dividing Regression Sum of Squares by Total Sum of Squares because; R-Square is the proportion of the variance explained by the independent variables.
- **Df:** They are degrees of freedom that are linked with the origin of variances. The total variance has N-1 degrees of freedom. In this case, there were N=120 students, so the DF for total is 119. The model of degrees of freedom is related to the number of predictors minus 1 (K-1). You may conclude that this would be 3-1, because there were three independent variables in the model. However, it includes an intercept. This intercept is automatically added to the model. Now, there are four variables including an inceptor. Therefore, the model includes 4-1=3 degrees of freedom. Note that you can omit the intercept. Similarly, the Residual degree of freedom is the total DF- the DF model, that is, 119-3=116.
- **Mean Square:** These are the Mean Squares, the Sum of Squares divided by their respective degree of freedom (**df**). For the Regression, the Mean Square is given by 2473.601/ 3 = 824.534. For the Residual, the Mean Square is given by 4404.365 / 116 = 37.969. You can compute the **F** ratio (21.716), dividing the Mean Square Regression (824.534) by the Mean Square Residual (37.969) to test the significance of the predictors in the model.
- **F** and **Sig.**: The F-value is the Mean Square Regression divided by the Mean Square Residual, yielding F=21.716. The p-value associated with this F value is very small (.000). These values are used to answer the question "Do the independent variables reliably explain the variations in the dependent variable?" The **p-value** is compared to chosen alpha level (typically 0.05) and, if smaller, one can conclude that the independent variables jointly explain variations in the dependent variable. If the **p-value** was greater than 0.05, then the group of independent variables does not show a statistically significant relationship with the dependent variable nor does it explain the variations in the dependent variable.

  Note that this is an overall significance test assessing whether the group of independent variables jointly explain the variations in the dependent variable, and does not test the significance of any of the particular independent variables to explain variations in dependent variable. The significance of each individual independent variable to explain variations in the dependent variable is shown below.

Coefficients table:

- **Model:** PASW facilitates you to assign numerous models in one regression command. This discloses the number of models being assigned.

  This column shows the predictor variables – **Constant, Hours spent on reading, Incidence of Absence.** The first variable (**constant**) represents the constant, also referred to in textbooks as the Y intercept, the height of the regression line when it crosses the Y axis. In other words, this is the predicted value of **Marks scored in First Year** when all other variables are 0.

- **B:** These represent the values for the regression. These values forecast the dependent variable from the independent variable. Moreover, they are evaluated in their natural units and that is why they are known as unstandardized coefficient. However, these coefficients cannot be assessed with each other as they can be evaluated on different scales. The regression equation can be presented in many different ways, for example:

  $$Y_{Predicted} = \beta_0 + \beta_1 x_1 + \beta_2 x_2 + \beta_3 x_3$$

  The column of estimates (coefficients or parameter estimates, from here on labeled coefficients) provides the values for β_0, β_1, β_2, and β_3 for this equation. Expressed in terms of the variables used in this example, the regression equation is:

  $$Y_{Predicted} = 60.029 + 0.457{*}x_1 - 0.489{*}x_2 + 0.005{*}x_3$$

  Y= Percentage Marks Scored in First Year, X_1 = Hours Spent on Reading, X_2 = Incidence of Absence, X_3 = Expenditure on Education

  These estimates tell you about the relationship between independent variables and dependent variable. These estimates tell the amount of increase in the Percentage Marks Scored in First Year that would be predicted by a 1 unit increase in the predictor. Note that the independent variables which are not significant, the coefficients are not significantly different from 0, which should be taken into account when interpreting the coefficients. (See the columns with the t-value and p-value about testing whether the coefficients are significant).

  The coefficient (parameter estimate) for Hours spent on reading is 0.457. So, for every unit increase in this variable will increase Percentage Marks Scored in First Year by .457 unit, holding all other variables constant. When the sign of the coefficient is + (plus) it shows positive relationship and – (minus) sign shows negative relationship between dependent and independent variable. Here in this example, there is positive relationship between **Percentage Marks Scored in First Year** and **Hours Spent on Reading**; and a negative relationship between **Percentage Marks Scored in First Year** and **Incidence of Absence**.

- **Std. Error:** These are the standard errors associated with the coefficients. The standard error is used for testing whether the parameter is significantly different from 0 by dividing the parameter estimate by the standard error to obtain a t-value (see the column with t-values and p-values). The standard errors can also be used to form a confidence interval for the parameter, as shown in the last two columns of this table.

- **Beta:** They are the standardized coefficients, that you would obtain if you standardized all of the variables in the regression, including the dependent and the independent variables, and ran the regression. When you have standardized the variables before executing the regression, you have arranged the entire variables on the identical scale. Moreover, you can observe the effective coefficient by comparing their magnitude. In addition, you find that the larger t-values have larger betas.

- **t and Sig.**: The t and Sig. columns give 2 tailed p-value and the t-value that are used to examine the null hypothesis. If a 2 tailed test is utilized, then the comparison of every p-value is done with the preselected value of alpha. The coefficients, which have alpha greater than p-value, then these coefficients are statically significant. For example, if you chose alpha to be 0.05, coefficients having a p-value of 0.05 or less would be statistically significant (which means, you can reject the null hypothesis and say that the coefficient is significantly different from 0). If you use a 1 tailed test (you predict that the parameter will go in a particular direction), then you can divide the p-value by 2 before comparing it to your preselected alpha level. The coefficient for **Hours Spent on Reading** is significant at 10% confidence interval because its p-value of 0.086 is less than 0.1.

In this example, the coefficient of **Hours Spent on Reading** is significant at 10% confidence interval and **Incidence of Absence** at 5%. The coefficient of **Expenditure on Education** is not statistically significant.

- **95% Confidence Limit for B Lower Bound** and **Upper Bound:** This shows a 95% confidence interval for the coefficient. This is very beneficial as it assists to comprehend how high and how low the literal population value of the parameter can be. The confidence intervals are dependent on p-values in such a way that if confidence interval is zero, then the coefficient is not statically significant. To get this information, it has to be selected in option while executing regression command. In some versions of PASW (earlier Statistical Packages for Social Sciences – SPSS), it is generated by default.

Summary

In this chapter we learnt:

- Assumptions of linear regression.
- Procedure for undertaking linear regression.

Chapter 14

Nonparametric Statistics

In this Chapter:

The term nonparametric was first used by Wolfowitz, 1942. To understand the idea of nonparametric statistics, it is required to have a basic understanding of parametric statistics. A parametric test requires a sample to be normally distributed. A nonparametric test does not rely on parametric assumptions like normality.

Nonparametric test create flexible demands of the data. To make standard parametric procedures legitimate, some provisions need to be fulfilled, especially for minor sample sizes. For example, the requirement of the one sample t-test is that the observation must be made from the ordinarily distributed population. In case, the provision is defied, then the resultants may not be credible. However, in case of the Wilcoxon signed rank to illustrate valid interference, normality is not required.

We can assume that the sampling distribution is normal even if we are not sure that the distribution of the variable in the population is normal, as long as our sample is large enough (for example, 100 or more observations).However, if our selected sample is too small, then those tests can only be utilized if we are assured that the variable is disseminated normally.

The applications of tests that are based on the normality assumptions are restricted by the deficiency of accurate measurement. For example, a study measures Grade Point Average (*GPA*) in place of Percentage Marks. This measurement scale does not measure the exact distance between the marks of two students. GPA allows us only to rank the students from "good" students to "poor" students. This measurement is called the ordinal scale. Statistical techniques such as Analysis of Variance, t- tests etc. assume that the data are measured either on interval or ratio scale. In such situations where data is measured on nominal or ordinal scale nonparametric tests are more useful.

Thus, nonparametric test are used when either:

- Sample is not normally distributed.
- Sample size is small.
- The variables are measured on nominal or ordinal scale.

There is at least one nonparametric equivalent for each parametric general type of test. Broadly, these tests fall into the following categories:

- Tests of differences between groups (independent samples);
- Tests of differences between variables (dependent samples);
- Tests of relationships between variables.

Many procedures have not been touched upon here. This chapter discusses the concepts and procedure to undertake Runs Test, Chi-square Test, Wilcoxon Signed Rank Test, Mann-Whitney Test and Kruskal-Wallis Test.

14.1 Runs Test

Runs test is used to examine the randomness of data. Many statistical procedures require data to be randomly selected. Runs test can be explained with the example of tossing a fair coin, where the probability of getting a head or a tail is equal, which is 0.5. Suppose we denote head by '1' and tail by '0' and record the outcomes as shown below, we can conduct Runs test to see whether the sample is randomly chosen or not. The null and alternative hypotheses for Runs test are:

- **H_0:** The sample is randomly selected.
- **H_1:** The sample is not randomly selected.

The Run length is calculated by counting the number of 0's or 1's in sequence. For example, the run length for 0 and 1 in the following sequence is 5 and 4 respectively and the number of runs is 2.

```
000001111
```

We shall conduct Runs test on our data set to examine whether the students belonging to different faculties (graduation) are randomly selected or not.

The procedure for undertaking Runs test is as follows:

1. Click on **Analyze** from the command menu as shown in Fig.PASW–14.1:

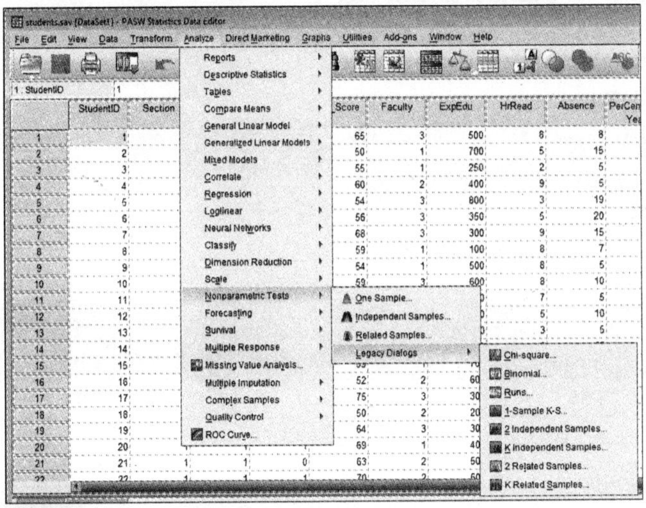

Fig.PASW–14.1

2. Click **Nonparametric**, **Legacy Dialogues** and then **Runs** to get the dialogue box as shown in Fig.PASW–14.2:

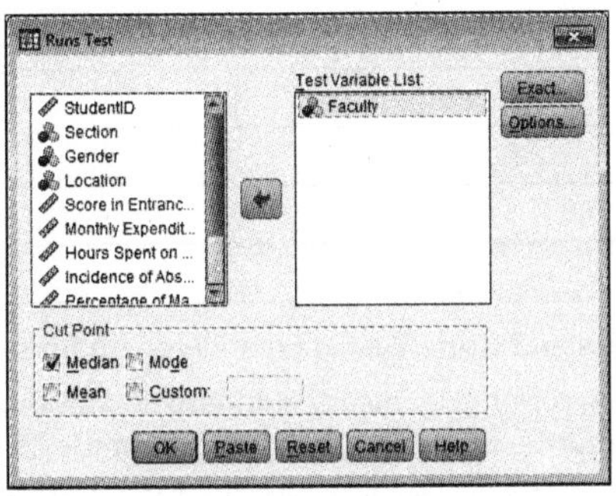

Fig.PASW–14.2

3. Select **Faculty** and move it to **Test Variable List** box.
4. Click **Options** button to get the dialogue box shown in Fig.PASW–14.3:

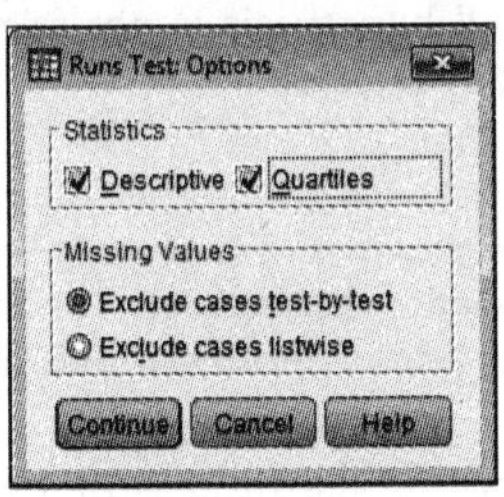

Fig.PASW–14.3

5. Check **Descriptive** and **Quartiles** check boxes.
6. Keeping all other options unchanged, click **OK** button to execute command. The output will be displayed in the output viewer window as shown below:

Command Syntax for Runs Test

```
NPAR TESTS
  /RUNS(MEDIAN)=Faculty
  /STATISTICS DESCRIPTIVES QUARTILES
  /MISSING ANALYSIS.
```

NPar Tests

Descriptive Statistics

	N	Mean	Std. Deviation	Minimum	Maximum	Percentiles		
						25th	50th (Median)	75th
Faculty	120	1.96	.726	1	3	1.00	2.00	2.00

Runs Test

	Faculty
Test Value[a]	2
Cases < Test Value	34
Cases >= Test Value	86
Total Cases	120
Number of Runs	43
Z	-1.523
Asymp. Sig. (2-tailed)	.128

a. Median

Two tables – **Descriptive Statistics** and **Runs Test** are displayed under the heading **NPar Tests**.

Descriptive Statistics table gives count (N), mean, standard deviation, maximum, minimum, 25th percentile (1st quartile), 50th percentile (2nd quartile or median) and 75th percentile (3rd quartile).

Runs Test table displays the Test Value, Cases less than Test Value, Cases greater than or equal to Test Value, Total Cases, Number of Runs, Z-statistic and associated Asymptotic Significance. The Test Value was specified to be the median and therefore, the test value is 2. The number of cases with values less than test value (median) are 34 and those having value greater than or equal to test value (median) are 86. The total cases represent the sample size, which is 120. Forty-three runs were recorded. The Z-value of -1.523 with asymptotic significance of .128 (less than 0.05), means that the null hypothesis is not rejected. Therefore, we say the number of cases belonging to different faculties is randomly selected.

14.2 Chi-Square Test

Chi-square is used to examine the association between two or more variables measured on categorical scales. Chi-square tests the hypothesis whether two or more samples drawn from the same population have similar characteristics or not.

Chi-square is used most frequently to test the statistical significance of results reported in bivariate tables, and interpreting bivariate tables is integral to interpreting the results of a chi square test.

Bivariate tabular (crosstabulation) analysis is used when trying to summarize the intersections of independent and dependent variables and to examine the relationship (if any) between those variables. For example, to know if there is any association between the **Gender** and their **Location**, Chi-square test can be applied. In this example, our independent variable is Location. We control the independent variable **Gender** and elicit as well as measure the dependent variable **Location** to test our hypothesis, whether there is some association between these two variables.

The Chi-Square test is a statistical technique to examine the association or statistical independence between the row and column variables in a two-way table. The null and alternative hypotheses for Chi-Square test are:

- **Ho:** There is no association between the row (Gender) and column (Location) variables.
- **H1:** There is association between the row (Gender) and column (Location) variables.

The procedure to conduct Chi-square test is as follows:

1. Click **Analyze** from the command menu as shown in Fig.PASW–14.4:

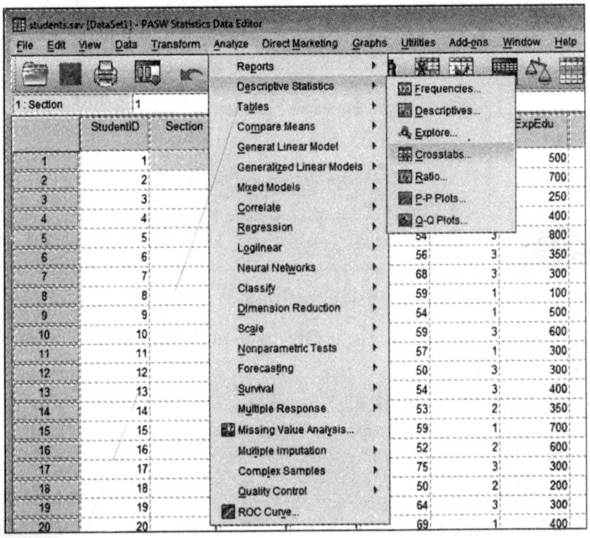

Fig.PASW–14.4

2. Click **Descriptives** and **Crosstabs** (Fig.PASW–14.4) to get the dialogue box shown in Fig.PASW–14.5:

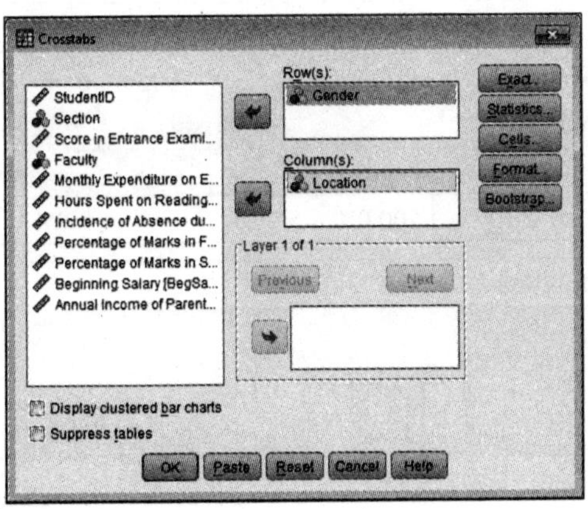

Fig.PASW–14.5

3. Select **Gender** and move it into the **Row** list box and **Location** in the **Column** list box.
4. Click **Statistics** button to get the dialogue box shown in Fig.PASW–14.6:

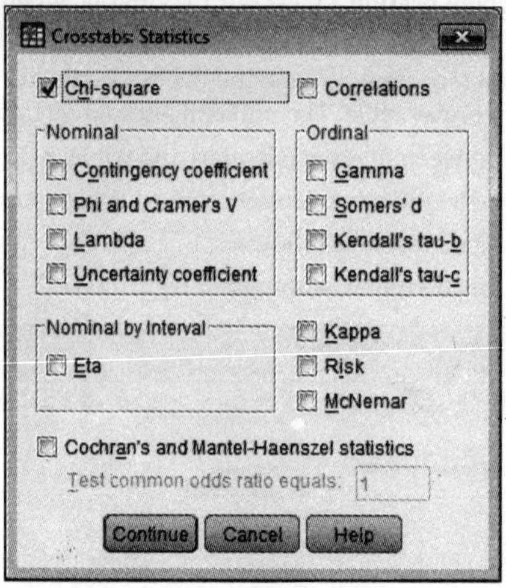

Fig.PASW–14.6

5. Select **Chi-Square** check box and then click **Continue** to return to the previous dialogue box.
6. Keeping all other options unchanged, click **OK** to execute command. The output will appear in output viewer window as shown below:

Command Syntax for Crosstabulations with Chi-Square

```
CROSSTABS
  /TABLES=Gender BY Location
  /FORMAT=AVALUE TABLES
  /STATISTICS=CHISQ
  /CELLS=COUNT
  /COUNT ROUND CELL.
```

Crosstabs

Case Processing Summary

	Cases					
	Valid		Missing		Total	
	N	Percent	N	Percent	N	Percent
Gender * Location	120	100.0%	0	.0%	120	100.0%

Gender * Location Crosstabulation

Count

		Location		
		Local	Commuter	Total
Gender	Male	33	33	66
	Female	39	15	54

Gender * Location Crosstabulation				
Count				
		Location		Total
		Local	Commuter	
Gender	Male	33	33	66
	Female	39	15	54
Total		72	48	120

Chi-Square Tests

	Value	df	Asymp. Sig. (2-sided)	Exact Sig. (2-sided)	Exact Sig. (1-sided)
Pearson Chi-Square	6.111[a]	1	.013		
Continuity Correction[b]	5.220	1	.022		
Likelihood Ratio	6.216	1	.013		
Fisher's Exact Test				.016	.011
Linear-by-Linear Association	6.060	1	.014		
N of Valid Cases	120				

a. 0 cells (.0%) have expected count less than 5. The minimum expected count is 21.60.

b. Computed only for a 2x2 table

Three tables – **Case Processing Summary**, **Gender*Location Crosstabulation** and **Chi-Square Tests** – are generated under the heading **Crosstabs** on executing the command for Chi-square test.

Case Processing Summary table gives the summary information (number of cases and missing values) of the variables.

Crosstabulation of **Gender** and **Location** is given in the second table. It shows that out of 66 males, 33 are locals and 33 are commuters. Out of 54 females, 39 are locals and 15 are commuters. This shows that there is association between **Gender** and **Location**. In order to examine the statistical significance of this result, we have to check the Chi-square statistic and its associated asymptotic significance value.

The third table provides required information of **Chi-square test**. The value of Pearson Chi-Square is 6.111 and associated significance value is .013 (which is less than 0.05). Therefore, the null hypothesis is rejected and we say there is association between **Gender** and the **Location**.

Many researchers often get confused between statistical significance and strength of the relationship. People tend to think that the more significant (the lower the p-value) relationship means stronger relationship. The significance level is influenced by the strength of the relationship and sample size. We require different measure to capture the strength of the relationship, or the effect size.

Many statistical packages do not include measures of strength of relationship. For Chi-square test, is easy to calculate. It is calculated by taking the square root of chi-square value divided by the sample size.

14.3 Mann-Whitney U Test

Generally, the *t*-test for independent samples is used, if two samples are compared over their mean value for some variable interest. Nonparametric alternatives for this test are the Wald-Wolfowitz Runs test, the Mann-Whitney U test, and the Kolmogorov-Smirnov two-sample test.

Mann-Whitney U test compares the sums of ranks of two independent groups. The null and alternative hypotheses for Mann-Whitney U test are:

- **H0:** There is no difference in sum of ranks between two independent groups.
- **H1:** There is difference in sum of ranks between two independent groups.

The procedure for undertaking Mann-Whitney U test is as follows:

1. Click **Analyze, Nonparametric** and **Legacy** as shown in Fig.PASW–14.1.
2. Click **2 Independent Samples** in **Legacy** Sub-Menu to get the dialogue box shown in Fig.PASW–14.7:

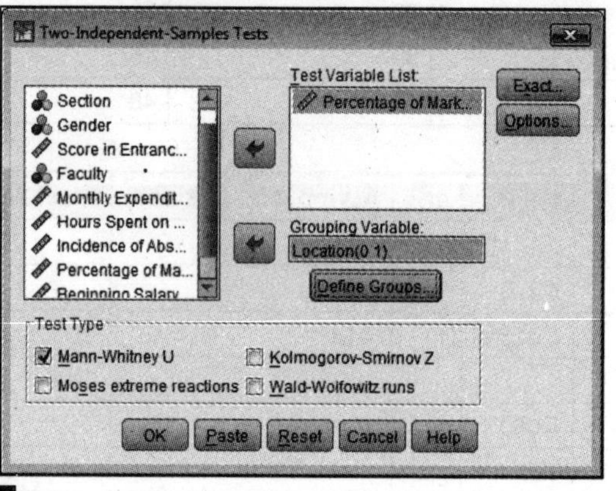

Fig.PASW–14.7

3. Select Percentage Marks Scored in First Test and move it to the Test Variables List box.
4. Select **Location** and move it to the **Grouping Variable** box.
5. Click the **Define** button and dialogue box shown in Fig.PASW–14.8 will appear on the screen:

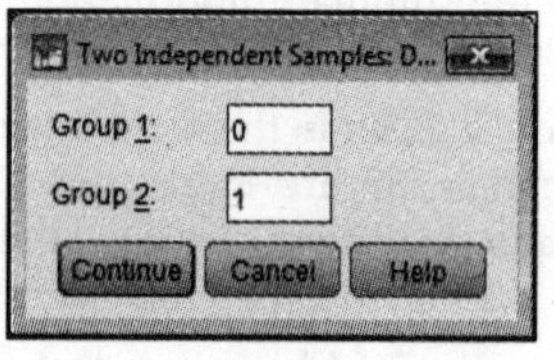

Fig.PASW–14.8

6. Type **0** in **Group 1** and **1** in **Group 2**. Click **Continue** to go back to the previous dialogue box.
7. Click **Options** to get the dialogue box shown in Fig.PASW–14.9:

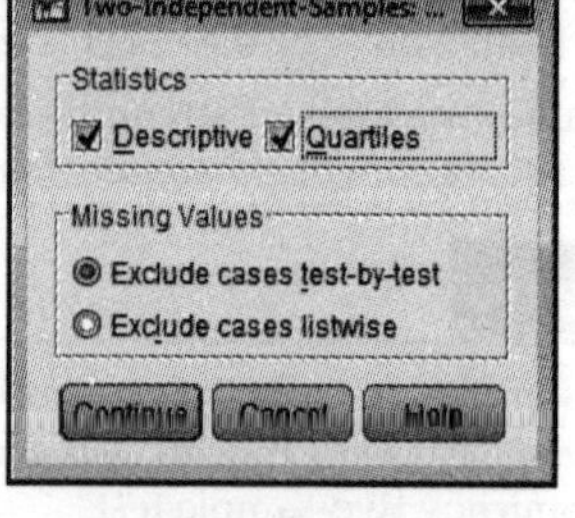

Fig.PASW–14.9

8. Select **Descriptive** and **Quartiles** options in **Statistics** frame by clicking them.
9. Click **Continue** button to go back to the previous dialogue box and keeping all other options unchanged, click **OK** o execute command. Following output will appear in the output viewer window:

Command Syntax for Mann-Whitney U Test

```
NPAR TESTS
  /M-W= PerCentFirstYear BY Location0 1)
  /STATISTICS=DESCRIPTIVES QUARTILES
  /MISSING ANALYSIS.
```

NPar Tests

Descriptive Statistics

	N	Mean	Std. Deviation	Minimum	Maximum	Percentiles		
						25th	50th (Median)	75th
Percentage of Marks in First Year	120	57.98	7.603	40	89	54.00	57.50	62.00
Location	120	.40	.492	0	1	.00	.00	1.00

Mann-Whitney Test

Ranks

	Location	N	Mean Rank	Sum of Ranks
Percentage of Marks in First Year	Local	72	60.32	4343.00
	Commuter	48	60.77	2917.00
	Total	120		

Test Statistics[a]

	Percentage of Marks in First Year
Mann-Whitney U	1715.000
Wilcoxon W	4343.000
Z	-.070
Asymp. Sig. (2-tailed)	.944

a. Grouping Variable: Location

Under the title – **Npar Tests,** a table – **Descriptive Statistics** are displayed. Just below this table, two more tables – **Ranks** and **Test Statistics** are displayed under the heading **Mann-Whitney Test.**

The **Descriptive Statistics** table gives count (N), mean, standard deviation, maximum, minimum and details about the quartiles.

The **Ranks** table displays the details about the mean ranks and sums of ranks for each category of **Location** – for ocals and Commuters. The sum of ranks of Locals is higher than the sum of ranks of Commuters.

The **Test Statistics** table gives information about whether the difference is statistically significant or by chance. The Mann-Whitney U test statistic is 1715.000 and the associated significance is .944. However, for large samples, we must check the z-value. The z-value -0.070 and the associated significance is .944 (which is much higher than 0.05). The null hypothesis is thus not rejected and we may say that the difference in sum of ranks for **Percentage of Marks Scored in First Year** is by chance. Simply, there is no significant difference in **Percentage of Marks scored in First Year** by locals and commuters.

The significance of z-statistic is examined by comparing the calculated z-value with the tabulated value. Predictive Analytic Software (PASW) provides information about significance value (2-tailed) and that helps in evaluating null-hypothesis. The most common procedure in statistical hypothesis testing is to establish a significance level, denoted by α, and to reject null-hypothesis when the p-value falls below it. Suppose, if α is set at 5%, in the preceding example the p-value is 0.944 and therefore, null hypothesis will not be rejected.

14.4 Wilcoxon Signed Rank Test

Wilcoxon Signed Rank test (also known as Wilcoxon Matched Pair Test) is the non-parametric version of dependent samples t-test or paired samples t-test. Sign test is the other nonparametric alternative to the paired samples t-test. If the variables of interest are dichotomous in nature (Male and Female or Yes and No) then McNemar's Chi-square test is used.

Wilcoxon Signed Rank test is also a nonparametric version for One-Sample t-test. Wilcoxon Signed Rank test compares the medians of the groups under two situations (paired-samples) or it compares the median of the group with hypothesized median (one-sample).

We shall focus our discussion on the paired-sample situation for understanding the Wilcoxon Signed Rank test. The null and alternative hypothesis for Wilcoxon Signed Rank test are:

- **H0:** There is no difference in median of the groups in two situations.
- **H1:** There is difference in median of the groups in two situations.

The procedure for undertaking Wilcoxon Signed Rank test is discussed below:

1. Click **Analyze, Nonparametric** and **Legacy** (Fig.PASW–14.1).
2. Click **2 Related Samples** in **Legacy** Sub-Menu to get the dialogue box shown in Fig.PASW–14.10:

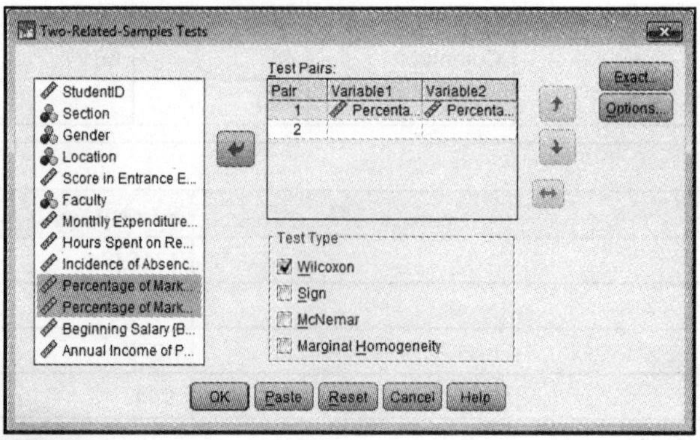

Fig.PASW–14.10

3. Select Percentage of Marks Scored in First Year and Percentage of Marks scored in Second Year simultaneously and move them to Test Pairs list box.
4. Click **Options** to get the dialogue box shown in Fig.PASW–14.11:

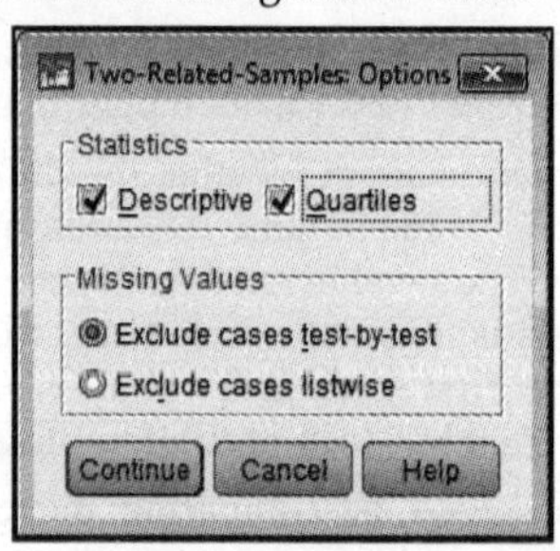

Fig.PASW–14.11

5. Select **Descriptive** and **Quartiles** by clicking on respective check boxes.

6. Click **Continue** to go back to the previous dialogue box.
7. Keeping all other values and options unchanged; click **OK** to execute the command. Following output will be displayed in the output viewer window as shown below:

Command Syntax for Wilcoxon Signed Rank Test

```
NPAR TESTS
  /WILCOXON=PerCentFirstYear WITH PerCentSecYear (PAIRED)
  /STATISTICS DESCRIPTIVES QUARTILES
  /MISSING ANALYSIS.
```

NPar Tests

Descriptive Statistics

	N	Mean	Std. Deviation	Minimum	Maximum	Percentiles 25th	Percentiles 50th (Median)	Percentiles 75th
Percentage of Marks in First Year	120	57.98	7.603	40	89	54.00	57.50	62.00
Percentage of Marks in Second Year	120	58.57	6.796	40	85	55.00	58.00	63.00

Wilcoxon Signed Ranks Test

Ranks

		N	Mean Rank	Sum of Ranks
Percentage of Marks in Second Year - Percentage of Marks in First Year	Negative Ranks	45[a]	57.44	2585.00
	Positive Ranks	69[b]	57.54	3970.00
	Ties	6[c]		
	Total	120		

a. Percentage of Marks in Second Year < Percentage of Marks in First Year

b. Percentage of Marks in Second Year > Percentage of Marks in First Year

c. Percentage of Marks in Second Year = Percentage of Marks in First Year

Test Statistics[b]

	Percentage of Marks in Second Year - Percentage of Marks in First Year
Z	-1.971[a]
Asymp. Sig. (2-tailed)	.049

a. Based on negative ranks.

b. Wilcoxon Signed Ranks Test

Descriptive Statistics table is displayed under the heading **NPar Tests** and two more tables – **Ranks** and **Test Statistics** are displayed under the heading **Wilcoxon Signed Ranks Test**.

The **Descriptive Statistics** table gives count (N) of negative ranks, positive ranks and ties; and mean, standard deviation, maximum, minimum and details about the quartiles for negative ranks, positive ranks and ties separately. The negative ranks are ranks assigned to those cases whose **Percentage Marks Scored in Second Year** is less than **Percentage Marks Scored in First Year**. Those cases whose **Percentage Marks Scored in Second Year** is more than **Percentage Marks Scored in First Year** are given positive ranks and those whose **Percentage Marks Scored in Second Year** is equal to the **Percentage Marks Scored in First Year** are called ties.

The **Test Statistics** table gives information about whether the difference is statistically significant or by chance. The Z-statistic is -1.971 and the associated significance is .049 (which is less than 0.05). The null hypothesis is thus rejected and we say the difference in sum of ranks for **Percentage of Marks Scored in First Year** is statistically significant. Simply, there is significant difference in **Percentage Marks Scored in Second Year** and **Percentage Marks Scored in First Year.**

14.5 Kruskal-Wallis Test

Kruskal-Wallis test is used with multiple groups. It is the non-parametric version of One-Way ANOVA. Median test is another nonparametric alternative to One-Way ANOVA.

Kruskal-Wallis compares medians of more than two independent groups. The null and alternative hypotheses for Kruskal-Wallis test are:

- **H_0:** There is no difference in median of the groups in two situations.
- **H_1:** There is difference in median of the groups in two situations.

The procedure for undertaking Kruskal-Wallis test is discussed below:

1. Click **Analyze, Nonparametric** and **Legacy** as shown in Fig.PASW–14.1.
2. Click **K Independent Samples** in **Legacy** Sub-Menu to get the dialogue box shown in Fig.PASW–14.12:

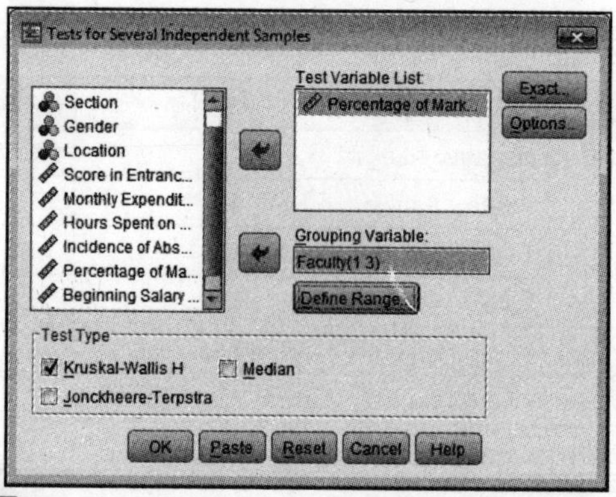

Fig.PASW–14.12

3. Select **Percentage of Marks in First Year** and move it into **Test Variable** List box.
4. Select **Faculty** and take it to **Grouping Variable** box.
5. Click **Define Range** to get the dialogue box shown in Fig.PASW–14.13:

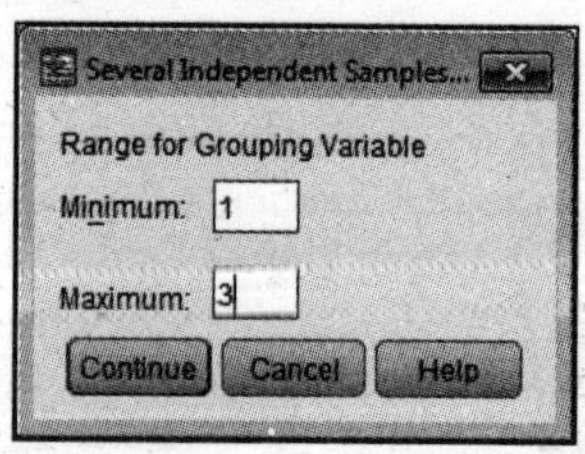

Fig.PASW–14.13

6. Type **1** in Minimum and **3** in Maximum; click the **Continue** button to return to the previous dialogue box.

7. Click **Options** to get the dialogue box shown in Fig.PASW–14.4 and select **Descriptive** and **Quartiles.**

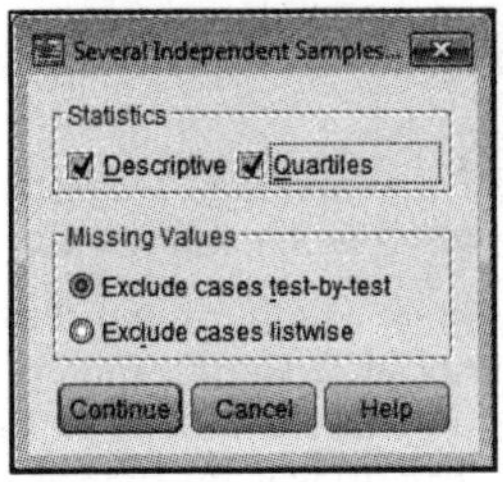

Fig.PASW–14.14

8. Click **Continue** to go back to the previous dialogue box and then click **OK** to execute command. The output will be displayed in the output viewer window as shown below:

Command Syntax for Krukal-Wallis Test

```
NPAR TESTS
  /K-W=PerCentFirstYear BY Faculty(1 3)
  /STATISTICS DESCRIPTIVES QUARTILES
  /MISSING ANALYSIS.
```

NPar Tests

Descriptive Statistics

	N	Mean	Std. Deviation	Minimum	Maximum	Percentiles 25th	50th (Median)	75th
Percentage of Marks in First Year	120	57.98	7.603	40	89	54.00	57.50	62.00
Faculty	120	1.96	.726	1	3	1.00	2.00	2.00

Kruskal-Wallis Test

Ranks

	Faculty	N	Mean Rank
Percentage of Marks in First Year	Arts	34	51.93
	Commerce	57	66.30
	Science	29	59.16
	Total	120	

Test Statistics[a,b]

	Percentage of Marks in First Year
Chi-square	3.711
df	2
Asymp. Sig.	.156

a. Kruskal Wallis Test

b. Grouping Variable: Faculty

Descriptive Statistics table is displayed under the heading **NPar Tests** and two more tables – **Ranks** and **Test Statistics** are displayed under the heading **Kruskal-Wallis Test.**

The **Descriptive Statistics** table gives count (N), mean, standard deviation, maximum, minimum and details about the quartiles.

The **Ranks** table displays the details about the mean ranks for each category of Faculty – Arts, Commerce and Science. The mean ranks of Commerce is highest (66.30), followed by Science (59.16) and Arts (51.93) is lowest.

The **Test Statistics** table gives information about whether the difference is statistically significant or by chance. The Chi-square statistic is 3.711 and the associated significance is .156 (which is higher than 0.05). The null hypothesis is thus not rejected and we may say that the difference **Percentage of Marks Scored in First Year** by students belonging to different **Graduation Faculties** is by chance .Simply, there is no significant difference in **Percentage of Marks scored in First Year** among students belonging to Arts, Commerce or Science faculty.

If there are more than two variables that were in sample, then we would use repeated measures ANOVA. The Friedman's two way analysis of variance and Cochran Q test are other nonparametric options to this method, which are used when the variable was calculated in categories, for example, Yes and No, Male and Female). Cochran Q is particularly useful for measuring changes in frequencies (proportions) across time. However, these techniques are not discussed here.

Summary

In this chapter we learnt:

- Runs test.
- Chi-square test.
- Mann-Whitney U test.
- Wilcoxon signed rank pair test.
- Kruskal-Wallis test.

Chapter 15

Logistic Regression

In this Chapter:

- Logistic Regression

Logistic regression analysis helps in predicting probability of occurrence of y (dependent variable) given the values of x (independent variables), when dependent variable is dichotomous. One can use dichotomous variable like health status (sick or not), employment status (employed or unemployed), labour force participation (part or not a part of labour force), family planning method(which type) etc. as a dependent variable. Independent variables can be continuous or categorical. It can also include interactions between continuous and categorical variables.

Logistic regression is a more flexible technique because it makes no assumptions about nature of relationship between independent and dependent variables. Moreover, independent variables are not required to be normally distributed. Please note, that the power of analysis is increased if variables are normally distributed.

When using logistic regression, it is important to note that if one variable predicts another, it does not imply causality; and statistical significance does not imply practical significance.

When dependent variable is dichotomous, we cannot directly apply linear regression. One of the assumptions of linear regression is that the relationship between variables is linear. When dependent variable is dichotomous, this assumption is violated. Logistic regression overcomes the problem of violating the assumption of linearity.

In logistic regression the dependent variable is the probability that an event will occur, hence y is constrained between 0 and 1. The predictors can be binary, a mixture of categorical and continuous or just continuous. The logistic model is defined as:

$$prob(event) = \frac{1}{1+e^{-z}}$$

where z is $b_0 + b_1x_1 + b_2x_2 + \dots b_px_p$ and x_is are predictors (independent variables).

The logistic equation can be rearranged into a linear form by converting the probability into a log odds or logit.

log [Prob(event)/Prob(no event)] = $b_0 + b_1x_1 + b_2x_2 + \dots b_Px_P$

This results a correlation, which is quite identical to that in numerous regressions, with an exception that now each one unit modification in a predictor is linked with the modification in log odds, rather than to react directly.

The maximum-likelihood method is employed to figure out the values of parameter. This method selects coefficients that make the observed values most likely to have occurred. The resulting value from the equation is a probability value that varies between 0 and 1. A value close to 0 means that y is very unlikely and a value close to 1 means that y is very likely to have occurred.

We shall try to understand logistic regression with the help of following example:

The health status (0=Not Sick and 1=Sick) is the dependent variable. The Smoking status (0=Not Smoking and 1=Smoking) and weight of the respondent measured in kilograms are independent variables (also called covariates). Hypothetical data for 25 persons is given in the following table:

Table 15.1: Example for Binary Logistic Regression

Health Status	Smoking	Weight (kg)	Health Status	Smoking	Weight (kg)
0	0	45	1	0	70
1	1	76	0	0	42
1	1	65	0	0	43
0	0	39	0	1	40
1	1	45	1	1	42
0	1	43	0	0	45
1	1	57	0	0	38

Table 15.1: Example for Binary Logistic Regression					
Health Status	**Smoking**	**Weight (kg)**	**Health Status**	**Smoking**	**Weight (kg)**
1	0	41	1	1	65
0	0	45	1	0	75
0	0	53	0	0	45
0	0	52	0	0	49
1	1	55	1	1	63
1	1	52			

Health Status: 0=Not Sick, 1=Sick

Smoking: 0=No Smoking, 1=Smoking

In this example we are interested in knowing the probability of a sickness of a person on the basis of his smoking habits and his body weight.

The procedure for undertaking logistic regression is as follows:

1. Click **Analyse** from command menu as shown in Fig.PASW–15.1:

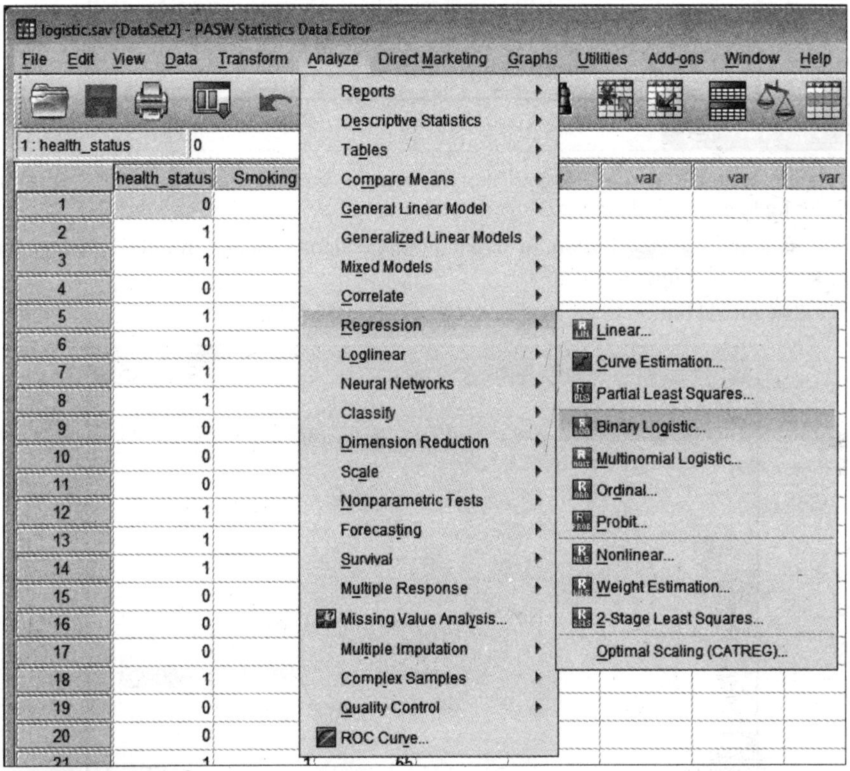

Fig.PASW–15.1

2. Click **Regression** and **Binary Logistic** as shown in Fig.PASW–15.1 to get the dialogue box shown in Fig.PASW–15.2:

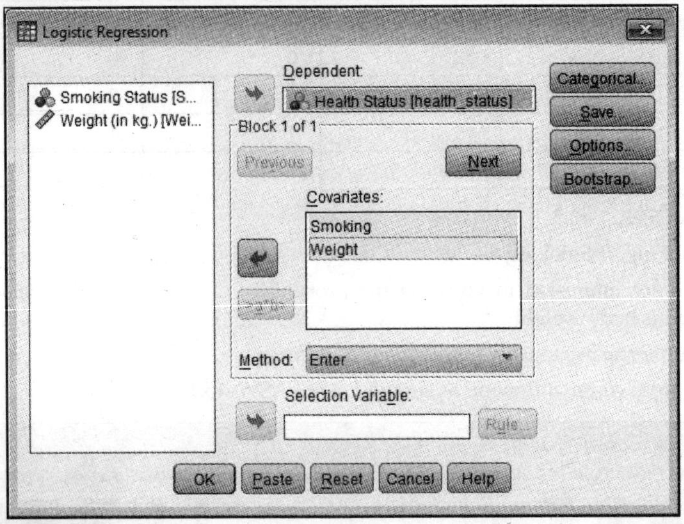

Fig.PASW–15.2

3. Select **Health Status** and move it into the **Dependent Variable** text box. Select **Smoking Status** and **Weight (in kg.)** and move them into **Covariates** list box.

   Note you must not use >a*b> button for moving independent variables into the covariate box. This button should used to test for interaction effect.

4. Click the **Categorical** button to get the dialogue box shown in Fig.PASW–15.3:

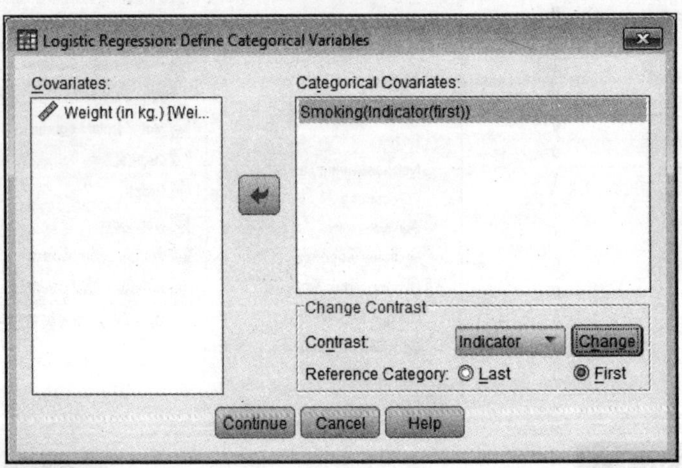

Fig.PASW–15.3

5. Since **Smoking** is a categorical variable, move **Smoking** into the **Categorical Covariates** list box.
6. In the Change Contrasts frame of the dialogue box, click on **First** to specify the **Reference Category** and then on **Change**.

Note

When we specify a covariate as categorical, a dummy variable is created. By default, k-1 dummy variables are created for k categories of a given covariate. In our example, we create a single dummy variable Smoking Status (1),it contains both categories of smoking and non smoking. The values are automatically assigned to it on the basis of specification of reference category. If the reference category is changed from last to first or vice versa, the values assigned to categorical variable – here, Smoking Status (1) changes. Since we have specified First as the reference category, the coding of original variable Smoking Status and the newly created dummy variable Smoking Status (1) is same. If we specify Last as Reference Category, the coding of Smoking Status (1) will be reversed. For simplicity and consistency, we have selected First as Reference Category.

7. Click **Continue** to go to previous dialogue box and then click **OK** to execute command. Following output will be generated in the output viewer window:

Command Syntax for Logistic Regression

```
DATASET ACTIVATE DataSet2.
LOGISTIC REGRESSION VARIABLES health_status
  /METHOD=ENTER Smoking Weight
  /CONTRAST (Smoking)=Indicator(1)
  /CRITERIA=PIN(.05) POUT(.10) ITERATE(20) CUT(.5).
```

Logistic Regression

Case Processing Summary

Unweighted Cases[a]		N	Percent
Selected Cases	Included in Analysis	25	100.0
	Missing Cases	0	.0
	Total	25	100.0
Unselected Cases		0	.0
Total		25	100.0

a. If weight is in effect, see classification table for the total number of cases.

Dependent Variable Encoding

Original Value		Internal Value
dimension0	Not Sick	0
	Sick	1

Categorical Variables Codings

		Frequency	Parameter coding
			(1)
Smoking Status	No Smoking	14	.000
	Smoking	11	1.000

Block 0: Beginning Block

Classification Table[a,b]

	Observed		Predicted		
			Health Status		Percentage Correct
			Not Sick	Sick	
Step 0	Health Status	Not Sick	13	0	100.0
		Sick	12	0	.0
	Overall Percentage				52.0

a. Constant is included in the model.

b. The cut value is .500

Variables in the Equation

		B	S.E.	Wald	df	Sig.	Exp(B)
Step 0	Constant	-.080	.400	.040	1	.842	.923

Variables not in the Equation

			Score	df	Sig.
Step 0	Variables	Smoking(1)	9.000	1	.003
		Weight	10.088	1	.001
	Overall Statistics		15.045	2	.001

Block 1: Method = Enter

Omnibus Tests of Model Coefficients

		Chi-square	df	Sig.
Step 1	Step	19.802	2	.000
	Block	19.802	2	.000
	Model	19.802	2	.000

Model Summary

Step	-2 Log likelihood	Cox & Snell R Square	Nagelkerke R Square
1	14.816[a]	.547	.730

a. Estimation terminated at iteration number 6 because parameter estimates changed by less than .001.

Classification Table[a]

	Observed		Predicted		
			Health Status		Percentage Correct
			Not Sick	Sick	
Step 1	Health Status	Not Sick	12	1	92.3
		Sick	1	11	91.7
	Overall Percentage				92.0

Classification Table[a]

	Observed		Predicted		
			Health Status		Percentage Correct
			Not Sick	Sick	
Step 1	Health Status	Not Sick	12	1	92.3
		Sick	1	11	91.7
	Overall Percentage				92.0

a. The cut value is .500

Variables in the Equation

		B	S.E.	Wald	df	Sig.	Exp(B)
Step 1[a]	Smoking(1)	3.284	1.433	5.251	1	.022	26.695
	Weight	.196	.094	4.363	1	.037	1.216
	Constant	-11.337	4.820	5.533	1	.019	.000

a. Variable(s) entered on step 1: Smoking, Weight.

Under the title **Logistic Regression**, three sets of tables are displayed. The first set comprises three tables – **Case Processing Summary, Dependent Variable Encoding** and **Categorical Variables Codings**. The second set is titled **Block 0: Beginning Block**. This comprises three tables – **Classification Table, Variables in the Equation** and **Variables Not in the Equation**. The third set is titled **Block 1: Method = Enter** and it comprises four tables – **Omnibus Tests of Model Coefficients, Model Summary, Classification table** and **Variables in the Equation.**

The **Case Processing Summary** table gives information on number of cases analysed, number of missing values and number of selected cases. In our example, there are no missing values and all cases are selected, therefore 25 cases are analysed.

The **Dependent Variable Encoding** table shows the value labels assigned to the dependent variable. The table shows that **0** is assigned to **Not Sick** and **1** is assigned to **Sick**.

The **Categorical Variable Encoding** table shows the values assigned to dummy variable **Smoking Status (1)** and the number of cases in each category. The value **0** is assigned to **not smoking** and **1** to **smoking**, which is similar to the value laels assigned to the original variable **Smoking Status**. We see from the table that 14 persons are non-smokers where as 11 are smokers.

In **Block 0: Beginning Block**, the logistic regression is estimated by simply including the constant. No covariates are included while estimating the equation. This model is called the base model. The **Classification Table** shows that the base model though, predicts correctly the number of **non-sick** persons it does not correctly predict the number of **sick** persons; there are 13 non-sick and 12 sick out of 25 respondents. This base model predicts those 12 sick persons also as non-sick. Thus, the models gives 100 per cent correct prediction for sick persons and 0 per cent correct prediction for non-sick persons. The overall percentage of correct prediction is 52 per cent.

The **Variables in the Equation** table shows the variables included in the equation and its estimated β-coefficient, standard error, Wald statistic, degrees of freedom, significance level and exponential (β).The squared ratio of estimated coefficient to its standard error is the Wald statistic and is used to examine the significance of parameters. If the Wald statistic is significant (its significance value is less than 0.05), then the parameter is significant. You see that the significance level of constant is greater than 0.05, and therefore base model is not adequate to predict the odds ratio for sickness.

The **Variables not in the Equation** table gives the score, degrees of freedom and associated significance level associated with those independent variables not included in the base model. The significance level associated with these independent variables (covariates) is less than 0.05 which indicates that these variables could be important in predicting the odds of health status.

In **Block 1: Method = Enter**, both– **smoking** and **weight** – are included in the model. Two more tables are generated in order to compare this model with the base model.

The **Omnibus Tests of Model Coefficients** table give the value of Chi-Square, degrees of freedom and associated significance level. The value of Chi-square indicates the change in -2LL (log likelihood) from base model to the present model. If Chi-square statistic is positive, it shows decrease in deviance in prediction of y from the previous / base model and if it is negative, it shows increase in deviance. Since the Chi-square is 19.802 and associated significance level is less than 0.05, the present model shows a decrease in deviance from the base model. Therefore, this model is a better fit compared to the base model.

The **Model Summary** table shows the values of -2Log Likelihood, Cox & Snell R^2 and Nagelkerke R^2. Since R^2 is not computed in logistic regression, -2LL, Cox & Snell R^2 or Nagelkerke R^2 are used to examine whether including an additional covariate is significant or not. Higher values of Cox & Snell R^2 and Nagelkerke R^2 indicate a better fit. Since we have used Enter method for estimating the regression model, we do not get

The **Classification Table** shows that overall model gives 92 per cent correct prediction. As shown in the table, out of 13 persons who are non-sick, this model predicts 12 to be non-sick and 1 to be sick. Out of 12 sick persons, the model predicts 11 to be sick and 1 to be non-sick. Thus, it predicts sick persons with 91.7 per cent accuracy and non-sick with 92.3 per cent accuracy.

The Variables in the Equation table shows the estimated coefficient of logistic regression with standard error. Exp(B) gives the change in odds for a unit change in the given covariate. The ratio of probability of occurrence to, the probability of non-occurrence of an event is termed as odds ratio. If p is the probability of occurrence of an event, then 1-p is the probability of non-occurrence of the same. Even (because sum of probabilities is always equal to 1), and odds ratio is given by:

$$OddsRatio = \frac{p}{1-p}$$

The positive Exponential of B-coefficients [Exp(B)] indicate that for each case moving from lower category to higher category, there is an increase in the odds ratio. This means that if a person starts smoking, his / her body weight remains same; the odds for being sick increases by 26.695 times and with unit (1 kg) increase in weight, the odds of being sick increases by 1.216 times.

Summary

In this chapter we learnt:

- Procedure to undertake logistic regression.
- Interpretation of results, especially the log odds ratio.

Chapter 16

Reliability Analysis

In this Chapter:

- Reliability Analysis

Reliability Analysis is a measure to check the internal consistency of an instrument constructed with multiple-item scales. Reliability analysis is undertaken by estimating a "true" score and comparing it with the observed score. It is used to examine whether the instrument measures the same thing irrespective of who administers the instrument and how.

Any instrument requires to be checked for internal consistency on four parameters:

- Internal consistency based on correlations among items (constructs) of the instrument. Cronbach Alpha is used to check this internal consistency.
- Internal consistency on the basis of administering two sets of items (constructs) measuring the same thing, at the same time, in the same instrument, to the same respondent. This is known as spilt-half reliability. It measures correlation between parts of the instrument. This type of internal consistency is also known as equivalence or parallel reliability. Cronbach's Alpha, Spearman-Brown coefficient, Guttman spilt-half coefficient and the Pearson correlation coefficient jointly measure this parallel reliability.
- Stability of instrument over time. If the same instrument is used to interview same respondents at different points of time and if the same items are interpreted in same manner even after the time interval of one week or one month, the instrument is said to be consistent. Spearman-Brown coefficient is used to test this consistency.
- Stability of instrument for different interviewers. If the same set of instrument is used by more than one interviewer, then the same respondents should give same responses to two interviewers. Cohen's Kappa is used to measure the inter-rate reliability.

We focus our discussion to internal consistency among items of the instruments. Therefore, we need to use Cronbach's Alpha. The null and alternative hypotheses for Cronbach's Alpha are:

- **H0:** the test is not reliable, that is, the observed score is not related to the true score.
- **H1:** the test is reliable, that is, the observed score is related to the true score.

The procedure for estimating Cronbach's Alpha is discussed below:

1. Open file **mobile phone.sav**.
2. Click on **Analyze** from the command menu as shown in Fig.PASW–16.1:

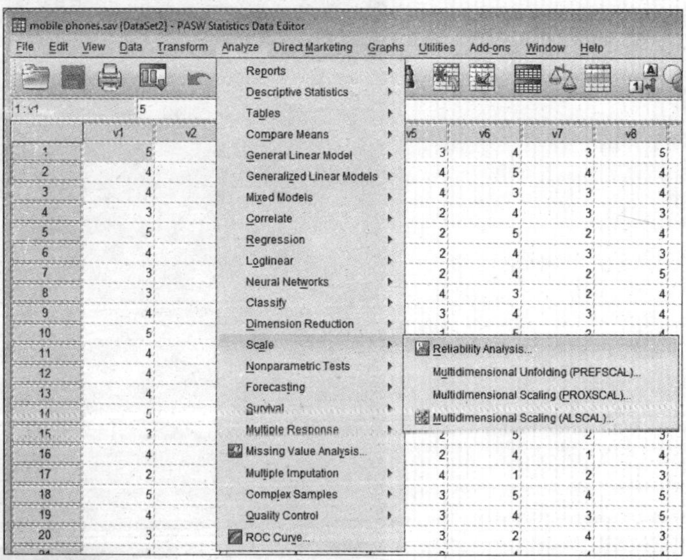

Fig.PASW–16.1

2. Click **Scale** and **Reliability Analysis** as shown in Fig.PASW–16.1 to get the dialogue box shown in Fig.PASW–16.2:

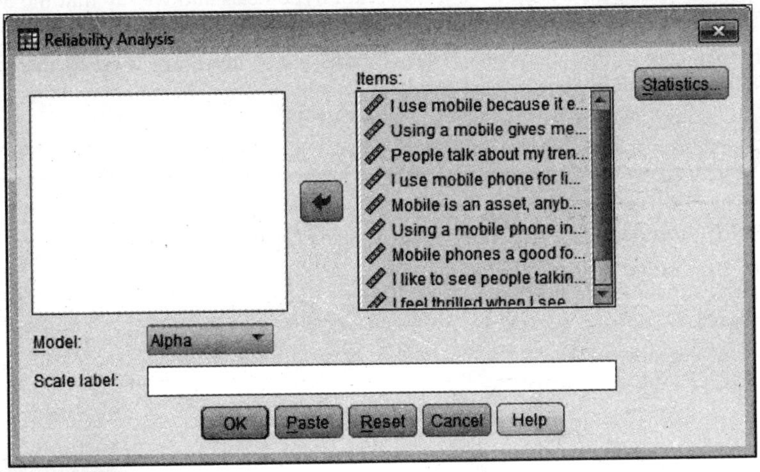

Fig.PASW–16.2

3. Select all the variables and drag it to **Items** list box.
4. In the **Model** dropdown box, select **Alpha** (the default selection).
5. Keeping all other options and values unchanged, click **OK** to execute command. Following output will be displayed in the output viewer window:

Command Syntax for Reliability Analysis

```
DATASET ACTIVATE DataSet2.
RELIABILITY
  /VARIABLES=v1 v2 v3 v4 v5 v6 v7 v8 v9 v10
  /SCALE('ALL VARIABLES') ALL
  /MODEL=ALPHA.
```

Reliability

Scale: ALL VARIABLES

Case Processing Summary

		N	%
Cases	Valid	50	100.0
	Excluded[a]	0	.0
	Total	50	100.0

a. Listwise deletion based on all variables in the procedure.

Reliability Statistics

Cronbach's Alpha	N of Items
.773	10

Two tables – Case Processing Summary and Reliability Statistics are displayed under main heading **Reliability** and sub-heading **Scale: All Variables**.

The Case Processing Summary table shows that out of 50 observations, all 50 observations are included in analysis. The value of Cronbach's Alpha is .773 and the number of items (questions) is 10. Since the value of

Alpha is higher than the accepted (.70), we reject the null hypothesis and we say that the instrument is reliable and can be used with other statistical procedures for further investigation.

However, if the data are multidimensional, that is, two sets of items are used to measure the same set of variables; the split-half reliability needs to be checked.

Summary

In this chapter we learnt:

- The procedure for undertaking reliability analysis using Cronbach's Alpha.
- Interpreting the results.

Chapter 17

Factor Analysis

In this Chapter:

Factor analysis is a method for reducing large number of variables to a small number of components or factors. Many studies are likely to have two or more variables that are highly correlated. Let us try to understand Factor Analysis with the help of following example:

The demand for mobile phones has increased manifold in past years. Infinity Inc., a mobile handset manufacturer wants to examine factors influencing purchase of mobile phones. They undertake a survey of 50 mobile phone users who were asked to rate 10 statements on their perceptions about their mobile handset and its uses on a 5-point scale. The datafile (**mobile phones.sav**) is given in Appendix–A.

In this example, the two statements **I use mobile phone because it enhances my personality** (**v1**) and **Using a mobile gives me a professional look** (**v2**)are likely to be strongly correlated. The concept of factor analysis is based on the fact that if two variables are correlated, since correlation does not imply causation, there exists a third variable termed here as **Factor** or **Component** that might explain the relationship between these two variables.

Note that the terms 'factor' and 'component' are used interchangeably. The term 'component' is used more frequently if extraction is done using Principal Components Method. If extraction is done using any other method, the term 'factor' is found commonly used.

In our example of mobile phones, the third variable used to describe the correlation between these two statements could be termed as **Self-Efficacy**. Extraction of factors reduces the number of variables, thereby making the dataset less bulky, manageable and cost effective. Here, **Self-Efficacy** is the derived variable and is termed as component or factor. This concept of data reduction is based on the fact that few components or factors explain most of the variance in the dependent variable (here, **factors influencing purchase of mobile phones**). The components explaining most of the variance in the model are known as principal components and the method for extracting these components is known as Principal Components Method.

Factor analysis is also used for classification of variables or detecting structure in relationship between variables; there are methods based on the assumption that some variability in data cannot be explained by all the components. However, we limit our discussion to use of factor analysis for data reduction and focus only Principal Components Method.

17.1 Principal Components Method

The underlying concept of Principal Components Method is that the extracted components explain most of the variance of the correlated variables. Since components are derived from strongly correlated variables, the components generated from Principal Components Method are likely to be uncorrelated or weakly correlated with each other. In our example, though **v1** and **v2** are highly correlated with each other, the extracted component **Self-Efficacy** will have weak correlation with the remaining variables / components.

The extraction of components follows a slightly complex process. We assume that there are only two variables and they are strongly correlated.

Note that three and more dimensional representation is required for three or more variables. Thus, for the sake of simplicity, the explanation involves only two variables.

The scatter diagram for these two variables is plotted and a regression line is fitted; this line is the extracted component. It explains maximum variability in the model; however, some variability remains unexplained by this regression line. This extracted component is treated as new X-axis. We define another line which explains the maximum out of the remaining variability in the dependent variable. This becomes the second component. The variance explained by this second component is less than that explained by the first component. The second component is now considered to be the X-axis and the process is repeated till most of the variability, though not 100 per cent is explained by successive components. This changing of X-axis after extracting each component is known as 'rotation'.

If the reference axes are kept unchanged after extraction of components, the components are referred to as 'unrotated components'. Rotation can be defined as a mathematical technique of arriving at simplest pattern of factor loading. Factor loading is defined as the coefficient of correlation between extracted components and the left out variables. But as more and more components are extracted, the remaining variables explain lesser and lesser variability in the model. Therefore, restrict the number of components to extract such that all the components explain maximum variation. It is not possible to explain 100 per cent variation in the model through extracted components; each component is extracted after rotation of axes, the extracted components are uncorrelated. Since the successive components are uncorrelated, the rotation is said to be orthogonal in nature. There are three types of orthogonal rotation – *varimax, quatrimax* and *equamax*. Since extraction in principal components method is based on variance maximization, *varimax* rotation is used to extract the components. *Direct Oblimin* and *Promax* are oblique rotation methods.

17.2 Necessary Conditions for Undertaking Principal Component Analysis

- Principal components analysis can be performed on ordinal, interval or ratio data. It is not possible to perform principal components analysis on nominal data.
- The variables should be normally distributed.
- The nature of relationship among variables should be linear.
- It is desirable that the number of observations meet the following criteria:
  - ➢ The number of observations should be at least double the number of variables.
  - ➢ The ratio of number of observations to number of factors should be 20:1.

17.3 Procedure for Undertaking Principal Component Analysis

1. Create the file – mobile phones.sav.
2. Click Analyze from command menu as shown in Fig.PASW–17.1:

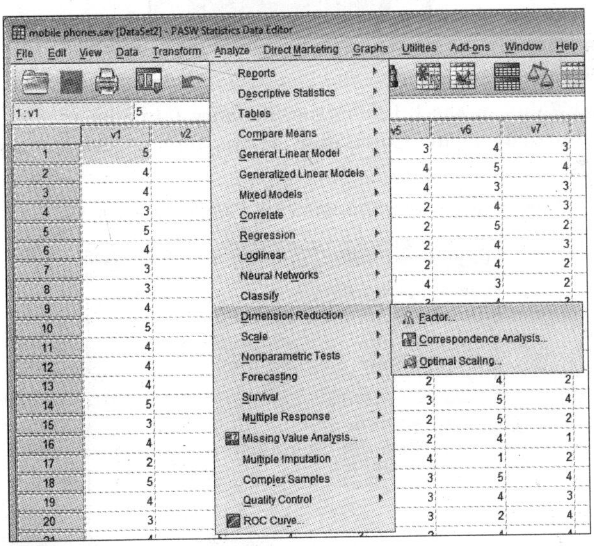

Fig.PASW–17.1

3. Click **Dimension Reduction** and **Factor** as shown in Fig.PASW–17.1 to get the dialogue box shown in Fig.PASW–17.2:

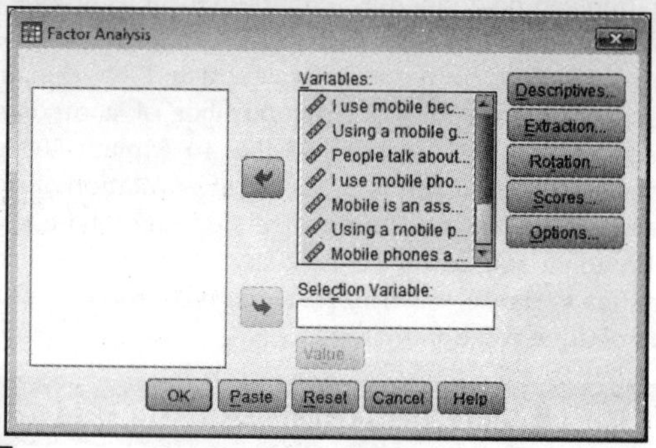

Fig.PASW–17.2

4. Select all the variables and take them to **Variables** list box and click **Descriptives** to get the dialogue box shown in Fig.PASW–17.3:

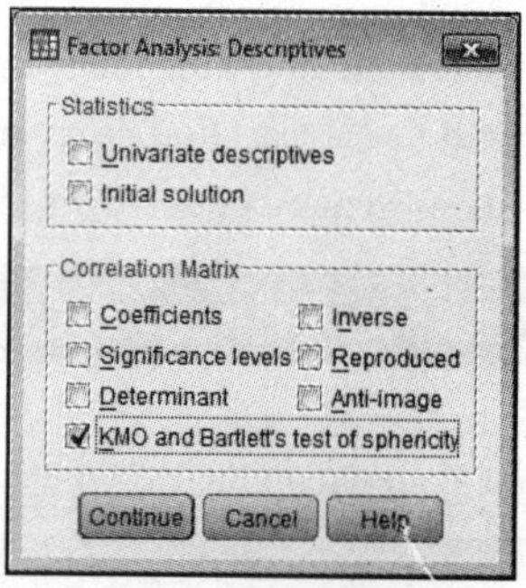

Fig.PASW–17.3

5. Uncheck the **Initial Solution** check box in the **Statistics** frame by clicking on it and click **KMO and Bartlett's test of shpericity** in the **Correlation Matrix** frame. Click **Continue** to go back to previous dialogue box.

6. Click **Extraction** to get the dialogue box shown in Fig.PASW–17.4:

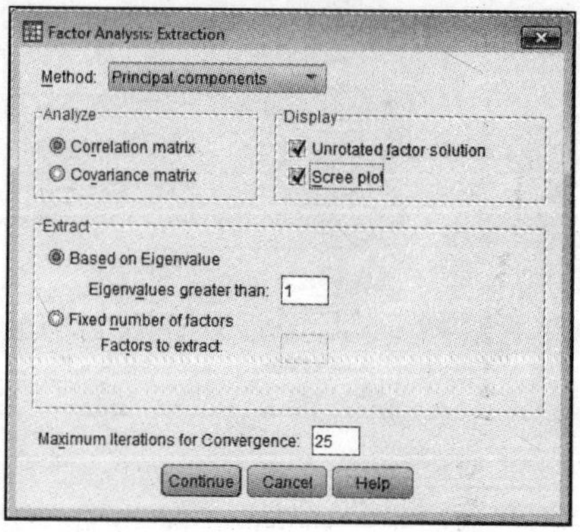

Fig.PASW–17.4

7. Keep all the default values and click the **Scree Plot** check box in the **Display** Frame. In the **Eigenvalues greater than** text box, we have retained the default value of **1**. This eigenvalue rule is known as the Kaiser's criterion. According to this criterion, only those factors with eigenvalue greater than 1 will be extracted. Eigenvalues are measure of total variation. The eigenvalue of a factor represents the total variation explained by that factor. Eigenvalue of 1 means the extracted components is equivalent to at least one original variable. Maximum iterations for convergence represent the number of iterations to be performed for fitting the regression line each time. Click **Continue** to return to previous dialogue box.
8. Click **Rotation** to get the dialogue box shown in Fig.PASW–17.5:

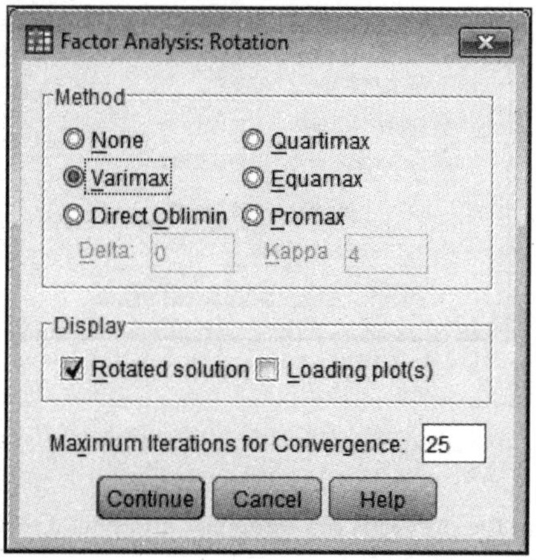

Fig.PASW–17.5

9. Click the **Varimax** radio button in the **Method** frame and check the **Rotated Solution** in the **Display** frame. In **Maximum Iterations for Convergence** text box, keep the default value of **25** and click **Continue** to return to previous dialogue box.
10. Click **Scores** to get the dialogue box shown in Fig.PASW–17.6:

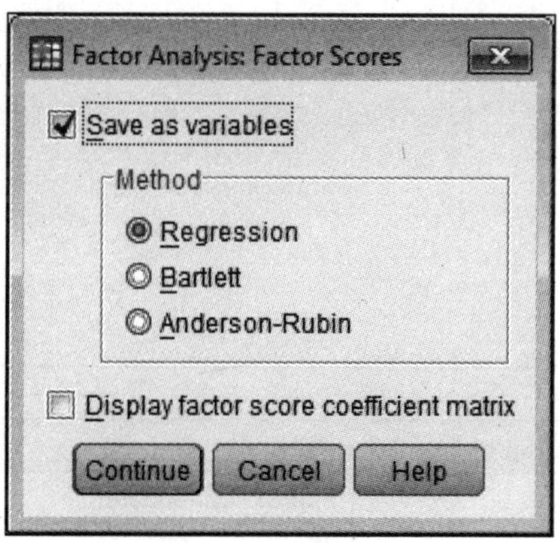

Fig.PASW–17.6

11. Click the **Save as variables** check box so that the extracted components are stored in the dataset. Keeping the default option of **Regression** in the **Method** frame, click **Continue** to go back to previous dialogue box.

12. Click **Options** to get the dialogue box shown in Fig.PASW–17.7:

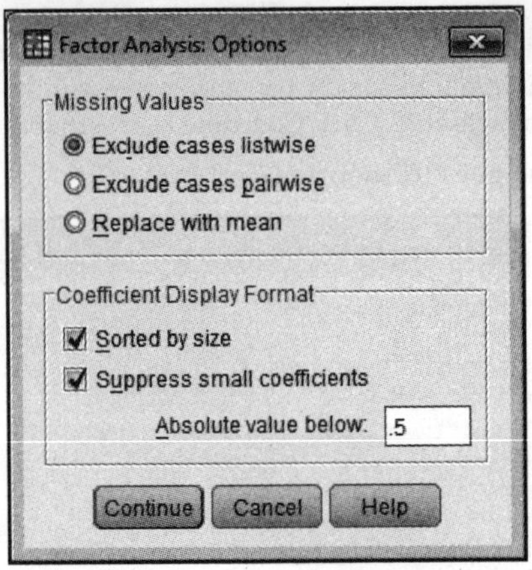

Fig.PASW–17.7

13. Click Sorted by size and Supress absolute values less than check boxes and type .5 in Absolute value below text box.
14. Click **Continue** to go back to the previous dialogue box and click **OK** to execute command. The output will appear in the Viewer window as follows:

Command Syntax for Factor Analysis using Principal Components Method

```
DATASET ACTIVATE DataSet2.
FACTOR
  /VARIABLES v1 v2 v3 v4 v5 v6 v7 v8 v9 v10
  /MISSING LISTWISE
  /ANALYSIS v1 v2 v3 v4 v5 v6 v7 v8 v9 v10
  /PRINT KMO EXTRACTION ROTATION
  /FORMAT SORT BLANK(.5)
  /PLOT EIGEN
  /CRITERIA MINEIGEN(1) ITERATE(25)
  /EXTRACTION PC
  /CRITERIA ITERATE(25)
  /ROTATION VARIMAX
  /SAVE REG(ALL)
  /METHOD=CORRELATION.
```

Factor Analysis

KMO and Bartlett's Test		
Kaiser-Meyer-Olkin Measure of Sampling Adequacy.		.670
Bartlett's Test of Sphericity	Approx. Chi-Square	268.673
	df	45
	Sig.	.000

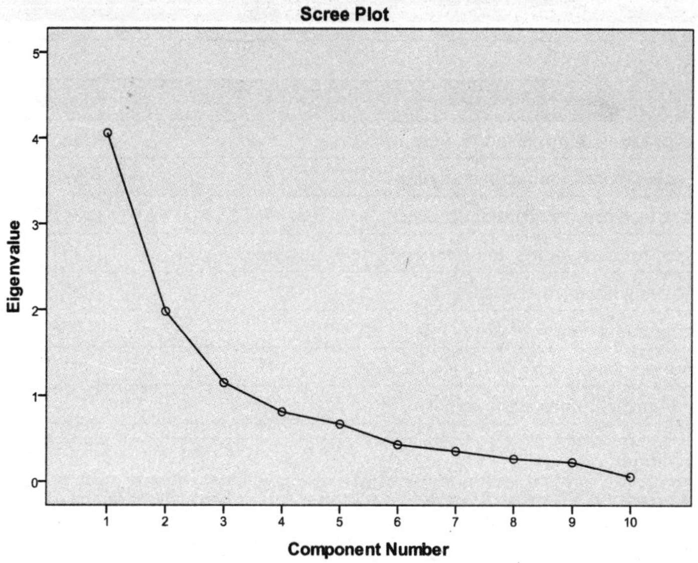

Component Matrix[a]			
	Component		
	1	2	3
I use mobile because it enhances my personality.	.930		
Having a mobile phone is an indicator of trendy lifestyle.	.888		
I feel thrilled when I see advertisement of my mobile on TV.	.814		
Using a mobile phone increases my confidence level.	.806		
Using a mobile gives me a professional look.	.707		
I like to see people talking about my handset.	.697		
People talk about my trendy ringtones.		.878	
Mobile phones a good for exchanging and forwarding text messages.		.762	
Mobile is an asset, anybody can contact me anytime.		.714	
I use mobile phone for listening music in free time.			.816
Extraction Method: Principal Component Analysis.			
a. 3 components extracted.			

Communalities	
	Extraction
I use mobile because it enhances my personality.	.899
Using a mobile gives me a professional look.	.668
People talk about my trendy ringtones.	.792

Communalities	
	Extraction
I use mobile phone for listening music in free time.	.686
Mobile is an asset, anybody can contact me anytime.	.530
Using a mobile phone increases my confidence level.	.712
Mobile phones a good for exchanging and forwarding text messages.	.737
I like to see people talking about my handset.	.577
I feel thrilled when I see advertisement of my mobile on TV.	.768
Having a mobile phone is an indicator of trendy lifestyle.	.816
Extraction Method: Principal Component Analysis.	

Total Variance Explained							
Component		Extraction Sums of Squared Loadings			Rotation Sums of Squared Loadings		
		Total	% of Variance	Cumulative %	Total	% of Variance	Cumulative %
dimension0	1	4.056	40.560	40.560	3.978	39.783	39.783
	2	1.979	19.790	60.349	1.981	19.815	59.597
	3	1.149	11.486	71.836	1.224	12.238	71.836
Extraction Method: Principal Component Analysis.							

Rotated Component Matrix[a]			
	Component		
	1	2	3
I use mobile because it enhances my personality.	.938		
Having a mobile phone is an indicator of trendy lifestyle.	.900		
Using a mobile phone increases my confidence level.	.827		
I feel thrilled when I see advertisement of my mobile on TV.	.755		
I like to see people talking about my handset.	.728		
Using a mobile gives me a professional look.	.655		
People talk about my trendy ringtones.		.882	
Mobile phones a good for exchanging and forwarding text messages.		.810	
Mobile is an asset, anybody can contact me anytime.		.689	
I use mobile phone for listening music in free time.			.823
Extraction Method: Principal Component Analysis. Rotation Method: Varimax with Kaiser Normalization.			
a. Rotation converged in 4 iterations.			

Component Transformation Matrix				
Component		**1**	**23**	
dimension0	1	.986	.086	-.143
	2	-.067	.988	.136
	3	.154	-.125	.980
Extraction Method: Principal Component Analysis. **Rotation Method:** Varimax with Kaiser Normalization.				

The output will comprise six tables and one chart. Under the title **Factor Analysis**, the **KMO and Bartlett's Test** table is displayed, followed by the **Scree Plot**. Five tables – **Component Matrix, Communalities, Total Variance Explained, Rotated Component Matrix** and **Component Transformation Matrix** – are displayed just below the **Scree Plot**.

The **KMO and Bartlett's Test** table displays the results for interpreting the adequacy of data for factor analysis. Kaiser-Meyer-Olkin (KMO) is a measure of sampling adequacy and its value should be greater than 0.6 for our sample to be adequate for undertaking factor analysis. Also, the p-value of Bartlett's test of sphericity should be less than 0.05.In this example the value of KMO test is 0.670 (higher than 0.6) and the p-value of Bartlett's test is .000 (less than 0.05), factor analysis can be undertaken using this dataset.

The **Scree Plot** determines the optimal number of components. It plots the eigenvalues of each component. The number of components which fall on the steep slope are extracted because the eigenvalues of those components are greater than 1. You may wonderhow many components to extract. At that time, it is this Kaiser criterion of extracting all components with eigenvalues greater that 1 can be resorted to. The components beyond the point where the curve changes its direction and becomes horizontal (eigenvalues less than or equal to 1), contribute very little to the variation and therefore, they can be eliminated. In our example of mobile phones, three components lie on the steeper side of the curve and all others lie on the flat portion of the curve. Therefore, scree plot suggests that optimal number of components is three.

The **Component Matrix** table shows the three components that are extracted. This is unrotated component matrix. The unrotated component matrix displays the correlation between variables and the extracted components. These correlations are known as factor loadings. Apparently, the first factor is more highly correlated with the variables than the second factor, and second factor is more highly correlated than the third factor. The reasons for the factor loading to appear like this are already discussed above.

The next table displays **Communalities**. Communalities mean the proportion of variance due to common factors and shared by several items. Communalities help estimate the variance that is unique to each variable; this uniqueness is calculated by total variance explained by that variable minus the communality of that variable.

The **Total Variance Explained** table displays the total variance, percentage variance and cumulative percentage variance for both – unrotated and rotated components. The first half of the table shows details of unrotated components and the second half shows the details of rotated components. The cumulative variance for both the unrotated and rotated components is 71.836 per cent. However, for unrotated components, the first component explains the maximum variance, followed by declining variance of the second and third components, where as in rotated components, the variance is uniformly distributed. Component 1 accounts for 39.783 per cent of total variance, component 2 accounts for 19.815 per cent and component 3 accounts for 12.238 per cent of the total variance in the model. The cumulative percentage of variance of unrotated as well as rotated components is always same.

In the **Rotated Components Matrix**, each number represents the partial correlation coefficient between variable and the rotated component. These coefficients help in identifying the component. All the variables that have large factor loadings for a given component define the component. In our example of mobile phones, the variables constituting **component 1** are:

- I use mobile because it enhances my personality.
- A mobile phone is an indicator of trendy lifestyle.

- Using a mobile phone increases my confidence level.
- I feel thrilled when I see advertisement of my mobile on TV.
- I like to see people talking about my handset.
- Using a mobile gives me a professional look.

The variables constituting **component 2 are:**

- People talk about my trendy ringtones.
- Mobile phones are good for exchanging and forwarding text messages.
- Mobile is an asset, anybody can contact me anytime.

Component 3 comprises only one variable and that is:

I use mobile phone for listening to music in free time.

Since we have checked the box for saving variables, three variables will be created in the **mobile phones.sav** file. Go to the **Data Editor** Window and scroll right to see the newly created variables. These are extracted components.

The **Components Transformation Matrix** table displays the specific rotation applied to the components. Rotated factor loadings are obtained by multiplying the unrotated factor loadings matrix with component transformation matrix.

The values displayed in data file for each component – for **Factor1_1, Factor2_1** and **Factor3_1** are obtained by multiplying the variable values matrix by factor score coefficients matrix. These components could be renamed by going to the Variable View Window and changing the name of the variable. Since **Factor1_1** can be renamed **Personality and Self-Efficacy**. **Factor2_1** can be renamed as **Asset Value** and **Factor3_1** can be called **Entertainment Tool.**

The results of Principal Component Analysis reveal that people associate possessing a mobile phone with following factors:

1. Personality and self-efficacy.
2. Asset Value
3. Entertainment tool.

Thus, Infinity Inc. should focus on these factors while launching an advertisement campaign to increase the sales of their mobile handsets.

Summary

In this chapter we learnt:

- The principal components method.
- Necessary conditions to undertake principal components analysis.
- Procedure to undertake principal components analysis.

Appendix–A: Dataset for students.sav

StudentID	Section	Gender	Location	Ent_Score	Faculty	ExpEdu	HrRead	PerCentFirstYear
1	1	0	0	65	3	500	8	69
2	1	0	1	50	1	700	5	60
3	1	1	1	55	1	250	2	55
4	1	0	1	60	2	400	9	69
5	1	0	0	54	3	800	3	56
6	1	0	1	56	3	350	5	54
8	1	1	1	59	1	100	8	62
9	1	0	1	54	1	500	8	59
10	1	0	1	59	3	600	8	50
11	1	1	0	57	1	300	7	55
12	1	0	0	50	3	300	5	52
13	1	0	1	54	3	400	3	55
14	1	0	1	53	2	350	2	55
15	1	0	0	59	1	700	7	60
16	1	0	1	52	2	600	3	46
17	1	1	0	75	3	300	8	50
18	1	1	0	50	2	200	2	52
19	1	1	0	64	3	300	7	65
20	1	1	1	69	1	400	8	70
21	1	1	0	63	2	500	8	60
22	1	1	1	70	2	600	9	68
23	1	1	0	50	1	200	5	54
24	1	1	0	55	3	400	9	56
25	1	1	1	64	2	800	9	60
26	1	1	1	60	2	600	8	68
27	1	1	0	65	1	700	7	60
28	1	1	1	70	2	800	6	65
29	1	1	0	62	1	300	5	61
30	1	1	0	53	1	200	3	55
31	1	0	1	55	1	600	3	45
32	1	0	0	60	2	200	8	68
33	1	1	0	65	3	500	3	40
34	1	0	0	55	3	100	4	54
35	1	0	1	53	3	1000	7	65

StudentID	Section	Gender	Location	Ent_Score	Faculty	ExpEdu	HrRead	PerCentFirstYear
36	1	1	1	59	3	500	7	89
37	1	0	0	53	1	400	3	40
38	1	1	1	62	1	450	3	46
39	1	0	1	68	1	650	6	65
40	1	0	0	65	2	250	6	62
41	1	1	1	54	2	350	3	40
42	1	1	0	63	2	800	8	65
43	1	1	1	58	2	650	5	60
44	1	1	0	64	2	700	5	70
45	1	0	1	69	1	750	3	49
46	1	1	0	70	2	300	3	55
47	1	0	0	57	2	650	6	64
48	1	0	0	67	3	400	6	63
49	1	0	1	50	2	300	5	69
50	1	1	0	55	2	350	4	49
51	1	1	0	70	1	650	8	65
52	1	0	0	60	1	750	5	55
53	1	1	0	55	2	500	3	69
54	1	1	1	50	3	450	8	62
55	1	0	1	65	3	575	4	54
56	1	0	0	75	2	690	5	57
57	1	1	1	45	1	580	9	60
58	1	0	0	80	2	475	7	65
59	1	0	0	55	3	630	8	68
60	1	0	0	65	3	520	4	59

Variable Values

Value		Label
Gender	0	Male
	1	Female
Location	0	Local
	1	Commuter
Faculty	1	Arts
	2	Commerce
	3	Science

Data for Incidence of Absence

Absence	Absence	Absence	Absence
8	15	6	20
15	25	2	9
5	20	30	13
5	9	25	15
19	9	30	25
20	15	1	8
15	4	20	15
7	20	30	5
5	5	15	5
10	25	8	19
5	9	30	20
10	15	9	15
5	12	15	7
25	17	5	5
24	24	26	10

Data for Add Cases

StudentID	Section	Gender	Location	Ent_Score	Faculty	ExpEdu	HrRead	Absence	PerCentFirst Year
7	1	0	1	68	3	300	9	15	60

Dataset for students_sec2.sav

StudentID	Section	Gender	Location	Ent_Score	Faculty	ExpEdu	HrRead	Absence	PerCentFirst Year
61	2	1	0	75	3	500	7	5	60
62	2	1	0	58	3	900	5	10	55
63	2	1	0	52	2	460	6	5	70
64	2	0	0	63	2	650	4	25	50
65	2	1	1	56	2	700	7	24	45
66	2	0	1	50	1	700	3	15	56
67	2	1	0	66	2	650	8	25	51
68	2	1	0	60	3	590	5	20	53
69	2	0	0	54	1	600	7	9	55

StudentID	Section	Gender	Location	Ent_Score	Faculty	ExpEdu	HrRead	Absence	PerCentFirst Year
70	2	0	0	59	1	550	8	9	59
71	2	0	0	70	2	450	8	15	65
72	2	0	1	50	2	660	9	4	69
73	2	1	0	55	1	580	5	20	47
74	2	1	1	65	2	460	9	5	58
75	2	1	0	69	3	560	9	25	54
76	2	0	0	51	3	600	8	9	69
77	2	1	0	56	1	650	7	15	60
78	2	0	1	65	1	550	6	12	55
79	2	1	0	57	2	450	5	17	69
80	2	0	0	63	2	490	3	24	56
81	2	0	1	50	2	560	3	6	54
82	2	0	1	45	2	630	8	2	60
83	2	0	0	59	2	540	3	30	62
84	2	0	0	49	1	620	4	25	59
85	2	0	1	65	2	560	7	30	50
86	2	0	1	80	2	700	3	1	69
87	2	0	0	67	1	250	3	20	52
88	2	1	0	85	1	400	4	30	55
89	2	1	0	58	2	800	6	15	55
90	2	0	1	70	2	350	4	8	60
91	2	1	0	60	3	300	3	30	46
92	2	0	1	55	1	100	8	9	50
93	2	1	0	59	1	570	5	15	52
94	2	1	0	67	1	600	5	5	62
95	2	1	0	62	2	300	3	26	57
96	2	0	1	49	2	300	3	20	54
97	2	1	0	58	2	490	6	9	59
98	2	0	1	68	2	460	9	13	50
99	2	1	0	62	2	700	4	15	59
100	2	1	0	54	2	600	2	25	54
101	2	0	1	50	2	690	9	10	56
102	2	0	1	57	2	700	3	5	62

StudentID	Section	Gender	Location	Ent_Score	Faculty	ExpEdu	HrRead	Absence	PerCentFirst Year
103	2	0	1	65	3	600	5	10	59
104	2	0	1	56	3	400	9	5	60
105	2	0	0	52	1	800	8	25	57
106	2	0	0	68	2	350	8	24	52
107	2	0	0	73	2	300	8	15	56
108	2	1	0	59	2	340	7	25	53
109	2	0	1	64	2	500	5	20	69
110	2	0	0	57	2	600	3	10	55
111	2	0	0	68	2	640	2	5	65
112	2	1	0	71	2	550	7	10	59
113	2	1	0	54	3	400	3	5	67
114	2	0	1	66	3	350	8	25	45
115	2	0	1	53	2	700	2	24	51
116	2	0	0	58	2	600	7	15	57
117	2	0	0	48	1	450	8	25	52
118	2	0	0	62	1	570	8	20	54
119	2	0	0	67	2	460	9	9	59
120	2	1	0	48	2	600	5	10	62

Dataset for students_sec1and2 more var.sav

StudentID	PerCentSec Year	BegSalary	Parent_Income	StudentID	PerCentSec Year	BegSalary	Parent_Income
1	75	16000	250000	61	57	12000	320000
2	59	15000	350000	62	56	12000	680000
3	58	9000	150000	63	68	17000	400000
4	65	12000	280000	64	55	12000	500000
5	58	8000	560000	65	47	7500	350000
6	56	9000	480000	66	59	9000	380000
7	59	10000	190000	67	55	9000	450000
8	64	12000	150000	68	54	11000	200000
9	56	13000	420000	69	51	8000	390000
10	53	9500	330000	70	54	8000	320000

StudentID	PerCentSec Year	BegSalary	Parent_Income	StudentID	PerCentSec Year	BegSalary	Parent_Income
11	58	14000	320000	71	61	17000	230000
12	53	9000	280000	72	68	17000	200000
13	54	9500	400000	73	47	8000	180000
14	57	10000	500000	74	62	15000	350000
15	62	15000	350000	75	56	12000	390000
16	48	8000	380000	76	69	17000	340000
17	53	8500	450000	77	58	12000	290000
18	56	8000	200000	78	56	12000	360000
19	63	11000	390000	79	64	15000	260000
20	69	14000	320000	80	56	15000	280000
21	63	13000	230000	81	59	15000	600000
22	65	15000	300000	82	63	17000	550000
23	56	11000	180000	83	65	15000	350000
24	59	10000	350000	84	62	12000	250000
25	63	13000	390000	85	48	8000	530000
26	64	16000	440000	86	67	8000	260000
27	56	11000	490000	87	54	8000	190000
28	63	15000	560000	88	59	8000	200000
29	65	15000	260000	89	52	8000	450000
30	58	11000	280000	90	57	8000	300000
31	46	7500	600000	91	48	8000	350000
32	69	20000	550000	92	52	8000	250000
33	42	6500	350000	93	55	9000	380000
34	56	7500	250000	94	68	10000	190000
35	62	9500	630000	95	65	10000	290000
36	85	16000	260000	96	52	10000	500000
37	46	8500	190000	97	53	12000	480000
38	50	8000	200000	98	52	12000	350000
39	66	15000	450000	99	58	12000	320000
40	62	15000	300000	100	52	8000	360000
41	40	12000	350000	101	53	15000	190000

StudentID	PerCentSec Year	BegSalary	Parent_Inco me	StudentID	PerCentSec Year	BegSalary	Parent_ Income
42	66	17000	550000	102	60	12000	200000
43	58	12000	380000	103	62	12000	450000
44	70	17000	390000	104	63	8000	300000
45	50	12000	290000	105	60	12000	350000
46	54	10000	300000	106	55	8000	250000
47	65	15000	480000	107	57	8000	380000
48	65	16000	350000	108	55	12000	190000
49	66	16000	220000	109	65	12000	290000
50	51	13000	360000	110	56	8000	500000
51	63	13000	350000	111	69	17000	480000
52	56	13000	550000	112	64	15000	350000
53	64	15000	150000	113	62	15000	320000
54	58	13000	280000	114	48	8000	360000
55	57	13000	560000	115	56	12000	200000
56	55	12000	480000	116	56	12000	450000
57	58	12000	190000	117	58	15000	300000
58	63	15000	150000	118	56	15000	350000
59	70	17000	420000	119	56	12000	250000
60	62	13000	330000	120	60	15000	380000

Dataset for Two – Way ANOVA (two-way ANOVA.sav):

Marks	cclasses	faculty	marks	cclasses	Faculty
76	1	1	67	2	1
75	1	2	64	2	2
92	1	3	77	2	3
77	1	1	66	2	1
72	1	2	62	2	2
95	1	3	76	2	3
76	1	1	58	2	1
73	1	2	60	2	2
93	1	3	72	2	3
79	1	1	62	2	1
68	1	2	61	2	2
96	1	3	78	2	3

In Variables view, give value labels **Marks Scored** to marks, **Coaching Classes** to cclasses and **Graduation Faculty** to faculty.

Dataset for Reliability Analysis and Factor Analysis (mobile phones.sav)

V1	V2	V3	V4	V5	V6	V7	V8	V9	V10
5	4	3	4	3	4	3	5	4	5
4	5	4	3	4	5	4	4	4	5
4	4	3	3	4	3	3	4	4	5
3	2	4	3	2	4	3	3	2	4
5	5	2	3	2	5	2	4	5	5
4	4	3	3	2	4	3	3	4	4
3	4	2	2	2	4	2	5	3	3
3	4	4	3	4	3	2	4	3	3
4	3	3	4	3	4	3	4	3	4
5	5	2	2	1	5	2	4	5	5
4	4	4	2	2	5	4	5	4	4
4	5	3	2	3	4	3	4	4	4
4	3	2	3	2	4	2	4	4	4
5	4	2	2	3	5	4	5	5	5
3	5	1	3	2	5	2	3	3	3
4	5	2	3	2	4	1	4	5	4
2	1	4	3	4	1	2	3	2	1
5	4	4	4	3	5	4	5	4	5
4	5	3	4	3	4	3	5	4	4
3	5	3	2	3	2	4	3	4	3
4	5	4	3	2	4	4	4	4	4
5	4	3	2	4	5	3	4	5	4
4	4	3	2	3	4	3	4	4	4
5	5	2	3	2	4	2	4	5	4
5	4	4	2	3	5	4	5	5	4
4	5	4	3	2	4	4	4	5	4
5	4	4	3	4	5	3	4	5	5
4	3	2	3	3	4	2	4	3	4
5	3	3	4	2	5	3	5	3	5
5	5	4	2	3	4	4	3	5	5
2	3	3	4	3	3	3	2	3	2

V1	V2	V3	V4	V5	V6	V7	V8	V9	V10
4	5	4	3	1	4	4	4	5	4
1	2	3	2	1	2	1	2	2	1
3	4	2	3	3	4	2	3	4	3
5	5	4	3	3	3	2	5	4	5
3	4	5	3	3	3	4	3	4	3
5	5	4	3	4	5	4	4	5	5
4	4	3	4	2	4	3	4	4	4
3	3	4	2	4	3	4	4	3	3
4	5	3	3	2	4	3	4	5	4
4	4	3	2	3	5	3	5	4	4
4	5	3	2	2	4	3	4	4	5
5	4	4	2	3	5	4	5	4	5
4	4	3	4	3	4	3	5	4	4
5	5	4	3	3	5	2	4	5	5
5	4	4	3	4	4	4	5	5	4
5	5	3	4	3	5	3	5	5	4
5	4	2	3	2	5	2	5	4	5
4	5	2	1	2	5	2	5	5	4
4	5	1	3	2	5	2	4	4	5

Variables	Value Labels
v1	I use mobile because it enhances my personality.
v2	Using a mobile gives me a professional look.
v3	People talk about my trendy ringtones.
v4	I use mobile phone for listening music in free time.
v5	Mobile is an asset, anybody can contact me anytime.
v6	Using a mobile phone increases my confidence level.
v7	Mobile phones a good for exchanging and forwarding text messages.
v8	I like to see people talking about my handset.
v9	I feel thrilled when I see advertisement of my mobile on TV.
v10	A mobile phone is an indicator of trendy lifestyle.

Values: 1-Strongly Disagree, 2=Disagree, 3=neutral, 4=Agree and 5=Strongly Agree